The Improvement of
Voice and Diction

THE MACMILLAN COMPANY
NEW YORK • CHICAGO
DALLAS • ATLANTA • SAN FRANCISCO
LONDON • MANILA
IN CANADA
BRETT-MACMILLAN LTD.
GALT, ONTARIO

The Improvement of Voice and Diction

JON EISENSON, Ph. D.

PROFESSOR OF SPEECH

DIRECTOR OF QUEENS COLLEGE SPEECH AND HEARING CLINIC

The Macmillan Company • New York

To Freda, Elinore and Arthur

Preface

It is probable that two kinds of students will use this book. The first group will include those with a strong interest in speech and in speaking. Because of their attitudes and aspirations, these students see an importance in learning to speak really well. Many of them are already confident and adequate speakers, but they are not satisfied with just passing competence. The student who is preparing to enter a profession such as law, the ministry, teaching, medicine, psychology, or politics—to name but a few—realizes that he can enhance his professional effectiveness by becoming skillful in speech. Speech will be a principal tool and medium in his profession. Knowledge that cannot be applied and transmitted does not translate itself into skill, and professional success demands skill as well as knowledge. When a profession requires ability to communicate, those who do not have this ability must acquire it, or be satisfied with lesser positions than they might otherwise attain. In many instances, they may have to change to other professions or vocations demanding less communicative skill in general, and effective voice and diction in particular.

The second group of students to use this text probably will include persons who were not self-motivated to study and improve their voice and diction. Someone—a teacher, counselor, or friend—

may have suggested, directed, or required that the student's speech be improved. Possibly the student may have had some awareness that his speech was not "just right." He may have intended to do something about the matter at some vague and indefinite time. He may even have tried to improve his voice, his diction, or both and may have succeeded to some degree. But now a decision has been made, by him or for him, that further improvement is necessary if he is to have adequate and effective speech. We hope that even if the motivation is external the student will not resist the instruction and the opportunity for training that will be his in a course in the improvement of voice and diction.

All of us have acquaintances or friends who do not speak as well as they might. On every campus there are students to whose speech we must "tune in" repeatedly over a period of time if we are to understand it. Most of these are native speakers; a few may be foreign born. There are also some students who have few friends because of real or imagined limitations associated with their speech. Our initial relationships are established through oral language. If oral language is inadequate in manner or in content, personal relationships may suffer. Fortunately, there are very few instances in which inadequate voice and diction need remain so. With proper motivation, and with knowledge and materials for the direction and application of such motivation, adequate voice and diction are possible for almost all of us and better than adequate voice and diction for many of us. We hope that the student is ready and willing (we have no doubt that he is capable) to work toward this objective.

In the development of this book, the author continues with a basic assumption made in others of his writings. The assumption is that intelligent human beings want to have some body of information about skills they are expected to acquire. Intelligent persons tend to have curiosity; they want to know something of the *what* as well as the *how* of activities they are expected to undertake. We hope that in the body of the text we have supplied enough of this kind of information about voice and diction to satisfy normal curiosity. Greater curiosity may be satisfied by an investigation of the references in the footnotes and in some of the suggested projects.

Where the student will begin in the study of this book and how he will proceed will depend upon the organization and objectives of his course. For students who are in a course devoted primarily to voice and secondarily to diction, the first part will be studied before the second. For students in a class with primary interest in voice, the first two chapters are likely to be followed by the material on speech sounds in the second part of the book. For students in a course in which voice and diction are given equal consideration, the order of study will be determined by the instructor's choice of approach. This, of course, need not be predetermined. The approach may well be decided by the particular needs of the students in a particular class and may vary accordingly.

We enjoyed writing the book. Some of the selections used as exercise material are borrowed or adapted. We are grateful to the individuals and to the sources that made this possible.

ACKNOWLEDGMENTS

The writer wishes to acknowledge with thanks the authors and publishers whose materials are quoted in this text. He is also deeply grateful to several of his colleagues with whom he conferred from time to time on aspects of the writing. Mardel Ogilvie, Wilbur Gilman, John Newman, and Elizabeth Scanlan all deserve thanks. The writer owes a special and large debt of gratitude to Professor Arthur Bronstein for his scholarly advice in the development of the material on diction. Professor Bronstein was willing to share his knowledge and skill in the field of phonetics, and the writer perhaps too often took advantage of this willingness.

Contents

Part One • VOICE

1 • Basic Considerations

EFFECTIVE VOCALIZATION

This section has several objectives. The first is to create awareness of what constitutes an effective voice; the second is to indicate how voice can be produced and controlled so that common faults are overcome or avoided; and the third is to suggest how voice can be improved as an instrument of communication.

Responsiveness

Beyond everything else, an effective voice is responsive to the intentions of the speaker. By being responsive, voice helps to communicate the speaker's feelings and thoughts so that he is readily able to let his listener know how he feels about what he thinks.

Appropriateness of Attributes

An effective voice is so intimately associated with what the speaker is saying that it attracts no attention to itself and therefore does not distract attention from what the speaker is trying to communicate. Distraction may result from either the characteristics of the voice or the manner in which the voice is produced. If the dura-

3

tion, quality, pitch, loudness, or any combination of these is faulty or in some way not consistent with the contents of the speech, an element of distraction is introduced. For example, matters of importance are usually spoken slowly rather than hurriedly. Unless secretiveness is to be suggested, they are uttered more loudly than items of lesser importance. Solemn utterances are usually associated with a relatively low pitch and lighter remarks with relatively higher pitches. A reversal of these pitch-contents relationships is likely to be either distracting or misleading. Excessive nasality, huskiness, or any other vocal characteristic which is striking may serve as a distraction. In a somewhat more fortunate way, a very fine voice may also be temporarily distracting if it directs the listener's attention to its unusual qualities. Most listeners, however, soon accept the fine voice and respond to the contents of the speech. On the other hand, a voice which includes a constant element of irritation may continue to distract and so impair the speaker's ability to communicate.

Manner of Production

A voice may have acceptable characteristics but still be ineffective if the speaker's manner of producing his voice attracts attention. If he is obviously straining to be heard, if his external throat muscles appear tense or his jaw tight, the listener may be distracted. If the listener must force himself to maintain attention, the effort may be unpleasant, and the listener may also become tense as a result of what he sees. On the other hand, the overrelaxed speaker, who seems almost too tired to vocalize and articulate, may fatigue his listener.

Sex, Age, and Physique

Another area of appropriateness is related to the sex, age, and physical build of the speaker. We expect men's voices to be different from women's. We expect mature persons' voices to sound different from children's. We expect persons who are big to have "big" voices. A high-pitched, "thin" voice may be acceptable from a small, delicate girl or a little boy, but it is not likely to be acceptable from either a man, a physically mature-looking woman, or a large boy.

Listener's Criteria

From the viewpoint of the listener, an effective voice is one which can be heard without conscious effort or strain. It is consonant with the speaker's message and helps make the message readily audible and intelligible. An effective voice is pleasant to hear, but the pleasure should be unconscious and should not dominate the listener's reactions as it might if he were listening to a good singer. To be effective, voice should be as loud as the specific speaking situation demands. If the speaker is talking to a group, his voice should be heard with ease by every listener, but none should be disturbed because of its loudness. In a conversational situation, the listener with normal hearing and normal power of concentration should not have to ask the speaker to repeat because of a failure to hear, nor should he wish to move away to avoid discomfort from overloudness. In summary, the listener, if he were inclined to be analytic, should be able to conclude that the speaker's voice, as well as his actions, suits the words, the over-all situation, and the speaker as an individual.

Objective Self-Listening

Although it is not always easy to see ourselves as others see us, the mechanics for hearing ourselves as others hear us are available to most of us. Tape or disc recordings of reasonable fidelity can be made at low cost at record shops, speech clinics, or agencies specializing in recording equipment. Although the most useful recording is one made when the speaker is not aware that he is being recorded and so is most himself, "candid" recordings are not always possible. If the recording is staged rather than candid, we recommend that it include conversational speaking as well as material read in a conversational voice and material spoken as if for a small audience. If the speaker frequently makes public addresses, he should also include some material spoken as if he were making a public address. Equipped with such a recording, the speaker about to be a self-listener should then hear himself on an instrument with playback fidelity at least equal to that of the recording instrument. So set, the speaker should ask himself these questions:

1. Is my voice pleasant to hear?
2. Does my voice have any characteristics I would consider undesirable in another speaker?
3. Does my voice reflect what I intended to convey in thought and in feeling?
4. Were the changes in pitch, loudness, duration, and quality consonant with the varying contents of my utterances?
5. Would I listen to this voice if I were not the speaker?
6. Does the voice reflect me as a personality?

If the speaker-listener is completely satisfied with all his answers, then he is one of the fortunate persons making the most of the gift of a good voice. If he is not entirely satisfied, then we assume he recognizes the need for improvement and is both ready and willing to do whatever is necessary to bring it about.

It is important to indicate at this point that what an individual hears when he listens to himself talking is different from what another person hears when listening to him. As Black and Moore point out:

> The two listeners—the one who is only listening and the one who is listening to himself while talking—do not have the same experience. The speaker who is monitoring his own voice hears a sound that no other listener hears. This is dramatically demonstrated as a person listens to a high-fidelity recording of his own voice. He is now an outside listener. The recordings of all his acquaintances' voices sound right, but the same apparatus when turned upon his own voice gives completely erroneous results! *

Because we are so close to the source of our voices we cannot hear how they sound as can a listener who is separated from us by physical distance. We hear ourselves through the tissues of our bodies, especially the bones of the head, as they directly conduct the sounds we produce to our hearing mechanism. We also hear ourselves through the initially external stimulation of the sound waves produced when we talk at the same instant that the sounds are conducted to our hearing mechanism. You can appreciate some of the difference between the two avenues of auditory stimulation if you stop up your ears while talking. You would then be hearing more nearly through bone conduction than you would with your

* J. W. Black and W. E. Moore, *Speech*, New York, McGraw-Hill Book Co., 1955, p. 57.

ears "open." Your voice sounds different and somewhat strange. You may contrast this immediately by repeating what you have said with your ears unstopped. You should, if at all possible, contrast this immediately by listening to a high-fidelity voice recording. Only then, making due allowance for subjective reactions, would you be able to hear yourself as others hear you. Among the important differences resulting from our multiple-conduction feedback system of listening to ourselves is that ". . . we misjudge our own pitch, loudness, and quality, and probably our rate." * Because we cannot hear ourselves as others hear us, it behooves us to accept the evaluation of others, especially if the others are objective and professionally trained voice teachers or therapists. Fortunately, despite the limitations of our self-monitoring system, there is considerable evidence to show that learning to listen is helpful in the improvement of both voice and diction.

Listening to Others

Before turning the mirror on ourselves it might help to do some directed listening to the voices that are part of our everyday living. We may find that some of our acceptances and rejections of individuals are related to their voices. Following are a few projects that should be useful.

Exercises for Listening to Others

1. Tune in to a "soap opera" and listen to the voices of the performers. Can you guess the hero or heroine through the medium of voice alone? Can you detect the villain? How about the family friend? What are the specific vocal attributes of each that influenced your decisions?

2. Compare the newscaster you habitually turn on with one you seldom hear. Do the vocal characteristics of the newscasters have anything to do with your choice? List the vocal characteristics you like and dislike for each. Which of the two has a more favorable balance?

3. Listen critically to two or three of your friends. Are there any characteristics of their voices you particularly like? Are there any you would like to have modified?

* *Ibid.*, p. 58.

4. Listen critically to some persons you do not particularly like. Do you hear any vocal characteristics that might account for your reaction to them?

5. Recall a teacher, present or past, whom you consider especially effective. Is the voice of the teacher an important factor in your judgment? Describe his vocal attributes. Contrast this teacher with one you consider ineffective. Describe the voice of this teacher and determine whether it was a factor in your evaluation.

6. Tune in to a radio or television round-table discussion on a controversial topic. Do you find yourself inclined to the point of view of any of the speakers because of the way he sounds? Do you find yourself disinclined to any for the same reason? List as specifically as you can the attributes and their effects on you. How would the following terms suit the individual speakers: agreeable, irritable, pompous, antagonistic, soft-spoken, firm, tired, energetic, pedantic, indecisive, weak, complaining, congenial, authoritative, warm, cultured, charming?

7. Listen to a radio or television network program in which there is a professional moderator and two or more participants. Compare the vocal tones of the moderator with those of the participants. Observe whether the moderator reveals any personal prejudices through his voice.

8. Listen to a group of friends or acquaintances engaged in a conversation or discussion on a controversial topic. Do the participants reveal their personalities as well as their viewpoints through their voices? What terms listed in project (6) or terms of your own choosing would you apply to them?

9. Do you know any public figures who have had voice training? (Many public figures have had such training and some prepare specifically for each important address.) Can you recall any changes resulting from this training?

Physical Health

For most speakers who are not especially aware of their speech and who are not trained self-listeners, voice is likely to reflect changes in both physical and mental health. In the absence of any specific and chronic condition affecting either aspect of health, vocal efforts will be adversely affected by such conditions as fatigue, ailments of the respiratory tract, and conditions which produce either hypertense or hypotense musculature.

Perhaps the single cause which most frequently affects our voices is the common cold. The cold, because it directly involves the nose and throat, impairs normal vocal reinforcement. In addition, if the larynx is involved, the vibrators (vocal bands) may be thickened and so may produce tones which are not adequately reinforced. If there is a significant amount of inflammation, we tend to avoid laryngeal pain by keeping our vocal bands apart, and as a result we produce breathy and husky tones.

Akin to the effects of the common cold are those produced by allergies which involve the respiratory tract. These may include nasal congestion, irritation of the throat and larynx, and coughing. If the coughing is persistent and severe, the vocal bands may become involved. We may begin to appreciate the effects of persistent coughing from the following:

> When you cough you force air through the windpipe at a speed approaching or exceeding that of sound, which is 732 miles an hour at sea level. . . . By the time the air reaches the level of the Adam's apple, its speed has dwindled to hurricane velocity of about 100 miles per hour. When it blows out of the mouth the air is moving at fifteen miles per hour, a mere zephyr.*

Most of us may be able to vocalize effectively despite the possible abuse to which our vocal bands are subjected when occasionally air is propelled at speeds which may be supersonic. It should be no surprise, however, that many of us cannot be chronic coughers and effective vocalizers, especially if the coughing is violent and hacking.

Good vocal hygiene calls for either avoiding the conditions which are conducive to poor vocalization or reducing vocal efforts when such conditions cannot be avoided. In regard to matters of physical health, persons who must speak often have an obligation to practice

---

* "Science Notes," New York *Times,* April 17, 1955. This note is presumably based on the experimental findings of B. B. Ross, R. Gramiak, and R. Hahn, "Physical Dynamics of the Cough Mechanism," *Journal of Applied Physiology,* 1955, 8:264–268. They found that, depending upon various external pressures and the size of the opening of the trachea, the velocity of air during a cough may range from a speed equivalent to a 15-mile per hour wind to that of a 100-mile per hour hurricane. "If . . . the tracheal lumen is compressed to one-sixth its normal cross section area, the linear velocity thus generated is 28,000 cm/sec., nearly 85% of the speed of sound."

good vocal hygiene. Dr. Brodnitz is succinct in his advice on how to maintain a healthy voice. He says ". . . keep your body in good shape to withstand the rigors of wind and weather; dress sensibly but do not undermine your resistance by pampering yourself; plan your meals in accordance with nutritional requirements; get as much rest and sleep as possible; exercise moderately." †

Mental Health

A mentally healthy person is one who is aware of what is going on about him and responds, without violence to his own integrity, to the demands of his environment. Mental health and the healthy, well-adjusted personality are attained through continuous effort. Speech and voice are both the tools and the results of the process of adjustment.

The young infant responds to his environment and expresses himself almost entirely through his voice. If a baby cries much of his waking time, he may be colicky. If he whines and is almost always on the verge of crying, he is an unhappy baby. If he coos to amuse himself but does little crying except for evident biological reasons, he is a happy or at least a satisfied baby. If he cries occasionally and coos sufficiently to amuse others as well as himself, he is a normal baby. Whatever his condition, whether it is temporary or chronic, he expresses it through his voice. And at each successive stage of his development, from babyhood to maturity, his voice continues to express—to reveal or to betray—his personality and his mental health.

Earlier in this chapter we suggested that the speaker become an objective listener and answer the question of whether the voice he heard reflected him as a personality. Another question to be answered was whether the voice had any characteristic which would be considered undesirable in another speaker. Here are some further questions we hope the listener, if he is a well-adjusted person, can answer in the negative. Does your voice suggest a whine when no whine is intended? Do you sound as if you are complaining about something when you intend to state a fact? Do you sound defeated? Do you sound aggressive rather than poised and secure? Do you sound chronically tired, bored, annoyed, or just too, too sophisticated

† F. S. Brodnitz, *Keep Your Voice Healthy*, New York, Harper & Brothers, 1953, p. 105.

for this mundane world in general and your associates in particular? If the answer is "yes" to any of these questions and there is no intention to suggest the trait which is expressed, insight and recognition should be of help in motivating a change.

Among the more frequent vocal problems associated with maturation is the failure of the voice to drop in pitch during physiological adolescence. Occasionally we meet chronological adolescents and postadolescents who still speak in their childhood pitch range. Sometimes we even find the habitual pitch level raised above that of preadolescence. Although in rare instances this vocal problem may be related to disturbances in motor control or in the glands, more often the cause is emotional. The chronological adolescent, whether boy or girl, who wants to continue to be mother's or daddy's child, or who is apprehensive for other reasons about growing up and assuming grown-up responsibilities, may be announcing the wish or the fear through an infantile voice.

Another adolescent problem frequently associated with vocal disturbance may arise from strong identification with an older person. As a result of this identification, an adolescent girl may imitate the pitch and other vocal characteristics of an idolized adult. Unfortunately, the voice of the adult may be the product of a vocal mechanism unlike that of the imitator. The woman teacher on whom the high school girl possibly has a "crush" may properly be a contralto with a pitch range too low for the larynx of the imitator. The effect may be a strained, husky voice. The problem for the boy in high school may be even more acute if he is intended by nature to be a tenor and his hero has a bass voice.

The author has had several male students who might have had good tenor voices, and possibly even been effective speakers within the baritone range, but who wanted very much to speak like bassos. Within the bass range, unfortunately, they were constanty hoarse and could not be heard beyond the first two or three rows of a classroom. Psychological investigation strongly suggested that the young men were overanxious to be recognized as men—and fearful that they might not be so regarded. The author has also had several middle-aged male voice patients with much the same problems of voice and associated psychodynamics. He has also had a number of women voice patients who were referred to him by laryngologists because of thickened vocal bands resulting from habitual vocalization in too low a pitch range. In several instances the women were working in professional areas which until recently had been considered the province of males. The suspicion of "masculine protest" was supported by the psychodiagnostic evaluation.

Sometimes, to the misfortune of the speaker, habits of voice may persist and so reveal the maladjustments, personality, and mental health of a past period. Voice production is a motor act, and motor acts which are repeated tend to become habitual. Thus, the once dependent person may still sound dependent, and the once aggressive "chip-on-the-shoulder" individual may still sound as if he were looking for trouble. With conscious effort, vocal habits can be modified so that we reveal ourselves as we are when we speak rather than as we were during a period of past adjustment difficulties. If, however, adjustment difficulties continue to be present, effective voice is not likely to be achieved unless therapy includes the problems for which the voice is a symptom.

The Effective Vocalizer

If we examine our reactions to individuals who have effective voices, we are likely to conclude that by and large they are also effective as persons. Voice, or any other attribute of human behavior, is not a free-floating essence or a blithe, disembodied spirit. It is on the contrary, an essential product and aspect of human behavior. It may sometimes be possible for a mentally or physically sick individual who has had considerable professional training to produce voice effectively for a specific purpose and for a limited time, as actors and some public speakers may be required to do. Even professional performers, however, cannot continue to vocalize effectively, act effectively, or in general pretend effectively for an indefinite period. In our discussion in subsequent chapters we shall assume that we are addressing ourselves to essentially healthy persons. This assumption permits leeway for the expression of a little bit of neuroticism which is or should be the privilege of all. It also allows for occasional physical ailments—even those which may be classified as psychosomatic because the body does protest what the mind sometimes must accept.

If the reader is at any time in doubt as to whether his lack of effective voice may be associated with either a temporary or a chronic state of subpar physical or mental well-being, proper medical consultation is in order. Certainly no person who has suffered from chronic hoarseness, or who has had any disturbance centered in the larynx, should undertake voice training without examination and clearance from his physician. If possible, the physician should be a specialist in diseases of the throat. Although voice training can improve most persons' vocal efforts, such training should not be undertaken when a physician prescribes vocal rest. We would also urge that no person become his own physician or use as a substitute for a physician a friend who has had what may appear to be similar voice symptoms. There is danger in using a friend's prescription. The individual who would be an effective vocalizer deserves a personal examination by his own physician.

2. The Mechanism for Speech

Early in life, normal human beings develop the ability to produce meaningful wave patterns in light and air. These patterns are known as speech symbols. The mechanisms by which the symbols are produced serve the biological functions of breathing and eating. Under voluntary control, however, these mechanisms can be modified in their functioning to serve the purposes of vocalization and articulation and thus the production of symbols used in speaking.

In this chapter we will discuss the mechanisms through which human beings achieve speech, are able to communicate their thoughts and feelings, or, when it suits their needs, are able to conceal rather than reveal their thoughts and feelings. We shall first consider how speech noise (voice) is produced and then how noise and breath are modified to produce articulated sound in a manner peculiar to human beings.

VOICE PRODUCTION

The mechanism for voice production has some close parallels to musical wind instruments. In most wind instruments, sound is produced when air is blown over a reed or through vibrating lips as in

14

the case of a trumpet and a trumpeter. The reed or the reed substitute (lips) is usually near the blowing end of an elongated tube. The quality of the sound produced with a wind instrument is determined partly by the size, shape, and nature of the material, partly by the length, thickness, and type of reed, and partly by the ability of the person doing the blowing. The human voice-producing mechanism permits even the average speaker to be a virtuoso. Without conscious practice, most of us become skilled in making our voice mechanisms respond to our wishes. We play our vocal apparatus through ranges of pitch, loudness, and quality not possible by any known combination of wind instruments. The extreme flexibility of the vocal mechanism is the basis for its superiority over musical wind instruments.

Requisites for Sound Production

In order to produce sound, whether it be music, noise, or voice, three essential conditions must prevail: (1) There must be a body capable of being set into vibration; (2) there must be an available force which may be applied to the body to set it into vibration; and (3) there must be a medium for transmitting the results of the vibration to individuals capable of awareness and response. The first two requisites are found in the normal human mechanisms for breathing and will be discussed subsequently. The third requisite is air.

With modifications which are brought about by recognition of need, a normal human being is readily able to make his breathing mechanisms serve for voice production while the function of respiration is sustained. We shall be able to understand how voice production is accomplished through a study of the nature and structure of the vocal mechanism. In our discussion an over-all view of the voice-producing mechanism rather than a detailed consideration of its component parts will be our objective.

The Vocal Bands

The vocal bands or vocal folds are bodies capable of vibration, thus meeting the first requirement for sound production. Biologically, the potential vibrators function as part of a valve mechanism to prevent foreign matter from entering the trachea and

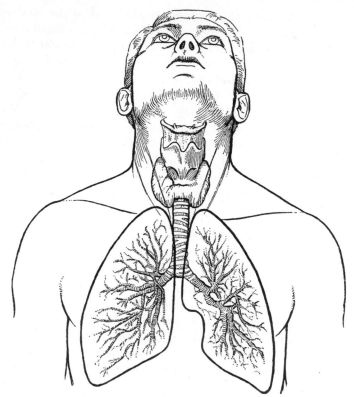

Fig. 1. View of the Larynx, Trachea, and Lungs.

involving the lungs. The vocal bands are two small, tough folds of connective or ligamentous tissue situated in the larynx or voice box at the top of the trachea (windpipe). The bands are continuous with folds of muscle tissue and are connected to cartilages of the larynx.

If we could view the vocal bands from above, as in Fig. 2, they would appear as flat folds of muscle which have inner edges of connective tissue. The vocal bands are attached to the inner curved walls of the thyroid cartilage at either side. At the midline, the bands are attached to the angle formed by the fusion of the two shields of the thyroid cartilage. At the back of the larynx, each band is attached to a pyramidal-shaped cartilage called the arytenoid.

Because of their shape and muscular connections, the arytenoid

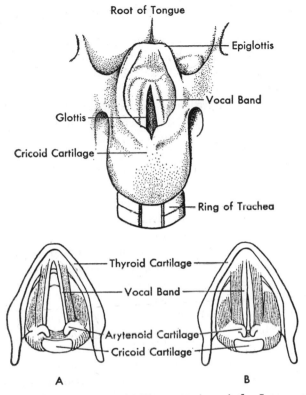

Root of Tongue

Epiglottis

Vocal Band

Glottis

Cricoid Cartilage

Ring of Trachea

Thyroid Cartilage

Vocal Band

Arytenoid Cartilage

Cricoid Cartilage

A   B

Fig. 2. View and Diagrammatic Representation of the Larynx and Vocal Bands Showing Attachments to Cartilages and Larynx.

Upper Diagram: The larynx viewed from above and behind (posterior aspect).

Lower Diagrams: A. Vocal bands shown in position for quiet breathing. B. Vocal bands in position for vocalization.

cartilages can move in several directions. In doing so, they directly influence the position and state of tension of the vocal bands. The arytenoid cartilages can pivot or rotate and tilt backward and side-wise. As a result of these movements, the vocal bands can be brought into a straight line along the midline position so that there is only a narrow opening between them (*B* in Fig. 2), or they can be separated for quiet breathing (*A* of Fig. 2). If the bands are brought together in a narrow "V," as in the upper part of Fig. 2, noisy whispering or possibly breathy voice would be produced if an effort were made to vocalize.

The small, tough vocal bands, ranging in length from ⅞ inch to 1¼ inches in adult males and from less than ½ inch to ⅞ inch in adult females, are directly responsible for the noise called voice produced by human beings.

The *frequency of vibration* of the vocal bands is determined by their length, thickness, and degree of tension when they begin to vibrate. Pitch is our subjective reaction to frequency changes or differences.* We think of pitch as being high, medium, or low or we use such terms as soprano, alto, tenor, baritone, or bass to designate ranges of vocal pitch.

Frequency of vibration varies directly (increases) according to the tension and inversely (decreases) according to the mass and length of the vibrating bodies. Because most men have longer and thicker vocal bands than most women, male voices are on the average lower in pitch than female voices. The average fundamental frequency for male voices is 128 cycles (waves) per second; it is 256 cycles per second for female voices.

Variation from our fundamental frequencies is, for the most part, a result of the changes in tension of our vocal bands. We have considerable control over their state of tension. Such control becomes evident each time we sing the musical scale or a song or raise or lower the pitch level of a sound or a word when talking. Variation also occurs as a result of involuntary changes in the vocal bands associated with over-all states of bodily tension. The tensions of the vocal bands vary as other muscles voluntarily or involuntarily become tense or relaxed. If you are habitually a tense individual, you are likely to vocalize at a higher pitch level than if you are habitually a relaxed person. Immediate responses to situations are productive of over-all changes in bodily tension which are likely to, be associated with tension changes in the vocal bands and therefore in their frequency of vibration. These changes become apparent in situations conducive to excitement and elation at one extreme and

---

*Technically, pitch may be considered as that attribute of auditory sensation in terms of which sounds may be ordered on a scale extending from low to high, such as a musical scale. (*American Standard Acoustical Terminology*, 1951, New York, American Standards Association.)

sadness or depression at the other. (This will be considered in some detail in our chapter on pitch.)

The Motive Force

The second requisite for sound production, the force which vibrates the vocal bands, is the column of air or expired breath stream. In ordinary breathing, the vocal bands are open in a wide-shaped "V" so that the stream of breath meets no resistance as it is exhaled. For purposes of vocalization, we recall, the vocal bands are brought together so that there is a narrow, relatively straight opening rather than a "V"-shaped one. The result is that the exhaled air meets resistance. In order for the air to be expired, the air column must be more energetically exhaled than it is in ordinary breathing. The energetic exhalation vibrates the vocal bands and voice is produced.

Vocalization for speech requires control. Control, which normally

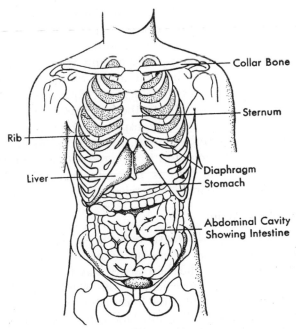

Fig. 3. The Chest (Thoracic) and Abdominal Cavities.

takes place without conscious effort on our part, is achieved usually by the action of the muscles of the abdominal walls and the muscles of the chest cavity.

The chest cavity (thoracic) consists of a framework of bones and cartilages which include the collarbone, the shoulder blades, the ribs, the breastbone, and the backbone. At the floor of the chest cavity, and separating it from the abdominal cavity immediately below, is the diaphragm. We can locate the large, double-dome-shaped muscle called the diaphragm by placing our fingers just below the sternum or breastplate and moving them around the front, sides, and back of the thoracic cavity to the spinal column. In breathing, the diaphragm rises toward the chest cavity during exhalation and descends toward the abdominal cavity during inhalation. In breathing for purposes of speech, both the normal respiratory rhythm and the extent of the upward and downward excursions may be modified according to the speaker's immediate needs.

The lungs function as air reservoirs. The lungs, which contain much elastic tissue, consist of a mass of tiny air sacs supplied by a multitude of air tubes and blood vessels. Because the lungs contain no muscle tissue, they can neither expand nor contract directly. They play a passive role in respiration, expanding or contracting because of differences in pressure brought about by the activity of the abdominal and rib muscles that serve to expand and control the thoracic cavity. Air is forced into the lungs as a result of outside air pressure when the chest cavity, expanded through muscle action, provides increased space for the air. Air is forced out of the lungs when the chest cavity decreases in size and the pressure of the enclosed air is increased. This is normally accomplished through action in which the diaphragm is passively but importantly involved.

Diaphragmatic Action

When the volume of the chest cavity is increased, air is inhaled into the lungs by way of the mouth or nose and the trachea. An increase in the volume of the chest cavity may be effected through a downward, contracting movement of the diaphragm, through an upward, outward movement of the lower ribs, or through a combination of both activities. During inhalation, the diaphragm is active in contracting, thereby lowering the floor of the thoracic cavity.

When inhalation is completed, the diaphragm becomes passive and relaxes. The abdominal organs then exert an upward pressure and so the diaphragm is returned to its former position. When it becomes necessary to control exhalation for purposes of vocalization and speech, the muscles of the front and sides of the abdominal wall contract and press inward on the liver, stomach, and intestines. These abdominal organs exert an upward pressure on the under-surface of the diaphragm. This pressure, combined with the down-ward-inward movement of the ribs, increases the pressure within the

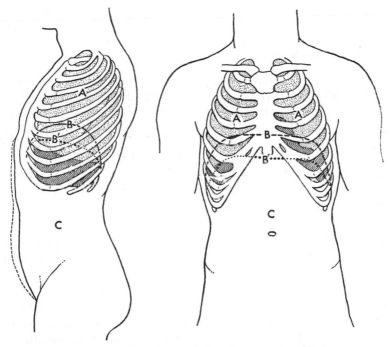

Fig. 4. *Diaphragmatic and Abdominal Activity in Breathing.*
A. *The thorax or chest cavity.*
B. *The diaphragm passive and "relaxed" as at the completion of exhalation.*
B'. *The diaphragm contracted as in deep inhalation.*
C. *The abdominal cavity. Note the forward movement of the abdominal wall which accompanies the downward movement of the diaphragm during inhalation.*
(*The cross-hatched portion of the lung represents the additional volume of the expanded lung as in deep inhalation.*)

thorax and so causes the air to be expelled from the lungs. Throughout the breathing cycle, the diaphragm is roughly dome-shaped. The height of the dome is greater after exhalation than after inhalation.

It is important to understand that the diaphragm, though passive in exhalation, does not relax all at once. If it did, breath would be expelled suddenly and in a manner which would make sustained vocalization impossible. Fortunately, the diaphragm maintains some degree of muscle tension at all times. When the diaphragm relaxes because of the pressure of the abdominal organs, it does so slowly and gradually as the air is expired. Thus a steady stream rather than a sudden rush of breath is provided for the purposes of speech.

Breathing for Speech

In breathing for ordinary life processes, the periods for inhalation and exhalation are approximately equal. Breathing for speech, however, usually requires that this regular rhythmic respiratory cycle be modified so that the period of exhalation exceeds that of inhalation. Normally, for speech, we inhale quickly between units of utterance and exhale slowly while speaking. This modification necessitates a degree of voluntary control not required for automatic breathing. Such control is usually achieved by abdominal activity.* This point will be considered in greater detail in our discussion on voice improvement.

In normal nonspeech breathing, an average of about a pint of air (500 cc.) is interchanged in each respiratory cycle. Conversational speech may require little or no more air; vigorous speaking may require more air. Seldom, however, do we use more than 10 to 20 per cent of the total amount of air our lungs are capable of holding. Control of breath and the appropriate use of our resonators for reinforcement of vocal tones rather than amount of breath are essential to adequate voice production.

---

* Stetson demonstrated that in the normal speaking act, short, individual breath pulses that correspond to the successive oral syllables result from the action of the rib-connecting (intercostal) muscles. (See R. H. Stetson, *Motor Phonetics,* 2nd ed., Oberlin College, Oberlin, Ohio, 1951, and R. H. Stetson and C. V. Hudgins, "Functions of the Breathing Movements in the Mechanism of Speech," *Arch. Neer. Phon. Exper.,* 1930, 5:1–30.)

Loudness and Reinforcement

The loudness of our vocal tones is determined in part by the vigor with which we force air from the lungs through the trachea and larynx. Fortunately, energy is not the only factor which determines how loudly we can vocalize. We also build up or reinforce vocal tones through the use of cavity resonators. The cavities that provide vocal reinforcement are the larynx, the throat (pharynx), the mouth (buccal cavity), and the nose (the cavity above the roof of the mouth). Because vocal tones produced in the larynx are reinforced by these resonators, considerably less energy is required for readily audible voice than would otherwise be necessary. The resonators also play an essential role in modifying the quality of vocal tones. The combination of size and shape of resonating cavities and the manner in which they are used give each of us a voice so individual that the recognition of a person by his voice alone is usually possible. The manner in which we use our resonators permits listeners to evaluate our vocal efforts as being *throaty, nasal, thin,* or *strident*; if we are more fortunate in our vocal efforts, we might merit more complimentary terms such as *full, colorful, rich,* or *vibrant*. With infrequent exception, the evaluation we earn for our vocal efforts is largely a matter of habit in the use of our vocal apparatus. Although it may not be possible for every vocalizer to have a beautiful voice, it is rarely necessary for any speaker to have an unpleasant or inadequate voice. In the absence of a specific defect in the structure or control of the vocal apparatus, or of a personality defect manifested in voice, acceptable voice should be possible because of the flexibility of our voice mechanisms.

The Larynx

Vocal tones, as soon as they are initiated, are reinforced in the larynx. If the larynx is free from organic pathology and not under strain and if the speaker initiates and maintains vocalization without abnormal tension, there is little he can or need consciously do about obtaining good laryngeal resonance. If the speaker has laryngitis, however, normal laryngeal reinforcement is not possible. If you suffer from laryngitis, it is best to reduce your talking to a minimum, and if possible, do no talking. If the condition is recurrent, or persistent, a visit to a physician is in order.

Tension of the extrinsic muscles of the larynx, as indicated, inter-
feres with the reinforcing function of the larynx. Such tension is also
likely to interfere with the free action of the vocal bands for good
tone production. The extrinsic muscles of the larynx are those which
connect it to the jaw and other bones and cartilages so that it will
maintain its normal position when at rest and be lifted upward and
forward for swallowing. Tension is necessary in the act of swallowing. You can feel the tension of the extrinsic muscles by placing your
hand on your throat as you swallow. Such muscular tension should,
however, be avoided in most speech efforts. We approximate such
tension for the vowels of *see* and *sue* but should avoid it for speech
efforts in general. The suggestions given for easy initiation of tone
may be reviewed here as practice to avoid unnecessary laryngeal
tension (see pages 52–59).

The Pharynx

The pharynx, or throat cavity, has the necessary attributes for
optimum sound reinforcement. How a cavity resonates (reinforces)
a given tone or range of tones is determined by several factors.
These include the size, shape, and nature (material, tension, etc.)
of the cavity walls and the size of its opening as related to the
source of sound (vibrating body) and/or other connecting cavities.
The pharynx, because of its size and the control we can exercise
over it to modify shape and tension, is much more important as a
vocal reinforcer than is the larynx. We modify the length of the
cavity each time we swallow or each time the soft palate is raised
or relaxed. We change the quality of vocal tones through changes in
the tension of the pharyngeal walls. Growths, such as enlarged
adenoids or tonsils, may damp vocal tones and modify loudness as
well as sound quality. When, because of infection or emotional
tension, the pharynx is abnormally tense, the voice quality tends to
become strident and metallic. Higher-pitched tones are reinforced
at the expense of low tones. The result is an unpleasant voice which
lacks adequate loudness and carrying power. When the pharyngeal
tensions are normal, the voice is likely to be rich and mellow—at
least as rich and mellow as the individual throat permits.

Our understanding of the action of the pharynx as a resonator can
be enhanced by a brief review of its structure. If we examine Fig. 5
we will note that the pharynx begins just above the larynx and

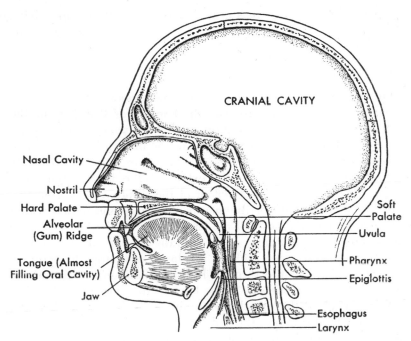

CRANIAL CAVITY

Nasal Cavity

Nostril

Hard Palate

Alveolar (Gum) Ridge

Tongue (Almost Filling Oral Cavity)

Jaw

Soft Palate

Uvula

Pharynx

Epiglottis

Esophagus

Larynx

Fig. 5. Section of Head Showing Principal Resonators and Organs of Articulation.

extends up to the entrance to the nasal cavity. The portion near the larynx—the *laryngopharynx*—is capable of considerable modification. The diameter can be changed for the reinforcement of fundamental tones and overtones produced in the larynx. The tones we identify as the vowels of our language are in part produced as a result of action of the laryngopharynx.

The *oropharynx* is the area just above the laryngopharynx. The oropharynx can pair with either the area below (the laryngopharynx), or above (the nasopharynx), or with the oral cavity (mouth), or with all three together to modify vocal tones. As a result, the oropharynx can act subtly or grossly to reinforce tones and to produce sounds of different qualities.

The *nasopharynx* is the uppermost part of the pharyngeal cavity. This area can in effect be separated from the mouth cavity and connected with the nasal cavity through the act of elevating the soft palate. When the soft palate is lowered, the nasopharynx can be paired with the lower part of the pharynx or with the oral cavity. The nasopharynx is directly involved in the reinforcement of the nasal consonants *n*, *m*, and *ng*.

The Oral Cavity

The mouth, or oral cavity, is the most modifiable of all the resonators of importance for speech. Except for that part of the roof of the mouth which constitutes the hard palate, all the parts which together form or are included in the oral cavity are capable of considerable movement. The lower jaw can move to create an oral cavity limited only by the extent of the jaw's action. The tongue, though attached to the floor of the mouth, can be elevated, flattened, extended out of the mouth, drawn up and curled within the mouth, or can almost fill the closed mouth. The lips can close tight along a straight line, open centrally or laterally to various-sized apertures, or open wide as the lower jaw drops to permit a view of the back of the throat. The soft palate and uvula can be elevated to increase the size of the back of the mouth or relaxed to make the back of the mouth continuous with the throat. Through these many modifications, the oral cavity not only produces the various sounds of our language but reinforces them as well.

The Nasal Cavity

Except when the nasopharynx is coupled with the nasal cavity, we have little direct control over the latter. Unfortunately, the linings of the nasal cavity and the cavity itself are considerably affected not only by physical illnesses involving the upper respiratory tract, but by emotional disturbances as well. The condition of the nose, it appears, is often an excellent indicator of what is wrong with us physically and emotionally. It fills up when we have a cold, when we are allergic, when we are very happy, and when we are acutely sad. When, for any of numerous reasons, the nasal cavity is not free, adequate reinforcement of nasal sounds in particular and nonnasal sounds in general is difficult if not impossible.

The Sinuses

The role of the sinuses as resonators has not been clearly established. We have four pairs of sinuses which drain into the nasal cavity. Most of us become aware of our sinuses when they are infected and drain the products of their infection into our respiratory tract. Short of trying to keep well so that we can avoid the unpleasant condition called sinusitis, there is little we can do about the sinuses to influence voice. Unlike most of the other cavities associated with the respiratory tract, we cannot control or modify the size, shape, or surface tension of the sinuses to affect the reinforcement of vocal tones.

Flexibility of the Vocal Mechanism

Earlier in the chapter we compared the voice mechanism with a wind instrument. In our comparison, the point was made that the vocal mechanism was considerably more flexible and therefore superior to any wind instrument as a producer of sound. The reeds of a wind instrument are fixed in size and degree of tension. Human vocal bands, however, can be changed in length and tension so that a comparatively wide range of pitch is possible. Through muscular contraction our resonating cavities can be modified so that the sound produced by the vocal bands can be variably reinforced. Normally, we can direct our voice through a combination of resonators so that sound emerges either orally or nasally. The manner in which we open and shape our mouths permits us to produce a variety of sounds that are most readily exemplified in the vowels of our language. When the lips, the tongue, and the palate become more actively involved in the modification of sound, articulation, an aspect of sound production peculiar to human beings, becomes possible. This aspect of sound will be considered after our discussion of the attributes of voice and some factors that are related to vocal changes.

✓ CHARACTERISTICS OF SOUND— AND VOICE

All sounds, including those which are vocal, have four fundamental characteristics or attributes. These are *loudness, pitch, duration,* and *quality.* When we respond to a given sound, whether it be the barely audible sound of a dropped pin or a clap of thunder, we are responding to a combination of attributes. The results of our experiences enable us to recognize certain sounds as belonging to the things which make them. So, also, we are usually able to associate voices with the persons who produce them. Tom's voice is a complex of his particular vocal attributes, as are the voices of Harry and Dick. If we know Tom, Dick, and Harry well, and have fair sensitivity to voice, we are likely to identify each by his voice. If we lack sensitivity to vocal differences, or if the sum of Tom's vocal attributes is much like Dick's or Harry's, we may occasionally make mistakes in our identification. Usually, however, one attribute of voice is likely to be different enough so that the sum produces a voice sufficiently individualized to permit reliable identification.

The human voice as a sound producer is not limited to one given pitch, loudness, duration, or even quality. The human mechanism with its subtle and complex neuromuscular controls is capable of a range of variation for each of the sound attributes. A baritone vocalizer may produce sounds that overlap the upper range of the bass and the lower range of the tenor. A female contralto may be able to overlap the high tenor and much of the soprano ranges. No speaker produces tones at a single loudness level. As we speak, we vary the intensity of our sounds from syllable to syllable, word to word, sentence to sentence, and, of course, from occasion to occasion. We vary the duration or time given to utterance as well as the pitch and loudness. We are able to speak rapidly, slowly, or at a moderate rate according to need as well as habit. Although our vocal qualities are relatively limited by the size and shape of our resonating cavities, these attributes can be modified. Some of us are even able to control vocal quality well enough to imitate other speakers. Most of us who do not habitually speak nasally or harshly can do so at will. All things and sound attributes considered, the normal human being can do considerably more with his sound-making apparatus than expert musicians can do with their musical instruments.

CORRELATES OF VOCAL CHANGES

Unless we consciously try to conceal our feelings as we talk, we are likely to reveal them by the way we sound. Voice, when not intentionally controlled, is a barometer of our affective states, our feelings and our moods. This is so essentially because voice is a product of muscular activity which in turn is intimately related to the emotional state of the organism. In a state of heightened emotion, as in anger or fear, we experience muscular tension. The muscles involved in voice production share in the increased total body tension. Thus when vocalization takes place it is on a higher pitch level than normal. Another involuntary change which accompanies heightened emotion is the addition of sugar to the blood stream. This enables us to engage in energetic activity which is sometimes an aspect of heightened emotion. The effect on a voice is to increase its loudness. The over-all effect of heightened feeling on utterance is that the voice becomes high pitched, loud, and rapid.

In contrast, depressed or let-down states are associated with vocal tones which are low in pitch level and relatively weak in loudness. This is so because the muscles of the body as a whole, and the vocal bands in particular, become overrelaxed or hypotonic, and energetic activity is reduced. The over-all effect on utterance is to make it relatively low in pitch and volume and slow in rate.

Voice which is dominated by intellect rather than emotion tends to be moderate in pitch as well as in loudness. This does not imply that intellectual efforts are devoid of feeling. It does imply that intellectual efforts accompanied by vocalization are normally not characterized by the exaggerated range and intensity of feeling which characterize emotional behavior. Under intellectual control, we are able to simulate emotion, to suggest how we would sound if angry, afraid, ecstatically happy, or depressed. When these pretenses are not necessary, we are ourselves. If we are our normal selves, we are usually moderate not only in our behavior in general but in the intensity of our feelings and in the manner in which our voices reveal (or sometimes betray) how we feel and think.

ARTICULATED SOUND

When breath which is set into vibration by the action of the vocal bands reaches the mouth as part of a speech effort, the breath stream is further modified by the action of the tongue, lips, palate, and/or cheeks to produce voiced articulated sound. If the breath stream is not set into vibration, then voiceless articulated sound may be produced. The organs of articulation serve essentially as interrupters or modifiers of the breath stream. The manner and place of interruption result in the production of articulated speech sounds. Each sound has its own characteristics or phonetic attributes. Oral speech consists of combinations of articulated sounds. When these sounds, produced according to the conventions of our language, are appropriately grouped and readily audible, we speak intelligibly.

The Articulators

Most of the articulated sounds of American-English speech are produced as a result of the activity of the lips and parts of the

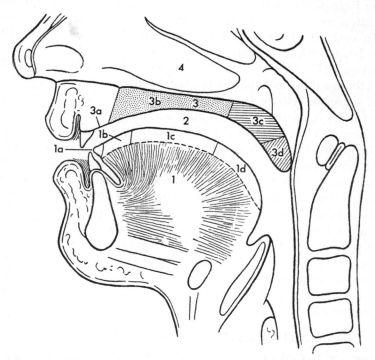

Fig. 6. The Oral Cavity and Its Articulators.

1. Tongue.	*1c. Front of Tongue.*
2. Mouth (oral) Cavity.	*1d. Back of Tongue.*
3. Palate.	*3a. Gum or Alveolar Ridge.*
4. Nasal Cavity.	*3b. Hard Palate.*
1a. Tongue Tip.	*3c. Soft Palate.*
1b. Blade of Tongue.	*3d. Uvula.*

tongue. These mobile articulators assume positions or make contact with fixed or relatively fixed parts of the upper jaw and the roof of the mouth (see Fig. 6).

The lips and teeth enclose the buccal (oral) or mouth cavity. The tongue lies within and almost completely fills the oral cavity. From the point of view of articulatory action the tongue may be divided into the following parts: the anterior portion or tongue tip, the blade, the mid-tongue, and the back. The roof of the mouth may be divided into the gum ridge or alveolar process (directly behind the upper teeth), the hard palate, the soft palate (velum), and the uvula.

The larynx also serves an articulatory function because the presence or absence of vocalization distinguishes many pairs of sounds such as *b* and *p* and *z* and *s*. The sound *h* is produced as a result of a degree of contraction within the larynx sufficient to produce audible friction.

Details as to the manner in which the articulators function to produce the different sounds of our language will be considered in Chapter 10. At the present time let us consider briefly the controlling mechanism through which man is enabled to make vocal noises, to modify these noises into distinguishable sounds and intelligible words, to use these words to express his feelings, his wishes, and his needs, and to become a member of a symbol-producing and symbol-responding culture.

THE NERVOUS SYSTEM

The Cerebrum

Many animals produce vocal noises, but only man can make sounds that make sense. We speak because we are able to integrate organs that biologically serve the functions of digestion and respiration for the nonbiological purpose of producing oral symbols. The achievement of speech is neurologically related to the development of the cerebrum in man. Except for the cerebrum of the brain, the nervous system of the human being is surprisingly like that of a dog and almost completely like that of an ape. The cerebrum is significantly different in man. It is larger in proportion to the nervous system as a whole than it is in animals, and it includes a bulge-like frontal area of greater size than that found in animals with otherwise comparable nervous systems. The brain is a coordinator and integrator of activity. In the brain, impulses set up by sounds and movements which are received by the ear, the eye, or other sense organs, are translated into images or into words which have significance and meaning.

The Cerebral Cortex

The gray outer covering of the brain is especially involved in the function of speech. The cortex contains ten billion or more nerve cells. Parts of the cortex have specialized functions which are involved in the peculiarly human ability to produce and understand oral (speech) or written symbols. These areas are indicated in Fig. 7. The marked areas include those for *hearing, seeing,* and *speech movement.* These areas are significant because of their evident capacity to evaluate specialized experiences *for the brain as*

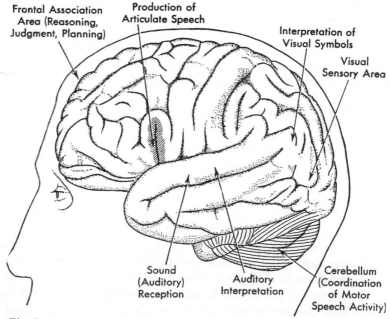

Fig. 7. *The Cerebral Cortex and Cerebellum and Some "Specialized" Areas Related to Speech.*

a whole. For example, the auditory area in the lower middle part of the brain evaluates sounds so that noises may be interpreted as *barks, wind in the trees,* or *words.* Similarly, the area in the back part of the brain (the occipital lobe) interprets impulses coming from the eye. Through this area we are able to recognize and identify objects we see and to read and so to make sense out of markings called letters and words.

The Central Nervous System As a Whole

In addition to the cerebrum, there are other parts of the central nervous system which are essentially involved in the production of speech. The parts are represented in Fig. 8. Briefly stated, the other parts serve the following functions in the integrated speech act.

The *cerebellum,* or little brain, receives impulses from higher brain centers. The impulses are sorted, arranged, and correlated so that the coordinated and precise muscular activity needed for speech becomes possible. Damage to the cerebellum may seriously impair the flow and control of coordinated speech activity. Damage of this sort is found in many cases of cerebral palsy.

The *medulla* contains the center essential for respiration, and damage to it may impair normal breathing. Bulbar polio involves such damage, and consequently the need for a mechanical respirator in cases of this disease should be clear.

The *bulb,* the *spinal cord,* and the nerves emanating from them control the muscles involved in the coordinated act of speaking. The *phrenic nerve* which emerges from the spinal cord in the region of the neck extends to the diaphragm. The phrenic nerve supplies the impulse which causes the diaphragm to contract and so brings about inhalation in breathing.

Other nerves which initiate movements involved in speech are the trigeminal (face and jaw muscles), the glossopharyngeal (tongue and pharynx), the recurrent laryngeal (larynx), and the glossal (tongue).

In the absence of pathology, the central nervous system, dominated by the cerebral cortex, controls the impulses involved in the act of speaking. Through this system, we are able to be articulate about our impressions, to reveal what we think and how we feel. Sometimes, if it suits our purpose, we conceal rather than reveal

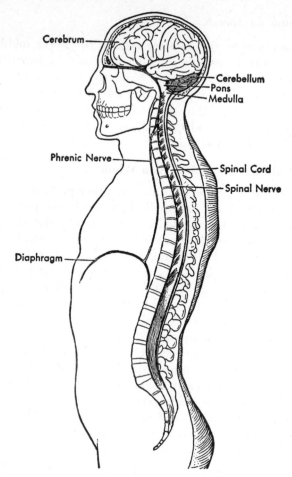

Fig. 8. The Central Nervous System in Relation to Speech.

The Cerebrum. Normal meaningful speech is dependent upon the integrative activity of the cortex of the cerebrum.

The Cerebellum "sorts and arranges" muscular impulses that come to it from higher brain centers. Impulses are here correlated so that precise muscular activity such as is needed for speech becomes possible.

The Pons is a bridge of nerve fibers between the cerebral cortex and the medulla.

The Medulla contains the respiratory and other vital reflex centers.

The Spinal Cord and its nerves control the respiratory muscles.

The Phrenic Nerve emerges from the spinal cord in the neck region and extends to the diaphragm. It supplies the impulses which cause the diaphragm to contract in breathing.

either our feelings, our thoughts, or both. The degree of expertness with which we use our speech apparatus varies considerably from person to person. All of us, however, with unimpaired physical mechanisms and with normal personalities, should be capable of speaking adequately. How to make the most of our mechanisms so that we fully utilize our capabilities to vocalize and articulate with ease and intelligibility will be considered in the chapters which follow.

3. Breathing for Effective Vocalization

Physicians specializing in the treatment of the throat, and those few who treat vocal disorders as well as diseases of the throat, recognize that most vocal disorders are a result of the use of any one or a combination of *inappropriate force, wrong pitch,* and *incorrect breathing.**

Although our experience does not show that most speakers necessarily breath incorrectly, use force inappropriately, or pitch their voices at wrong levels, a knowledge of what can be done to improve voice may be helpful to all of us. Certainly the speaker who wants a better than ordinary voice or who aspires or needs to use voice as an instrument for his vocation or profession has an obligation to himself as well as to his listeners to know what students in the field of voice recommend as to the use of force, pitch, and breathing. We shall begin with a consideration of breathing.

BREATHING FOR VOICE PRODUCTION

Earlier, in our discussion of the mechanism for speech, we pointed out that breathing for speech calls for a modification of the normal respiratory cycle so that (1) the inspiration-expiration ratio

* For a discussion of this viewpoint by a physician, see F. S. Brodnitz, *Keep Your Voice Healthy,* New York, Harper & Brothers, 1953, Ch. XII.

is changed to provide a much longer period of exhalation than of inspiration and (2) a steady stream of air is initiated and controlled by the speaker to insure good tone. These modifications, we have found, are usually achieved most easily by the type of breathing which emphasizes abdominal activity.

At the outset, we would like to point out that good breathing for vocalization is by no means synonymous with deep breathing. Many good speakers use no more breath for vigorous speaking, or public speaking, than they do for conversational speech. Seldom is it necessary for any person to employ more than one-fifth of his breath capacity for any vocal effort.

Abdominal Breathing

If we observe the breathing of a person or an animal who is sleeping on his back or side, we should be able to note that during inhalation the abdominal area moves upward or forward while during exhalation the abdominal area recedes. Figure 4, p. 21, visualizes what we can see in the way of abdominal activity as well as what we cannot see in the way of diaphragmatic activity for breathing which emphasizes abdominal control.

The essential point for us to appreciate is that in breathing which is characterized by action of the abdominal muscles, the muscles of the abdomen relax in inhalation and contract in exhalation. When we learn how to contract or pull in the abdominal walls consciously, and how much and how fast to control such contraction, breathing for speech becomes *voluntary if needed*. If the reader is now exercising such control unconsciously, the suggested exercises which follow are not particularly important for him. If he is not, or if he finds that he cannot easily sustain a hum or a gentle whisper for from twenty to thirty seconds, then the exercises should be followed. These exercises are designed to create awareness and conscious control of abdominal action in breathing.

Exercises for Control of Abdominal Action in Breathing

1. Lie on a couch or bed with a firm mattress. Spread your hands on the abdominal area immediately below the ribs so that the thumbs point to the rear and the fingers point forward. Inhale for normal, nonspeech breathing. Your hands should rise during inhala-

tion and fall with the abdomen during exhalation. If the action is reversed, then the breathing is incorrect and should be changed to bring about the suggested activity. Repeat until the suggested action is accomplished easily. Be sure that you have on no tight belt or clothing while doing this and the following exercises.

2. Sit in a relaxed position in a comfortable chair with a firm seat. Your feet should be flat on the floor. Place your hands as in exercise (1). Now the abdominal walls should push forward on inhalation and pull in on exhalation.

3. Repeat as in exercise (2). Then inhale gently for about five seconds and exhale slowly, sustaining the exhalation for ten seconds. If you find yourself out of breath before the end of the ten-second period, then you have probably exhaled too quickly. Try the exercise again, intentionally slowing down the exhalation.

4. Inhale fully and then breathe out slowly and completely. Your hands should still be following the movement of the abdominal walls. Repeat, but this time press gently but firmly with your hands to force the expulsion of air from your lungs. Repeat, counting to yourself while exhaling. At this point you should be able to count for about thirty seconds before becoming uncomfortable.

5. Repeat, but this time vocalize a clear *ah* while exhaling. *Start your vocalization the moment you begin to exhale.* Stop before becoming uncomfortable. Repeat, vocalizing a sustained *hum* while exhaling. The *ah* and *hum* should be sustained longer than a nonvocalized exhalation.

6. Inhale deeply and then count out evenly and slowly until you feel the need for a second breath. Maintain even pitch and loudness levels. Repeat, but this time keep your hands at your sides and concentrate on a gradual pulling in of the abdominal wall during the counting. You should be able to count to at least twenty on a sustained exhalation. In any event, continue to practice until a count of at least fifteen is attained. With continued practice, a count of twenty to thirty (at the rate of two numbers per second) should become possible after a normal inhalation and a full thirty-second count after a deep inhalation.

7. With hands at your sides, repeat the above exercise on two successive breaths. Be certain that you do not exhale to a point of discomfort. Nor should you inhale so deeply that some air has to be exhaled for the sake of comfort.

8. Repeat, reciting the alphabet instead of counting. Avoid wasting breath between utterance of the letters. Note how far you are able to go on a single normal breath and on a single deep breath.

9. Repeat, whispering the alphabet. Note the letter you reached before requiring a second breath. Depending upon the degree of whisper, this might be only a third or a half of the number of letters of your vocalized effort. This is normal. A whisper is wasteful of breath.

10. Count, with vocalization, in groups of three. Avoid exhalation during pauses. Did you come close to the number you reached in counting without grouping? If you did not, then you probably exhaled between groups of numbers. Try it again until the two counts are about even.

11. Repeat exercise (10), using the alphabet instead of counting.

12. Recite the months of the year with pauses after March, June, and September. You should have no difficulty reciting all twelve months even with "seasonal" pauses.

13. Try to say each of the following sentences on a single breath.

   a. Let all who enter here beware!
   b. The road is long that has no turning.
   c. Alone, alone, all, all alone.
   d. One-two, one-two, forward march.

14. If you had no difficulty with the single sentences, then try uttering these longer sentences and complete each on a single, sustained breath. Do not, however, force the expulsion of air beyond a point of comfort.

   a. He that falls in love with himself will have no rivals.
      BENJAMIN FRANKLIN

   b. Plato held that rhetoric was the art of ruling the minds of men.

   c. Her blue eyes sought the west afar,
      For lovers love the western star.
      SIR WALTER SCOTT
      —The Lay of the Last Minstrel

d. For he who fights and runs away
   May live to fight another day;
   OLIVER GOLDSMITH
   —*The Art of Poetry*

e. Upon what meat doth this our Caesar feed,
   That he is grown so great?
   WILLIAM SHAKESPEARE—*Julius Caesar*

f. The day is cold, and dark, and dreary;
   It rains, and the wind is never weary;
   HENRY WADSWORTH LONGFELLOW
   —*The Rainy Day*

The following exercises involve the use of speech sounds which have a whispered quality. They are normally more wasteful of breath than most of the previous exercises. They are, however, important in establishing breath control because much of what we say includes nonvocalized (voiceless) sounds as well as those which have a definite whispered or fricative quality.

Exercises for Establishing Breath Control

1. Inhale normally and then release the breath while producing the sound *s*. Be sure the sound is evenly maintained. Try to sustain the *s* for ten seconds. Repeat with the sound *sh*, then *th* as in *think*, and *f* as in *fall*.

2. Inhale deeply, but avoid discomfort. Repeat exercise (1). Compare these efforts with the length of time for a sustained *m* or *ah*. You are not likely to sustain any of these breathy sounds as long as *m* or *ah*, but you should come fairly close.

3. Try saying each of the following sentences on a single breath. If you do not succeed the first time, try a deeper inhalation on successive trials. Do not intentionally whisper.

a. Harry had heroic inclinations.
b. Fido, his friendly dog, shared Harry's inclinations.
c. Heaven helps those who help themselves.
d. What is truth for most of us is not truth for all of us.

   e. The crisp and crackly leaves fell from the tree.
   f. Listen in respectful silence for the wisdom you may hear.
   g. The rushing stream washed the shrubbery along with it.
   h. Some critics hold that plays attributed to Shakespeare
      were really written by Marlowe.

4. If you have been successful with all of the sentences, then try these couplets on a single breath. If you pause at the end of the line, try not to exhale at the pause.

> a. Double, double, toil and trouble;
>   Fire burn and cauldron bubble.
>   WILLIAM SHAKESPEARE—*Macbeth*

> b. My only books
>   Were women's looks,
>   And folly's all they've taught me.
>   THOMAS MOORE
> —*The Time I've Lost in Wooing*

> c. Where'er I wander, boast of this I can,
>   Though banished, yet a trueborn English man.
>   WILLIAM SHAKESPEARE—*Richard II*

> d. Was this the face that launch'd a thousand ships,
>   And burnt the topless tower of Ilium?
>   CHRISTOPHER MARLOWE—*Faustus*

> e. I always voted at my party's call,
>   And I never thought of thinking for myself at all.
>   W. S. GILBERT—*H. M. S. Pinafore*

Clavicular Breathing

Older readers, or readers who have had older teachers, may have been exposed to a type of breathing which emphasized movement of the upper part of the rib cage and the clavicles. It is difficult now to understand the rationale of this type of breathing for speech. If there was a rationale, it was somehow based on the belief that by expanding the least expandable part of the thoracic cavity, more space for air and, with deep breathing, more air could be brought into the lungs. With the additional hard-to-get quantity of air, better physical hygiene in general and better voice in particular were then supposed to be readily achieved. Now, with our understanding that it is not the amount of breath but the control of the breath stream which is important, any technique which emphasizes quantity of air is not held in high regard. Even if quantity of air were important, it could be more easily increased through deep breathing with abdominal and lower rib-cage activity than with clavicular breathing which, at best, merely elevates the chest as a whole. In fact, clavicular breathing tends to be shallow rather than deep and requires more frequent inhalation than does abdominal breathing. Beyond this, clavicular breathing has definite disadvantages in that it has been found to be associated with a marked tendency of the muscles of the larynx and throat to become too tense for proper vocalization and reinforcement of tone.

To check on any tendency toward clavicular breathing, stand before a full-length mirror and breathe in deeply. Relax, then exhale fully. Repeat twice. Note, and correct, any tendency of the shoulders to be appreciably elevated or of the chest as a whole to be raised. Abdominal breathing, which we recommend, would call for little or no movement of the shoulders or upper chest. Movement, if it is to be discerned, would be of the lower chest and abdominal areas. Usually this will require a profile rather than a full-front view.

An added check, as well as an exercise to correct the tendency toward clavicular breathing, is the following: Place your hands on your chest with your fingers spread and the thumbs pointing toward the collarbone. Take a deep breath, then say the days of the week. Observe, and, if necessary, use the pressure of your hands to prevent any appreciable upward movement of the upper chest and shoulders. For variety, the exercise might be done with counting from one through ten or reciting the alphabet in sequences from *a* through *l* and *m* through *z*. If upper chest movement is inhibited, the normal compensatory action will bring about the desired movement of the abdominal and the lower chest muscles. Be certain that the movement is forward during inhalation and inward during exhalation.

Breathing and Phrasing

In the exercises to establish abdominal breathing and the awareness of breath control, our emphasis was on sustaining a sound, a series of words, or a sentence on a single breath. For ordinary conversational speech, and for most public speaking purposes, length of uninterrupted utterance is not as important as the interruption of a unit of thought because of the need for additional breath. The occasions are infrequent when a speaker will need to utter more than twelve to fifteen syllables on a single breath. The speaker must learn to anticipate inhalation and to stop at an appropriate point to inhale. If he learns this, he will avoid having to stop at an inappropriate point because he cannot continue speaking without another breath. The appropriate or natural stopping places are at the ends of units of thought, *between phrases or sentences.* Unless the speaker is reading or reciting verse with regular meter, the units of thought are likely to be of varying lengths. Breathing must therefore be adjusted to anticipate needs. For example, if the speaker cannot comfortably quote Emerson on a single breath to the effect that "His heart was as great as the world, but there was no room in it to hold the memory of a wrong," he has a choice of at least two stopping places. He may, without doing violence to the thought, stop at the places indicated by the vertical lines: "His heart was as great as the world, || but there was no room in it || to hold the memory of a wrong." We might note, incidentally, that some but not all units of thought are marked off for us by punctuation. Some units of thought have no punctuation marks. The reader must, on the basis of meaning, decide where and whether to phrase. The good vocal phraser uses punctuation as a guide but is not a slave to it.

A speaker with a fair breath capacity and good breath control might easily go as far as the second vertical line before stopping for a breath. Unless he feels that he is equal to the entire sentence, however, he should not try to go beyond the second vertical line because to do so would mean interrupting a unit of thought in order to inhale.

In exercises (1)–(5) immediately following, possible stops for inhalation are indicated by vertical lines. In terms of your own breath capacity, mark off the places at which you plan to inhale. Inhale briefly at these places so that there is no suggestion of awkward pausing. Try to inhale as infrequently as possible so that the reading does not become jerky. Maintain abdominal control of breathing. If necessary, place your hands on the abdominal wall to feel the pushing away at the inhalations and the pulling in at the exhalations while reading aloud.

Exercises for Abdominal Breathing and Phrasing

1. Breathe in as you would for inhalation during casual conversation, then count at the rate of two numbers per second, pausing, and if necessary inhaling, at the marked places.

1-2-3-4-5-6-7-8-9-10-11 || 12-13-14-15-16-17-18-19-20-21

The first grouping should have been produced easily on a single breath; the second would be somewhat more difficult because of the additional syllables.

2. Repeat as above, but this time pause and renew your breath supply after fourteen; then count from fifteen through twenty-one.

3. Count as long as you can on a single deep breath, but avoid becoming uncomfortable either because of too deep an inhalation or too exhaustive an exhalation. Note the point at which you pause for breath. Then count again, but this time intentionally pause and inhale two numbers in the sequence earlier than you had to pause the first time. Count again to the same number.

4. Recite the alphabet, pausing, and inhaling if necessary, only at the marked places. Be sure to pause if you do not need to inhale.

a-b-c-d-e-f-g-h || i-j-k-l-m-n-o-p-q || r-s-t-u-v-w-x-y-z

Were you able to go beyond the first group? With practice, the entire alphabet should be recited easily after a single, moderate inhalation.

5. Read the following sentences aloud, pausing, and breathing if necessary, at the marked places. In addition to the initial breath, it should not be necessary to inhale more than once per sentence.

a. The thought is attributed to Plato || that a boy || of all wild beasts || is the most difficult || to manage.

b. A bore has been defined || as a person who talks || when you wish him to listen.

c. Mark Twain advised || that there are two times in a man's life || when he should not speculate. || When he can't afford it || and when he can.

6. In the following exercises, read the material aloud to determine where you need to stop for breath. Pause to indicate phrasing, but inhale only when you cannot go on comfortably to the next phrase on the remaining breath.

a. Lord Chesterfield advised "Never hold any one by the button or the hand in order to be heard out; for if people are unwilling to hear you, you had better hold your tongue than them."

b. "What a blessed thing it is," said Holmes, "that nature, when she invented, manufactured and patented her authors, contrived to make critics out of the chips that were left!"

c. Oscar Wilde, who helped to make cynicism an English fashion, held that though education was an admirable thing it was well to remember from time to time that nothing that was worth knowing could really be taught. Perhaps what Wilde really meant was that what is worth knowing is what is left after the specifics we have been taught have been forgotten.

Avoiding Waste of Breath

If while executing the exercises earlier in the chapter the reader had difficulty in counting up to fifteen on a single breath, it may have been that too much breath was wasted in the vocal effort. The most likely cause of wasted breath is a failure to bring the vocal bands close enough together to prevent leakage of air during vocalized speech efforts. Whispered or semiwhispered speech is necessarily wasteful of breath because then the vocal bands are kept fully or partially open. This may be noted in an examination of Fig. 9 which shows the positions of the voice bands in quiet breathing, whispering, and vocalized speaking. In order to overcome breathiness, it will help first to become aware of a speech effort which, by nature of the sounds employed, is necessarily breathy. The

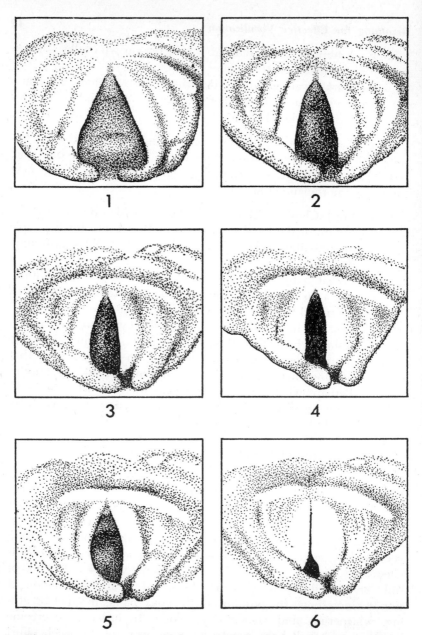

Fig. 9. *Diagrams Based on High Speed Photos Showing Changes in Positions of Vocal Bands from Quiet Breathing (1, 2), to Whispering (3, 4, 5), to Vocalization (6).*

46

following sentences contain a number of voiceless fricative and plosive sounds which are normally and appropriately characterized by a breathy quality. Hold your hand, palm turned in, about six inches in front of your mouth, as you say:

1. Pots and pans came flying through the open door.
2. Sheila and Tom took a short stroll through the forest.
3. The spray froze as it spattered over the hull of the ship.

In contrast with the above sentences, the following contain only voiced sounds and few which have a plosive quality. Say the following, again holding your hand in front of your mouth to feel the difference in breathiness.

1. Leon ran a mile.
2. We rowed down the river.
3. The old man was ill.

The following sentences contain a few sounds which are normally breathy. Try to say them with as little waste of breath as possible. Shorten all *f, v, th, s, z,* and *sh* sounds to reduce the length of these fricative-breath consonants. With good breath control, each sentence should be said on a single inhalation.

1. The meaning of "no news is good news" is not always clear.
2. Sam and Lillian walked hand in hand along the lake.
3. The siren warned that a house was on fire.
4. The ship set out to sea despite the storm.

Excessive breathiness may be a result of carrying over the aspirate quality of a sound to the succeeding vowel. This effect may be avoided, or reduced, by taking care not to prolong the aspirate sounds and to emphasize the full vocalization of the vowels and diphthongs. Especial caution is necessary when the initial sound is an *h* as it is a particularly breath-consuming sound. With these thoughts in mind, try to say the following pairs of words so that there is no more aspiration on the vowel or diphthong of the second word of the pair than there is on the first. There should, of course, be no aspirate quality in the first word of each pair.

I	high	out	bout
ale	hale	are	tar
oar	four	eel	wheel
air	hair	old	hold
awe	saw	ease	cheese
ire	tire	ate	hate
ear	tier	ohm	home
at	that	am	cam
am	tam	awl	shawl

In each of the following sentences emphasize the production of the vowel or diphthong sounds. Despite the temptation provided by initial aspirate sounds, avoid any carry-over of breathiness to the succeeding sounds.

1. Hail, hail, the gang's all here!
2. A policeman's life is not a happy one.
3. All are not born kittens which purr like cats.
4. He honked his horn as he sped down the street.
5. Harry hiked three miles up the hill.
6. Home came the sailor, home from the sea.
7. The poet Goethe held that he is happiest, be he king or peasant, who finds peace in his home.
8. George Eliot believed that because a woman's hopes are woven of sunbeams, a shadow can quickly annihilate her hopes.
9. He who hopes against hope is hoping still.
10. A wife can be most comfortable with a husband who is taller, stronger, heavier, homelier, and of course older than she.
11. Paul Bunyan characterized the hypocrite as one who is a saint abroad and a devil at home.
12. Some of the envious critics of Ben Franklin characterized the creator of Poor Richard as a shabby, penny-pinching soul.

Affected or Imitative Breathiness

Many persons vocalize with a breathy quality out of choice. The choice is not always a conscious one. Frequently it had its beginning in imitation born of admiration of a popular figure. Often the figure is a performer, a star of radio, screen, and television. So called "sultry-voiced" singers have influenced the vocal efforts of many high school and college adolescents who wanted to be sultry-voiced whether or not they could sing. Many young children have husky and breathy voices because of unconscious imitation of their mothers, and a few, perhaps, of their fathers. Unfortunately, excessive breathiness frequently has an adverse affect on the laryngeal mechanism as well as on the ability of the speaker to maintain as long a series of phrases or sentences as the nonbreathy speaker. The over-all result is a vocal habit which loses its attractiveness in the postadolescent period. The breathy vocalizer then finds himself, or more frequently, herself, a fatigued speaker, and occasionally one with thickened vocal bands. If this becomes the case, then considerable vocal reeducation is in order. Good voice production is achieved with good breath control. With such control, clear rather than breathy quality should be established throughout the normal pitch range. Clear tones are produced with a minimum use of air for a maximum vocal effort.

The following exercises are intended as a general review opportunity for the practice of breath control. In doing them, make certain (1) that there is no evidence of clavicular breathing; (2) that abdominal activity and lower chest activity characterize the breathing for vocalization; (3) that inhalations are correlated with units of meaning; and (4) that there is no waste of breath either at pauses for phrasing when there is no need for inhalation, or because of excessive aspiration on specific speech sounds, or as a characteristic of the vocal effort as a whole.

Exercises for Practice of Breath Control

1. A rainbow in the morning
   Is the Shepherd's warning;
   But a rainbow at night
   Is the Shepherd's delight.
   Old Weather Rhyme

2. Bulwer-Lytton advised: "In science, read by preference, the newest works; in literature, the oldest. The classic literature is always modern."

3. Clarence S. Darrow, a famous trial lawyer, never gave up fighting for causes he considered deserving. Yet he did not always ex-

pect to win. Darrow believed it proper for a man of twenty to be full of fight and hope, to want to reform the world. When the man becomes seventy, he should still want to reform the world, but he should also know that he can't.

4. In one of his famous *Sun Dial* columns, the journalist Don Marquis expressed his belief that "Publishing a volume of verse is like dropping a rose petal down the Grand Canyon and waiting for the echo."

5. A wise, but unfortunately anonymous man observed of men and the weather in general that:

> As a rule man is a fool,
> When it's hot he wants it cool,
> When it's cool he wants it hot,
> Always wanting what is not.

> 6. O woman! in our hour of ease,
> Uncertain, coy, and hard to please,
> And variable as the shade
> By the light quivering aspen made;
> When pain and anguish wring the brow,
> A ministering angel thou!
>
> SIR WALTER SCOTT—*Marmion*

4 • Production of Clear Tones

Voice, we now realize, is a product of integrated muscular activity. The combination of tendinous tissue and muscles which constitute the vocal bands is set into vibration as a result of integrated activity of the muscles of respiration and those controlling laryngeal action. When the integration is right and the approximated vocal bands are brought together closely enough so that there is sufficient resistance to the column of air being forced up from the lungs, voice is produced. When the vocal bands are not approximated so that there is adequate resistance to the column of air, then the result is either a semivocalized effort or unvocalized breathing, depending upon the degree of approximation (see Fig. 9, page 45). Our immediate concern will be to establish the concept and technique for the initiation of good, clear tones.

Good tones are free from the effects of tension or strain. Good tones are initiated with ease, appropriately reinforced by the resonating cavities, and sustained with ease. Tonal (vocal) impurities result most frequently from tensions of the muscles of the throat and neck that interfere with the free action of the muscles of the larynx, and so of the vocal bands. Tonal impurities may arise indirectly from incorrect breathing habits which, we recall, may be

51

associated with laryngeal tension. Tonal impurities may also be caused by inappropriate resonance.

In the absence of any structural defect of the voice-producing mechanism, a defect of hearing that makes vocal monitoring difficult, or any emotional disturbance associated with either excessive or inadequate muscular tonicity, reasonably good vocal tones should be possible for all speakers. Some speakers, we realize, will have mechanisms whose parts are so well combined that excellent voices are theirs without effort or training. Others may not be so fortunate in the structure of their vocal mechanisms. For them, effort and training are necessary to make the most of their vocal instruments. Our immediate concern will be to suggest how we can use what we have so that, without too much effort, most of us will be able to initiate and sustain good vocal tones.

Initiation of Tone

To initiate a good tone, the vocal mechanism must be *ready for vocalization.* Readiness implies anticipation and preparation. For voice production, this means that the vocal bands must be aligned (approximated) a moment before the column of air is forced up from the lungs to set them into action. If the column of air precedes the approximation of the vocal bands, then the vocal product will begin with a whisper or an unvocalized breath. The vocal bands must be tense enough to set up resistance to the column of air, but not so tense as to be fully successful in their resistance. With excessive tension (hypertension), the vocal bands may not be able to vibrate. With a lack of sufficient tension (hypotension), vibration may take place, but with an accompanying air leakage or breathiness.* What is needed is sufficient tension to require a forceful, sustained column of air to set and maintain the vocal bands in action. In brief, the resistance should be just under the amount required to be successful. Although voice can be produced as the laryngeal tensions become excessive, the vocal tones become strained and generally unpleasant.

The exercises that follow will help to establish awareness of *proper laryngeal tension* as well as *readiness for vocalization.*

* Review the discussion in the chapter on breathing for avoidance of breathiness (pages 45–50).

Exercises for Developing Readiness to Vocalize

1. Contract the throat muscles as you would to swallow some food or water. Note the sensation of the contracted muscles. Now open your mouth as if to produce a gentle *ah* sound. Do your throat muscles feel more or less tense than they did when you pretended to swallow? Unless they are more relaxed than for swallowing, they are likely to be too tense for the initiation of a good tone. Note the sensation of the contracted muscles so that you will know what to avoid. Be sure that your *ah* production is gentle.

2. *Yawn gently* with your mouth half open. Breathe in and out through your mouth. Note the feeling of air in the back of the throat. Now swallow, and contrast the easy breathing sensations with those in swallowing. If the yawning is gentle and the breathing easy, your throat muscles should be relaxed. This is the state of muscle tension (tonus) needed for vocalization.

3. Sit comfortably in a chair with your feet flat on the floor. Permit your head to drop to your chest as if your head were a dead weight. Yawn gently and then breathe in and out three or four times through your mouth. Note the sensation. Now swallow, and again contrast the tonus of the throat muscles in swallowing with that in gentle yawning. Repeat the gentle yawning and easy mouth breathing until the sensation of relaxed throat muscles is fixed in your mind.

4. Stand erect but at ease. Repeat exercise (3) in a standing position.

5. In a standing position, with throat muscles relaxed, say the *vowels* only of the following words, each to a slow count of from one to three: *alms, all, Alps, ooze, eel.* Now vocalize from one vowel to the next without interruption. You should be able to note somewhat increased throat and laryngeal tension for the vowels of *ooze* and *eel* compared with those for *alms, all,* and *Alps.* This is proper if the different vowel values are to be produced. Try, however, to avoid excessive tension.

6. Get ready to say *all* but do not produce any sound until your mouth is open and shaped for the vowel of *all.* Then produce the word. Now, by contrast, intentionally begin vocalizing *before your mouth is open* and you are set to articulate the word *all.* Did you

hear or feel a difference? Unless your vocal habits are so good that you could not follow a direction to do the wrong thing, the first effort should have been clearer and easier than the second. The second effort might have been characterized by initial tension, and possibly by a "click" in the larynx.

7. Repeat the first half of exercise (1) with three to four successive utterances of the words *one, my, ah,* and *eel.* For each word, produce the successive utterance without intervening pauses. Check for initial tension or laryngeal click at the initiation of the effort. If your timing is right and you are prepared to vocalize before you set your vocal folds into vibration, the tone should be clear.

8. Open your mouth as though for a gentle yawn, but instead of yawning say *ha, how, ho, ha, haw, ho.* Next, try the sentence *Who am I?* These efforts should begin with some breathiness for the words which begin with an *h* sound, but the breath should not be carried over to the vowel which follows. Be sure that you maintain a relaxed throat throughout the exercise.

9. With a relaxed throat, count from one to ten, emphasizing activity of the lips and tongue. Try to become aware of oral activity in the *front of your mouth.* Now, count from one to twenty. Do not force your exhalation beyond a point of comfort. If you note any tendency for the throat muscles to tighten, it may be because you are attempting too much speech on a single exhalation. Pause to inhale before tension sets in.

10. Say the alphabet while emphasizing activity in the front of the mouth. Do not attempt to go beyond the letter *k* on your first attempt. On successive attempts go as far as you can in the alphabet up to the point of laryngeal or throat tension. You may note a feeling of lip fatigue. If so, it is likely that you do not habitually articulate with sufficient activity at the front of the mouth. With practice, the feeling of fatigue should disappear.

11. Read the following materials aloud, always maintaining a relaxed throat. Make certain that you are *set for vocalization* before you begin to speak. If at any time your throat muscles become tense, or you become aware of laryngeal tension, return to exercises (1)–(8).

    a. Albert and Ann strolled down the lane.
    b. I am not inclined to argue established facts.

c. All that glitters is not gold.
d. My weariness is not because of work.
e. The snow fell softly in the quiet air.

f. Sweet day, so cool, so calm, so bright!
The bridal of the earth and sky—
The dew shall weep thy fall tonight;
For thou must die.
GEORGE HERBERT—*Virtue*

g. Sweet Auburn! Loveliest village of
the plain,
Where health and plenty cheered the
laboring swain,
Where smiling Spring its earliest visit paid,
And parting summer's lingering blooms
delayed;
OLIVER GOLDSMITH—*The Deserted Village*

h. The ring is on my hand
And the wreath is on my brow;
Satins and jewels grand
Are all at my command
And many a rood of land
And I am happy now.
EDGAR ALLAN POE
—*Bridal Ballad*

i. Shall I, wasting in despair,
Die because a woman's fair?
Or make pale my cheeks with care
'Cause another's rosy are?

Be she fairer than the day,
Or the flow'ry meads in May!
If she think not well of me,
What care I how fair she be?
GEORGE WITHER
—*The Lover's Resolution*

Avoidance of the "Glottal Attack"

Several times in our discussion and in the exercises for the proper initiation of clear tones, we referred to vocalization characterized by a throat click. Vocalization produced with an overtense larynx is frequently accompanied by a glottal (laryngeal) click, stop, or shock. The glottal shock results from an attempt to start vocalization when the larynx in general and the vocal bands in particular are hypertense. The result of the hypertension is that more than a normal amount of energy is needed for the breath column to set the vocal bands into sustained action to produce voice. Unless the vocal bands are somewhat relaxed, vocal efforts are likely to be accompanied by an initial click or single, cough-like blast when the breath column succeeds in getting through between the vocal bands. Except when glottalization is an accepted characteristic of the speech of a national or cultural group—as it is among the Scots—voice accompanied by glottal clicks strongly suggests that the speaker's throat and larynx are hypertense and under strain. Added evidence of this condition is the presence of a high, narrow pitch range.

Glottal attacks are most likely to occur at the beginning of sentences or phrases with initial vowels. Some speakers, however, glottalize on almost all initial voiced sounds. The over-all result tends to be detrimental to the speaker and unpleasant to listeners for whom glottalization is not an accepted speech characteristic.

For readers who are still uncertain about their tendency to initiate vocalization with a glottal attack, the following added explanation should illustrate what should generally be avoided. A glottal stop noise is normally and appropriately produced when you clear your throat with a light, unvocalized cough. You can feel this stroke, click, or flapping of the vocal bands by gently placing your thumb and index finger just below the Adam's apple as you cough. If voice is added to the light cough, the result is likely to be the production of an *ugh* sound.

The exercises to establish proper laryngeal tension, readiness for vocalization, and easy initiation of tones should be reviewed by readers who have a tendency to initiate voice with a glottal attack. In addition, the following exercises should be of help.

Exercises for Overcoming Glottal Attack

1. Produce the sound *aw* as in *awful* with intentional breathiness (semiwhisper). Repeat, prolonging the *aw* for the equivalent of a count of six. Decrease the breathiness so that on the final two counts the *aw* is fully vocalized. Maintain a relaxed throat so that there is neither glottal initiation nor tension as vocalization increases.

2. Repeat exercise (1), using the vowels of *alms, ooze, ohms,* and *ease.* Be especially careful that on the last vowel there is no excessive strain or glottal shock.

3. Try to say each of the following words without initial glottalization. If you note a glottal attack, prefix a lengthened *h* before each of the words, and move from the *h* to the word without increasing the laryngeal tension and without glottalization.

arm	ohm	ale	eat
asp	own	at	am
all	ill	ace	and

4. Repeat exercise (3), prefixing the sound *m* if there is any tendency to a glottal attack. Repeat with an initial *n*.

5. Try each of the following sentences, being especially careful to avoid glottalization on the initial vowels. Words which begin with vowels *within a phrase* should be pronounced as though they were actually linked or blended to the last sound of the preceding word. The sounds which are most likely to be glottalized are in italics.

   a. On *occasion* each man must construct his *own island.*
   b. *Ideals* cannot *always* be shared.
   c. A man may be *alone even in* a crowd.
   d. *Attitudes* cannot *always* be taught, *even* to those who *are attentive.*
   e. An *electric eel is* not *in* need *of* guile.
   f. *All* who go *aboard are* not *equally* good travelers.

6. The following phrases may be somewhat more difficult because they contain many normally tense vowels in initial positions and so provide opportunities for glottal attacks. If you initiate the vocaliza-

tion with just enough tension for the proper articulation of the
vowel, but with no more than that much tension, the glottal stop
should be avoided.

each and every	Irma is ill
ever and ever	eels are edible
each to his own	east of Eden
it's an ill wind	Ed is insistent
at each opportunity	anger and anguish
alias Amy	allegiance is often alleged

7. The following verses offer opportunity for additional practice.

    a. All the world's a stage,
       And all the men and women merely players:
       They have their exits and their entrances;
       And one man in his time plays many parts,
       WILLIAM SHAKESPEARE—*As You Like It*

    b. Out upon it, I have loved
       Three whole days together!
       And am like to love three more,
       If it prove fair weather.
       SIR JOHN SUCKLING
       —*The Constant Lover*

    c. With thee conversing I forget all time,
       All seasons and their change; all please alike.
       JOHN MILTON—*Paradise Lost*

    d. I reached the Alps: the soul within me burned,
       Italia, my Italia, at thy name:
      And when from out the mountain's heart I came
    And saw the land for which my life had yearned,
    I laughed as one who some great prize had earned:
       OSCAR WILDE—*Sonnet on Approaching Italy*

    e. The air broke into a mist with bells,
       The old walls rocked with the crowd and cries.

Had I said 'Good folks, mere noise repels
But give me your sun from yonder skies!'
They had answered, 'And afterward, what else?'
ROBERT BROWNING—*The Patriot*

The Glottal Stop As an Articulatory Fault

Although many persons initiate voice without a glottal attack, they may have a glottal quality in their speech because of an articulatory habit. The habit or fault is one of substituting a glottal grunt or click for a *t* or a *d* in words in which either of these sounds is followed by an *l* or an *n*. This sound substitution will be considered in somewhat greater detail in our discussion of specific sound improvement. For the present, we suggest that the reader test himself on the list of words that follows. If he can feel or hear himself produce a glottal explosive for the *t* or *d* on more than one or two of the words, he should make a special effort to articulate a clear but light and not exaggerated *t* or *d* to avoid giving his speech an over-all glottal quality.

bottle	fettle	button	ladle
kettle	rattle	mutton	paddle
settle	written	patent	saddle
metal	bitten	mountain	hidden

5 • Making Yourself Heard

CONTROL OF LOUDNESS

Adequate loudness, we pointed out earlier, is an essential attribute of an effective voice. For most of us, adequate loudness usually means being easily heard in conversation. Sometimes it means competing with surrounding noises, both human and mechanical. Occasionally, however, we must speak to a group which by virtue of its size, demands louder than normal conversational voice. Sometimes we must speak under conditions that demand more loudness than is ordinarily needed; we may have to yell a warning, issue a command, or address a group indoors or outside without the assistance of an electronic amplifier.

Loudness is best regulated through breathing control. One of the ways to speak loudly is to increase the energy with which the breath stream vibrates the vocal bands. The greater the amplitude, or the more extensive the swing of the vocal bands, the louder the sound. In addition, loudness is also related to the way our resonating cavities reinforce our vocal tones. It usually requires less energy than we think to vocalize loudly enough to be readily heard.

If we recognize that the vocal attribute we think of as loudness is a result of the amplitude or swing of the vocal bands *and* the amount of reinforcement afforded the initiated tone by the resonating cavities acting as amplifiers, we will not overstress the force or energy it takes to speak as loudly as the occasion requires. The danger in using added energetic action to produce loud tones is that a strain of the pharyngeal and laryngeal walls is likely to result. The effect of such strain is to reduce the efficiency of the cavities of the pharynx and larynx as reinforcing cavities. Because of this the vocal tones are less loud than they might otherwise be. In carrying out the suggestions for increasing loudness, the reader should avoid increasing tensions of the larynx or throat. In addition to the physical feeling of strain, listen for elevation of pitch. If the vocal tones are higher in pitch than normal for you, the likelihood is that the muscles (walls) of your resonating cavities are excessively strained.

To understand the change in action of the abdominal wall for loud vocalization, place your hands on the abdomen and shout aloud "All out!" You will (or should be able to) note that there is a sudden pulling in of the abdominal muscles and that the pulling in is greater than for normal conversation. If this does not occur, and you are not readily able to speak as loudly as you would like and should reasonably expect, then the following exercises should be of help in establishing adequate loudness.

Exercises for Developing Adequate Loudness

1. Review the exercises for proper breath control (see pages 40–45). This should create awareness of abdominal action established for conversational voice needs.

2. Place your hands on the abdomen and say *ah* as you might for a throat examination. Then take a moderately deep but comfortable breath and again begin to say *ah*. This time apply pressure suddenly with your hands. The tone should increase in loudness. If you have not caught yourself by surprise, and exhaled without vocalization, the *ah* should have become appreciably louder. Whether or not you have caught yourself by surprise, repeat the exercise and produce a loud *ah*.

3. Repeat exercise (2), producing three loud *ah*'s without straining. Breathe in if necessary after each *ah*. Loud voice production requires more breath than normal conversation, so that more fre-

quent inhalation becomes necessary to maintain loud voice without strain.

4. Repeat, except that this time exert direct control over the abdominal muscles as you produce your loud *ah's*.

5. Say the following short commands, each on a single breath, without strain and without an increase in pitch level toward the end of the phrase.

    a. All aboard!
    b. He's out!
    c. Be gone!
    d. Come here!
    e. Away with you!

6. Try the following sentences, on a single breath if possible. Speak as if there were a need to use a loud voice to assert yourself.

    a. I'll go when ready!
    b. Be gone my man!
    c. I mean what I say!
    d. Once more and you're through!
    e. There you go again!

The following exercises are intended to help in the building up and control of degrees of loudness rather than in the sudden production of loud voice. Such practice is closer to the normal use of loudness for emphasis and vocal variety in speaking.

Exercises for Controlling Loudness

1. Initiate an *ah* in a tone which is barely audible, gradually increase the loudness of the *ah* until it is louder than your usually conversational voice, and then reduce the loudness until the tone is again barely audible. Do not change the pitch or force the length of exhalation beyond a point of comfort.

2. Count from one to five increasing the loudness on each number. Begin with a barely audible one and end with a five which can easily be heard across a forty-foot room.

3. Count to seven, increasing the loudness up to four and then decreasing loudness from five through seven. Maintain the same pitch level throughout the count.

4. Say each of the following phrases or sentences three times, increasing loudness from a normal conversational level to one which can easily be heard across a forty-foot room.

     a. I'll go!
     b. Come back!
     c. Please!
     d. No!
     e. I won't!
     f. Enough!
     g. Who's there?

5. Read each of the following sentences, first in an ordinary conversational tone and then as if you were trying to address a person in the tenth row of a crowded room.

     a. I'll go in a few minutes.
     b. The time is now.
     c. I'll say this for the last time.
     d. Listen if you wish to understand.
     e. Are you John Jones?

Strengthening the Voice

Up to this point our discussion of loudness has been based on the assumption that the speaker could make himself heard under normal conditions but might be in need of help to make himself readily heard under difficult conditions. Occasionally, however, we find persons whose habitual loudness levels are too weak for easy hearing even under relatively good speaking conditions. Such speakers need help to be heard even in quiet conversation.

In some instances, the cause of a weak voice is physical and may be attributed to a structural disturbance or anomaly of the vocal mechanism. Such instances are comparatively rare and require specialized treatment rather than self-help to improve the voice as much as possible. Sometimes a weak voice is a carry-over from a physical state during sickness or the subsequent period of convalescence. A sick person may not have the energy to make himself heard, and in the early stages of recovery he may not care whether or not he can be heard. When the patient is finally well enough to care he may somehow decide that perhaps making others strain to hear him is not without advantage. So a habit of weak vocalization may persist. There is also a possibility that as a child the speaker was brought up in a home with an ill relative, or a crotchety one who believed that children should be seen, if necessary, but were not worthy of being heard. The barely audible voice may then have become the safer one, the one that did not bring isolation or a scolding.

Occasionally, the barely audible voice characterizes the individual who feels that what he has to say is unworthy of a listener or that as a speaker he lacks value. His weak sounds may be interpreted as apologetic noises or noises which are produced because he feels a social need to say something but entertains fear that if he is heard he may be held responsible for what he says.

Such physical and mental conditions, however, are not the usual causes of weak voice. Much more frequently, a weak voice is the result of poor vocal habits such as poor breath control, excessive tension of the vocal mechanism, inappropriate pitch, or improper use of the resonating cavities to reinforce vocal tones. If the reader has no reason to believe that there is anything physically wrong with his vocal apparatus, if he is not longing for the advantages and immunities of the sick bed or the attentions associated with his convalescence, if he is a reasonably well-adjusted person, audible voice should be his for the trying.

The earlier discussion on how to control loudness through breath control obviously holds for the person with a weak voice. In addition, the following exercises should be of help.

Exercises for Strengthening Weak Voice

1. Drop your jaw for a gentle but open-mouthed yawn. Inhale with your mouth open, and then pull in slowly but firmly on the abdominal muscles. Now permit a yawn to escape as you exhale as a "by-product" of the position of mouth and the controlled breathing.

2. Repeat exercise (1) five times, making the yawn louder each time but maintaining the same pitch.

3. Now, instead of yawning, prepare to say *aw* as in *awful*. Maintain an even pitch. Repeat five times.

4. Repeat exercise (3), but this time with the sound *oh*.

5. Say *oh* (a) as if surprised, (b) as if horrified, (c) as if pleased, and (d) as if you are shouting a warning.

6. Pretend you are imitating a siren on a fire truck, increasing and decreasing the loudness of your voice on the sound *oh*. Repeat, using the sound *aw*. Avoid any feeling of tension of the throat or larynx, and do not extend the length of vocalization to a point of discomfort.

7. Imagine yourself a drill sergeant and give your platoon the following orders.

  a. Forward, *march!*
  b. Platoon, *halt!*
  c. About *face!*
  d. At ease!
  e. Rest!

8. Count from one through five, increasing the loudness on each count but maintaining the same pitch level. Repeat three times.

9. Practice each of the following in a voice loud enough to be readily heard across the length of your living room.

  a. Break, break, break,
  On thy cold gray stones, O Sea!
  And I would that my tongue could utter
  The thoughts that arise in me.
  ALFRED, LORD TENNYSON
  —*Break, Break, Break*

  b. Ah. Faustus,
  Now hast thou but one bare hour to live,
  And then thou must be damn'd perpetually!
  CHRISTOPHER MARLOWE—*Faustus*

  c. Are you done? Are you completely done?

  d. A horse! A horse! my kingdom for a horse!
  WILLIAM SHAKESPEARE—*Richard III*

  e. Blow, winds, and crack your cheeks! rage! blow!
  WILLIAM SHAKESPEARE—*King Lear*

f. Roll on, thou deep and dark blue Ocean—roll!
    Ten thousand fleets sweep over thee in vain;
    Man marks the earth with ruin—his control
    Stops with the shore;
        LORD BYRON—*Childe Harold's Pilgrimage*

g. If a word
    Our orators let fall, save what pertains
    To peace, I'll raise a storm of words,
        and rain
    A very tempest of abuse upon them!
        ARISTOPHANES—*The Acharnians*

h. Let the great world spin forever down
        the ringing grooves of change.
        ALFRED, LORD TENNYSON—*Locksley Hall*

i. He flung himself from the room, flung himself upon
    his horse and rode madly off in all directions.
        STEPHEN LEACOCK—*Gertrude the Governess*

j. Shrill and high, newsboys cry
    The worst of the city's infamy
        WILLIAM VAUGHN MOODY
            —*In New York*

k. Lay on, Macduff
    And damn'd be him, that first cries,
    "Hold, enough!"
        WILLIAM SHAKESPEARE—*Macbeth*

l. Pour the sweet milk of concord into hell,
    Uproar the universal peace, confound
    All unity on earth.
        WILLIAM SHAKESPEARE—*Macbeth*

m. 'My name is Ozymandias, King of Kings.
    Look on my works, ye Mighty, and despair!'
        PERCY BYSSHE SHELLEY—*Ozymandias*

n. The cataract strong
Then plunges along,
Striking and raging
As if a war waging
Its caverns and rocks among—

ROBERT SOUTHEY
—The Cataract of Lodore

10. If you have no difficulty making yourself heard across your living room, try the same selections again but this time pretend that your room is forty feet long and as many feet wide. If you are successful in this exercise, then repeat the selections as if you were addressing an audience from the stage of a moderate-sized theater.

11. Read the following as if you were addressing four hundred persons waiting for your announcements in an auditorium.

a. The meeting is adjourned. Return in two hours.
b. Tomorrow's meeting will begin at 9 A.M.
c. Refreshments will be served in the recreation hall.
d. John Smith is the winner.
e. There will be no school tomorrow.

FORCE

In our earlier discussion of loudness and force, our emphasis was on producing voice so that it is audible in varying speaking situations. At this time we shall assume that the speaker has no problem in making himself heard and is controlling the loudness of his voice so that it is adequate to meet the needs of a small conversational group or of a larger formal audience. The speaker is now concerned with the use of loudness or force to give color and meaning to what he wishes to say.

Syllable and Word Stress

Force is regularly used in American-English speech as the way of establishing syllable stress in polysyllabic words. Except for compound words such as *bookcase, fireplace,* and *mankind,* one syllable of a polysyllabic word is stressed (spoken more forcefully) than the other syllables. Word stress is regularly, perhaps too regularly, used to emphasize a word within a phrase or a phrase within a sentence. When used as the only technique for emphasis, speech begins to sound immature. When used, along with pitch, quality, and duration, as one of several ways of emphasizing speech content, force becomes a useful technique and monotony is avoided.

Variety

Except for public speaking situations in which the speaker does not have the help of mechanical amplification, large differences in force are rarely necessary. Change in the use of force rather than amount of force is the factor of variety which permits the speaker to give import to one idea and to subordinate other related ideas. Sometimes a desired effect in giving special meaning is better achieved when the significant words are spoken with reduced rather than increased volume. Such would be the case for the sentence, "Please, my love, *be still*." If the words *be still* are spoken so that they are barely audible, they are given more complete meaning than might otherwise be possible.

Change in force may be used to achieve dramatic as well as subtle, intellectual effects. A deliberate, degree-by-degree increase in force from a low to a high level of intensity helps to produce a dramatic effect. So also may a reduction in force from a moderately high to a low intensity. It may be both dramatic and sophisticated if the content is worthy of the technique.

The exercises that follow will help to bring out some of the meanings which can be communicated through the use of controlled changes in vocal force.

Exercises for Changes in Force

1. What are the differences in the meaning of the following words when the syllable stress is shifted from the first syllable to the second?

*con*duct	con*duct*
*con*vict	con*vict*
*de*coy	de*coy*
*di*gest	di*gest*
*ob*ject	ob*ject*
*re*bel	re*bel*

2. Read the following sentences, changing the stress from the first word of the sentence to each succeeding word. Do not, however, stress articles, conjunctions, or prepositions.

a. You and I are going.
b. I am poor but honest.
c. One or the other must leave.
d. I like Bill.
e. Is he the man you like?
f. What is your answer?
g. This is your reward.
h. Joe is a brilliant man.
i. We thought he returned.
j. He is not long for this world.
k. Thursday was the day of reckoning.
l. She can do anything.

3. Use controlled and moderate stress to bring out the essential meaning of the following:

a. Never in the field of human conflict was so much owed by so many to so few.
   WINSTON CHURCHILL—1940 Speech

b. George Bernard Shaw observed that an Englishman thinks he is moral when he is only uncomfortable.

c. "I hope you have not been leading a double life, pretending to be wicked and being really good all the time. That would be hypocrisy."
   OSCAR WILDE—*The Importance of Being Earnest*

d. Democracy is based upon the conviction that there are extraordinary possibilities in ordinary people.
   HARRY EMERSON FOSDICK—*Democracy*

e. Peace is not an ideal at all. It is a state attendant upon the achievement of an ideal. The ideal itself is human liberty, justice, and the honorable conduct of an orderly and humane society. Given this, a durable peace follows naturally

as a matter of course. Without this, there is no peace, but
only a rule of force until liberty and justice revolt against it
in search of peace. To regard peace as an end in itself and
as something to be achieved at all hazards, is in effect to
labor for the indefinite continuance of war.

NICHOLAS MURRAY BUTLER—*A World in Ferment*

f. A foolish consistency is the hobgoblin of little minds,
adored by little statesmen and philosophers and divines.
With consistency a great soul has simply nothing to do. He
may as well concern himself with his shadow on the wall.
Speak what you think now in hard words and to-morrow
speak what to-morrow thinks in hard words again, though it
contradict everything you said to-day—'Ah, so you shall be
sure to be misunderstood.'—Is it so bad, then, to be misunderstood? Pythagoras was misunderstood, and Socrates,
and Jesus, and Luther, and Copernicus, and Galileo, and
Newton, and every pure and wise spirit that ever took flesh.
To be great is to be misunderstood. . . .

RALPH WALDO EMERSON—*Essays*

g. Today the guns are silent. A great tragedy has ended. A
great victory has been won. The skies no longer rain death—
the seas bear only commerce—men everywhere walk
upright in the sunlight. The entire world is quietly at
peace. The holy mission has been completed, and in report-
ing this to you, the people, I speak for the thousands of
silent lips, forever stilled among the jungles and the beaches
and in the deep waters of the Pacific which marked the
way. I speak for the unnamed millions homeward bound
to take up the challenge of that future which they did so
much to salvage from the brink of disaster. . . .

We have known the bitterness of defeat and the exulta-
tion of triumph, and from both we have learned there can
be no turning back. We must go forward to preserve in
peace what we won in war.

DOUGLAS MACARTHUR
—*The Surrender of Japan*, September 2, 1945.

4. Use more marked changes in force to communicate the meanings of the following passages.

a. Is life so dear, or peace so sweet, as to be purchased at the price of chains and slavery? Forbid it, Almighty God! I know not what course others may take; but as for me, give me liberty, or give me death!

   PATRICK HENRY—Speech in Virginia Convention

b. We shall go on to the end, we shall fight in France, we shall fight on the seas and oceans, we shall fight with growing confidence and growing strength in the air, we shall defend our Island whatever the cost may be—

   WINSTON CHURCHILL—Speech, June 4, 1940

c. From Berlin, Rome, and Tokyo we have been described as a nation of weaklings—"playboys"—who would hire British, Russian, or Chinese soldiers to do our fighting for us.
   Let them repeat that now!
   Let them tell that to General MacArthur and his men.
   Let them tell that to the sailors who today are hitting hard in the far waters of the Pacific.
   Let them tell that to the boys in the Flying Fortresses.
   Let them tell that to the Marines!

   FRANKLIN DELANO ROOSEVELT—Speech, 1942

d. What! drawn, and talk of Peace? I hate the word
   As I hate hell, all Montagues, and thee.
   Have at thee, coward!

   WILLIAM SHAKESPEARE—*Romeo and Juliet*

e. Blow, winds, and crack your cheeks! rage! blow!
   You cataracts and hurricanes, spout
   Till you have drench'd our steeples, drown'd the cocks!
   You sulphurous and thought-executing fires,
   Vaunt carriers of oak-cleaving thunderbolts,
   Singe my white head! And thou, all shaking thunder,
   Strike flat the thick rotundity o' the world!

   WILLIAM SHAKESPEARE—*King Lear*

f. Read the following stanza with increased but controlled
   force up to the next to the last line; try reading the last
   line with a marked reduction in force to achieve dramatic
   contrast.

O masters, lords and rulers in all lands,
How will the future reckon with this man?
How answer his brute question in that hour
When whirlwinds of rebellion shake the world?
How will it be with kingdoms and with kings—
With those who shaped him to the thing he is—
When this dumb terror shall reply to god,
After the silence of the centuries?

EDWIN MARKHAM—*The Man with the Hoe*

6 • Reinforcement of Tone Through Resonance

The material and exercises in the preceding chapter stressed the well-controlled and energetic use of breath for the purpose of making ourselves readily heard when more than conversational loudness was required. As we recall (see page 23), the loudness of our voices is also determined by resonating cavity reinforcement. Because of this effortless and energy-conserving physical phenomenon, most of us are able to speak at length, even under less than optimum conditions, without experiencing fatigue. With the mechanical assistance of microphones and electronic amplifiers, we seldom need to speak at more than conversational levels. But even conversational voice level would be difficult for all of us to maintain, as it is for some of us, without resonating cavity reinforcement.

The chief resonators are the cavities of the larynx, pharynx (throat), mouth, and nose.* If these cavities are not temporarily irritated or inflamed by a respiratory ailment or obstructed by organic growth such as enlarged tonsils or adenoids, good reinforcement of tone should be possible. Muscular tension may also impair tone, but unless such tension is chronic or regularly associated with some speech efforts, the effect of tension is likely to be transitory.

* This is a good point to review our earlier discussion of the resonating cavities (see pages 23–27)

73

Improvement of Resonance

The manner in which the combination of our resonators reinforces our vocal tones produces that attribute of speech by which the
quality or timbre of our voices is identified. Unless we make a conscious attempt to disguise our voice, and frequently despite such an
attempt, we are revealed by our vocal tones. Some of us are fortunate
and have voices that are naturally pleasant to hear. A few of us, by
misuse, do harm to our vocal apparatus. A very few may not have
been generously endowed by nature and have mechanisms that at
best are only fair. In this small number may be persons whose combination of laryngeal, pharyngeal, oral, and nasal cavities do not
adequately reinforce the basic tones to produce acceptable vocal
qualities. Fortunately, most of us, including the members of the last
group, can learn to treat our mechanisms with respect. By doing so
we can make the most effective use of what we have. The discussion
that follows should be of help along this line.

In our earlier discussion of the initiation of tones we considered
the relationship of physical and emotional tension to voice production. Specific suggestions and exercises were presented to establish
proper initial vocalization. Our present concern will be to create
awareness of resonance as one of the objectives for voice improvement. As we continue our discussion of resonance we must bear in
mind that none of our resonating cavities acts independently of
the others. Changes of the oral cavity are likely to affect the
pharynx, and changes in the pharynx are likely to affect oral
cavity, the larynx, and/or the nasal cavity. Despite this interde-
pendence, specific modifications in one of the resonating cavities can
result in vocal qualities which may be described by such terms as
oral, guttural, and nasal.

Oral Resonance

Oral resonance is likely to be improved if the speaker makes a
conscious effort to emphasize lip and tongue activity while speaking.
Such activity helps to accomplish the objective of the singing teacher
who directs his student to "place his tones forward in the mouth."
In our attempt to achieve oral resonance, however, we must not so
exaggerate articulatory activity as to make it obvious to our listener-
observer, and so make us self-conscious.

Optimum oral resonance can be obtained only when the back of the oral cavity is open and relaxed so that we are able to initiate and maintain vocalization with an open throat. The following exercises should be of help for this purpose.

Exercises for Oral Resonance

1. To establish the open throat, drop your head toward your chest. Permit your jaw to drop open, and then breathe easily through your mouth. If your mouth was not forced open and your head is hanging relaxed from your neck, you should be able to feel your throat at ease and relaxed as you breathe through your mouth.

2. Breathe in through your mouth and then yawn gently. Avoid all suggestions of muscle strain of the lower jaw or throat as you yawn. As you continue to breathe through your mouth, note the feeling of air in the back of the mouth and throat. Inhale and exhale only as deeply as for normal respiration. Continue for about ninety seconds.

3. Repeat exercise (2), but this time produce a relaxed *ah* on each exhaled breath. Do this five times.

4. Begin as in exercise (3), but this time add an *m* to the *ah* so that the result is *ahm*. Repeat five times.

5. With an open throat and relaxed lower jaw, say each of the following three times. Say each slowly, and stop for a breath between vocalizations.

Mah, bah, dah, nah, hah, pah, fah, thah, shah, yah

In the immediately succeeding exercises, it will not be possible to keep your throat as relaxed as for exercises (1)–(5). Make certain, however, that your throat and mouth muscles are as relaxed as they can be while producing the indicated sounds. The exercises will emphasize oral activity and articulation in the front of the mouth.

6. Observe your mouth in a mirror as you produce the following words in pairs. Note the change in lip and jaw positions.

he	who	elf	off
it	hook	am	ought
ate	oat	alp	alm

7. Observe lip and tongue activity as you say each of the following:

a. Tic, tac, toe, away we go.
b. Peter was fond of picking peppers.
c. Who are you and who am I?
d. Amy tip-toed up the hill.
e. The wind played a tune in the trees.
f. The silvery moon shed its light on the lake.
g. A wag once defined an American college as a football stadium with a few academic buildings attached.
h. Is basketball replacing baseball as the most popular American sport?
i. Poets are fond of picking on December as a time for dreariness.
j. A university must be both a place and a state of mind for ideals and ideas and opportunities to put them into practice.

8. The following selections should be read with emphasis on articulatory action in the front of the mouth.

a. The essayist and critic, William Hazlitt, held that only those deserve a monument who do not need one.

b. The lilies of the field whose bloom is brief;—
   We are as they;
   Like them we fade away
   As doth a leaf.
   CHRISTINA ROSSETTI—*Consider*

c. The grey-ey'd morn smiles on the frowning night,
   Chequ'ring the eastern clouds with streaks of light.
   WILLIAM SHAKESPEARE—*Romeo and Juliet*

d. And, after all, what is a lie?
   'Tis but
   The truth in masquerade.
   LORD BYRON—*Don Juan*

e. Man passes away; his name perishes from record and recollection; his history is as a tale that is told, and his very monument becomes a ruin.
   WASHINGTON IRVING—*The Sketch Book*

Nasal Resonance

We have already suggested that the importance of the nasal cavities for vocal reinforcement can be appreciated when we are suffering from a head cold. This condition not only deprives us of the ability to produce proper nasal sounds but generally and adversely affects all vocal efforts. We become especially aware of the need for nasal reinforcement when we try to produce nasal sounds —*n*, *m*, and *ng* [ŋ]. These American-English sounds are articulated orally but are resonated in the nasal cavities and are emitted through the nose. In order for the sound to enter the nasal cavities, the soft palate must be relaxed and lowered. Lowering the soft palate produces a large opening at the posterior entrance of the nasal cavities (the nares) and a narrow avenue through the nares for the sound to be resonated as it emerges from the nostrils. The characteristic differences in the three nasal consonants result from modification in the oral cavity. For the sound *m*, the entire cavity is used because the tongue lies comparatively flat at the floor of the mouth; for *n*, the tongue is raised so that a smaller part of the mouth is used; for the *ng*, only a narrow area at the back of the mouth behind the raised tongue is used as a supplemental reinforcer.

Although only three English sounds are characteristically nasal, there is little doubt that, in connected speech, sounds in close proximity to the nasals are also partly reinforced nasally. It is virtually impossible to avoid some degree of nasality on the vowels of words such as *nine, mine,* and *ring.* How to avoid excessive nasalization of vowels will be considered later. At the present time we prefer to make a case for proper nasal reinforcement rather than to create anxiety about excessive nasality.

Appropriate nasal reinforcement provides both roundness and carrying power to the voice. It permits us to be heard with relatively little expenditure of energy. We can become aware of these effects by sustained, easy humming. To hum easily, make certain that the throat muscles, the tongue, and the soft palate are relaxed. The jaws should be almost but not quite together. The lips should barely touch so that a slight tickling sensation is experienced on humming. An easy, properly produced hum should be felt as well as heard. You should be able to feel it not only on the lips but at the sides of the nostrils if your thumb and index finger are placed gently at these spots.

The fullness of tone and vibrating effects associated with proper nasal reinforcement can be appreciated by contrasting a phrase or sentence with many nasal sounds with another containing no nasals, such as the following:

Amanda enjoys candy.
Tilly likes fish.

Mabel may marry.
Bill will tarry.

Mary murmured in the moonlight.
Ted was tight lipped.

The following exercises should help to create awareness of nasal resonance as well as to afford an appreciation of the fullness of tone and carrying power which may be obtained with the careful production of nasal sounds. At first exaggerate the length of each nasal sound, but avoid any intentional increase of energy in vocalization. Also be certain that each exercise is performed with a relaxed throat and jaw. Sustain your tones evenly through controlled, gradual abdominal contraction on exhalation.

Exercises for Nasal Resonance

1. Hum gently for the equivalent of a count of four on a sustained breath. Repeat five times.

2. Drop your jaw and bring the tip of the tongue in position for *n*. Produce *n* for the equivalent of a count of four. Repeat five times.

3. Blend a hum with the sound *ah* (*mah*). Make certain that the soft palate is raised for the *ah*. Repeat five times.

4. Blend a lengthened *n* with *ah*, then do the same for *n* and *aw*. Repeat each five times.

5. Blend a lengthened *m* with *ah* and follow by another *m* (*mahm*). Do the same for *m* and *aw* (*mawm*). Repeat each five times.

6. Repeat exercise (5) with *n* before and after the sounds *ah* and *aw* (*nahn* and *nawn*). Repeat each five times.

7. Exaggerate the length *but not the intensity* of the nasal sounds in each of the following:

a. morning at seven   once upon a time
    meandering at noon   mournful moaning
    mind your manners   a man's man
    more and more   many a long month
    none may mind   universal longing

b. Man cannot live on bread alone.
    Most men can chant better than they can sing.
    Mabel had a phantom mind.
    Oriental dances employ meaningful pantomime.
    Tom was fond of ocean fishing.
    The lame may lead the blind.
    Friends are proven on rainy days.
    Napoleon maintained that most men are only grown children.
    Kipling considered Gunga Din to be a better man than the master who flayed him.
    Individual man may be less predictable than mankind in general.

c. Man's inhumanity to man
    Makes countless thousands mourn!
          ROBERT BURNS
    —*Man Was Made to Mourn*

d. Know then thyself, presume not God to scan;
    The proper study of Mankind is Man.
          ALEXANDER POPE—*Essay on Man*

e. Voltaire maintained that doctors are men who prescribe medicine of which they know little, to cure diseases of which they know less, in human beings of whom they know nothing.

f. If the mountain won't come to Mohammed,
    Mohammed must go to the mountain.
          English proverb

g. Alexander Pope held that an obstinate man does not hold
opinions, but they hold him.

h. Sunset and evening star,
    And one clear call for me!
And may there be no moaning of the bar,
    When I put out to sea,
ALFRED, LORD TENNYSON—*Crossing the Bar*

i. Here, where the world is quiet;
    Here, where all trouble seems
Dead winds' and spent waves' riot
    In doubtful dreams of dreams;
I watch the green field growing
    For reaping folk and sowing,
    For harvest-time and mowing,
    A sleepy world of streams.
ALGERNON CHARLES SWINBURNE
—*The Garden of Proserpine*

j. . . . sweet is every sound,
    Sweeter thy voice, but every sound is sweet;
Myriads of rivulets hurrying through the lawn,
The moan of doves in immemorial elms,
And murmuring of innumerable bees.
ALFRED, LORD TENNYSON—*The Princess*

k. And all my days are trances,
    And all my nightly dreams
Are where thy gray eye glances
    And where thy footstep gleams—
In what ethereal dances,
    By what eternal streams!
EDGAR ALLAN POE—*To One in Paradise*

NASALITY

Our orientation in this book has been to emphasize the positive.
We preferred, for example, to explain how vocal tones could be
produced clearly, with adequate loudness and proper breath con-

trol, than to discuss how to overcome hoarseness, breathiness, or any other vocal inadequacy or defect. This was also our approach in considering resonance and the reinforcement of tone by the nasal cavities. As a precautionary measure, however, we believe it advisable at this point to discuss separately the prevalent fault of *excessive nasality*. Fortunately, when we have learned either to avoid or to overcome excessive nasality, we shall have attained the positive objective of establishing appropriate nasal reinforcement.

Causes of Excessive Nasality

The most common cause of excessive nasality is failure of the soft palate to rise when necessary to block off the stream of breath (sound) as it enters the oral pharynx. If the soft palate is elevated, the sound is directed forward and emitted orally. A relaxed soft palate permits the sound to enter the nasal cavities where it is reinforced to become qualitatively nasal.

If failure to elevate the soft palate has a physical basis, medical attention is in order. If the failure is caused by a general indifference to speech efforts, to listener reactions, and superficially at least to the world in general, psychotherapy may be indicated. Excessive nasality is frequently associated with articulatory sluggishness. Often the jaw, lips, and tongue as well as the soft palate move without precision and alertness. The over-all result is speech that sounds slovenly and voice that sounds tired, monotonous, and nasal.

For the most part, excessive nasality is a manner of speech which has been learned unconsciously. Even if this manner of speaking at one time reflected an attitude of thinking or of behavior, change for the better can take place if the will to change is present.

The following exercises are based on the assumption that there is no organic basis for the excessive nasality and no psychological need for its persistence.

Exercises for Awareness of Palatal Action

1. Stand before a mirror and yawn with a wide-open mouth. Note the upward movement of the soft palate and uvula while the yawn is maintained. Stop the yawn and relax. Repeat and note the feeling as well as the action of the elevated palate.

2. Hum gently, then think but do not vocalize a lengthy *ah*. Be

certain that your mouth is open and the tongue flat. Observe the action of the soft palate as it is elevated and maintained for the *ah*. Now, by way of contrast, permit the soft palate to relax and produce a nasalized *ah*. Again, raise the soft palate for an appropriately vocalized *non-nasal ah*. Capture the feeling of the elevated soft palate when the *ah* is properly vocalized and orally reinforced. Repeat for the vowels of *all* and *ooze*.

3. Close your nostrils by pinching them. Say *ah*. Repeat with open nostrils. Whether the nostrils are pinched or free there should be little or no difference in the sound. Repeat for the vowels of *whose, hull, home, haw, hog, harm*.

4. Say *n* while noting the action and position of a relaxed soft palate. Then say *ah* and again note the action and position of the elevated palate. Alternate between the two sounds until you have an immediate awareness of the difference in palatal position.

5. Place a clean, cold hand mirror under your nostrils and produce a lengthy *ah*. If the soft palate is elevated, there should be no clouding of the mirror. Practice until there is no clouding, then repeat for all the vowels of exercise (3).

6. Repeat exercise (5) with the vowels of *eel, if, ail, elf, at, ask*. Check with a mirror for nasalization. Be especially careful about the vowels of *elf* and *ask*.

7. Pinch your nostrils closed as you say each of the following sentences. (If you note a feeling of stuffiness in your nose, or a feeling of pressure in your ears, then you are being excessively nasal. Lift your soft palate to block off the entrance of air to the nasal cavity.)

a. This is what I wish to see.
b. The ship is about to leave the port.
c. The letter I expected was posted too late.
d. The tree reached up to a fiery fall sky.
e. Who has courage to speak has courage to be free.
f. Will you have tea or coffee?

8. Say the following pairs of words with your attention focused on the avoidance of nasality in the second member of each pair. Make certain that your soft palate is elevated immediately after the nasal consonant is produced in the first member of each pair and

through the production of the second member. It may also help to lessen any tendency toward nasality if you exaggerate the articulatory activity of the lips and the front part of the tongue.

knee	tea	new	too
knit	sit	nook	took
nail	tail	note	tote
net	wet	nought	bought
mat	bat	not	tot
mask	task	ma	pa
nerve	serve	mare	dare
mud	dud	near	dear
mile	pile	muse	fuse
now	how	noise	poise

Associated or Assimilated Nasality

Earlier we learned that there are three sounds in American and English speech which appropriately require nasal reinforcement for their production. These sounds are *m*, *n*, and *ng* (ŋ). In connected speech, unless there is almost anxious care to avoid the effect, sounds in close proximity to nasal consonants are likely to be slightly nasalized. The nasalization is a "contamination by association" resulting from the manner of the articulation of the nasal sounds. Specifically, one of the following may happen.

1. The lowered soft palate may not be raised in time to prevent the following sound from being somewhat nasalized. Delay in raising the soft palate after the production of a nasal consonant probably accounts for the nasalization of the vowels that succeed the nasals in words such as *my, may, mate, new,* and *note.*

2. The soft palate may be lowered while the sound preceding the nasal is articulated as in words such as *aim, and, whom, only, sing,* and *young.* Here the nasalization is in anticipation of required articulatory movement (the lowering of the soft palate for appropriate reinforcement of a succeeding nasal sound).

3. The soft palate may not be sufficiently elevated because of the influence of preceding as well as succeeding nasal consonants as in *name, man, among, number* and *singing.*

There is no reasonable objection to some traces of nasalization resulting from the assimilative influence of nasal consonants. What needs to be avoided is an over-all effect of dominant nasality merely because some nasal sounds are present.

The exercises recommended earlier for gaining awareness and control of the soft palate are, of course, applicable for overcoming the effects of excessive nasalization resulting from the influence of nasal consonants. Here also emphasis on front of the mouth (tongue and lip) activity is important. The following additional exercises should also be helpful.

Exercises for Assimilative Nasality

1. When the nasal consonant precedes the vowel, lengthen the nasal consonant. Lengthening the consonant will afford you the extra moment of time needed to elevate the soft palate. This should reduce the "contaminating," assimilative effect of associated nasality and permit you to give appropriate reinforcement to the nasal sound.

    a. Practice on the following sound combinations. At the outset, exaggerate the length of the nasals to a marked degree. Then reduce the degree of exaggeration, but maintain the actual duration of the nasal sound for a time you consider about twice as long as normal. Finally, reduce the length of the nasals so that they are of normal duration, or as close to normal as possible, without nasalizing the succeeding sounds.

m	ee	n	ee
m	oo	n	oo
m	ay	n	ay
m	ah	n	ah

    b. Practice saying the following words, at first exaggerating the length of the nasal sounds. Then practice with the same words, this time with as little exaggeration as possible consistent with the avoidance of assimilated nasality.

meal	mood	neat	noose
mill	mull	nill	nook
mell	mote	nail	note

mate	maul	never	nought
mat	mock	nack	not
mask	moth	nap	nock
mud	mirth	nut	nerve

c. Practice with the following phrases, being careful at first to lengthen the nasal sounds and to avoid excessive nasality on the sounds that follow. Go over the same phrases, this time lengthening the nasals only as much as necessary to avoid assimilated nasality.

a man of moods	no news
more and more	move the map
new to me	not my meat

d. Practice saying the following sentences, exercising the same precautions as in the preceding exercise.

Mabel moved to the next city.
The mail brought the needed material.
Moods without thoughts are empty.
May is the time for new bloom.
The new needs to be measured against what once was new.

2. Emphasize oral activity for the sounds that precede the nasal consonants in the following exercises.

am	rant	lounge	turned
aim	town	hunch	joined
end	any	round	found
own	only	yearn	haunt
on	anger	hunger	penny

3. Incorporate the words of the preceding exercise into short sentences such as the following:

a. There is nothing without an end.
b. Big Jim owned the town.
c. Courage is not only for the strong.
d. We joined the group in song.

4. The following exercises emphasize combinations in which the nasal consonants both precede and follow vowels or diphthongs.

They therefore provide an opportunity for careful control to avoid temptation and inclination to excessive assimilative nasality. Nasality of the nonnasal sounds can be minimized if you lengthen the first nasal consonant and emphasize oral activity for the succeeding vowel or diphthong. Your objective should be only as much lengthening of the nasals as is necessary to avoid assimilated nasality.

a. Practice on words such as the following:

mean	nine	rumbling	Neanderthal
nimble	meander	underneath	known
main	numerous	crowning	mentor
meant	numb	ambition	mince
moan	mournful	grinding	minnow

b. In sentence contexts, the tendency to assimilative nasality is increased. Practice careful enunciation of the following:

Most men are more mindful of their own misfortune than they are of their neighbors'.

Winter became spring, and spring almost summer before the January snows were gone.

Mournful sounds are sometimes made by nonmournful men.

Neanderthal man is believed to have belonged to a race of ancient cave dwellers.

A baseball team conventionally includes nine men.

Nathaniel Newton could avoid almost anything but temptation.

Dreams furnish opportunities for men who are meek to become potent and to crown their ambitions without qualms and anxiety.

Man is a subject of thought, of scorn, of controversy and of near divinity. Poets and thinkers through ancient times to the present have expressed their views. Here are some of them.

Carlyle maintained that Man was the miracle beyond all miracles, "the great inscrutable mystery of God."

Mark Twain, not entirely in humor, once proclaimed, "There are times when one would like to hang the whole human race, and finish the farce."

Man that is born of a woman is of a few days, and full of trouble.

Job, XIV:1

Emerson believed that "Man is a piece of the universe made alive."

Napoleon held that men, in general, are but great children.

5. As a test of your ability to resist the temptations of assimilated nasality, use the materials of exercises (1), (2), and (4), intentionally exaggerating the over-all nasality of your speech. Then, to demonstrate your control, go over the exercise materials without yielding to the temptation to commit assimilated nasality. By way of variety, try the same technique for the following:

a. One precedent creates another. They soon accumulate and constitute law. What yesterday was fact, today is doctrine.

The Letters of Junius

b. There is no man so good, who, were he to submit all his thoughts and actions to the laws, would not deserve hanging ten times in his life.

MICHEL DE MONTAIGNE—*Of Vanity*

c. The whole art of teaching is only the art of awakening the natural curiosity of young minds for the purpose of satisfying it afterwards.

ANATOLE FRANCE—*The Daughter of Clementine*

d. Opinions cannot survive if one has no chance to fight for them.

THOMAS MANN—*The Magic Mountain*

6. Review the discussion and practice the exercises on nasal resonance (see pages 77–80).

7 . Pitch and Voice Improvement

In our discussion of the mechanism for voice production the point was made that vocal pitch should be related to properties inherent in the individual's mechanism. We are not free to choose an habitual pitch level or pitch range according to our attitudes, tastes, or whims or to change the pitch level and range according to mood or fashion. An essential task for a speaker who wants to be certain that he is making the best use of his vocal instrument is to determine the pitch level and range most appropriate for him. Fortunately, most speakers normally vocalize at pitch levels and within pitch ranges appropriate for them. Under abnormal conditions, with or without conscious awareness of the pitch level and range which we shall consider optimum, vocalization may suffer because control is lost. A few persons, however, may habitually vocalize at pitches which are not natural or optimum, and so their voices are less effective, less pleasant, and frequently much less comfortable than they could be. We will therefore proceed almost immediately to a consideration of how to determine the optimum pitch level and the most suitable pitch range. Before this is done, however, we will pause for a few working definitions.

Optimum pitch is the level at which voice can be initiated with greatest ease and effectiveness. It is the pitch at which one can achieve the best quality and the necessary loudness with the least expenditure of energy. It is the pitch at which the individual's vocal mechanism functions with greatest efficiency. Because optimum pitch is related to the structure of the vocal apparatus, optimum pitch is sometimes referred to as the *structural pitch*. Because optimum pitch would be the likely product of "doing what comes naturally" if there were no contrary internal or external physical, emotional, or cultural pressures, the term *natural pitch* is also used.

Habitual pitch is the level at which an individual most often vocalizes. *Habitual range* refers to the pitch levels most frequently employed in speaking. *Range* itself refers to the pitch levels which a speaker is capable of producing below and above his habitual pitch level. It is obviously desirable that the speaker's optimum pitch and optimum range be the ones habitually used. If this is not the case, then changes need to be made. The changes will be directed toward (1) becoming aware of optimum pitch and learning to produce this pitch level at will, (2) establishing this pitch as a habit, and (3) developing a pitch range with optimum pitch as the basic level.

Determination of Optimum Pitch

For most speakers, optimum pitch is likely to be the level one-fourth to one-third above the lowest level within the entire pitch range.* If, for example, the speaker has a twelve-level pitch range (musical tones and half-tones according to the scale), his optimum pitch would probably be the third or fourth level above his lowest. If his pitch range were wider and were to include fifteen levels, his optimum pitch would most likely be about level five. For a speaker with a twenty-one-level pitch range, optimum pitch would be about level six.

There are several approaches and techniques that may be used to arrive at optimum pitch. Ultimately, the best technique is the one which works successfully for the individual; it should not be limited by any voice or speech teacher's personal prejudices. We

---

* G. Fairbanks, *Voice and Articulation Drillbook*, Harper & Brothers, 1940, p. 168, says: "The most satisfactory method that has been devised thus far for the calculation of the *natural* pitch level of an individual involves the determination of that pitch which lies 25 per cent of the way up that individual's total singing range including falsetto."

shall consider the techniques we personally have found useful and easily demonstrable without any pretense of having a monopoly on all the workable ones. For most cases, the first of the techniques is usually sufficient to establish awareness of optimum pitch.

Techniques for Achieving Optimum Pitch

1. Relax the throat muscles. Take a moderately deep breath and vocalize an evenly sustained *ah* at whatever pitch comes out naturally. Do not think of the pitch until after you hear yourself produce it. Do not attempt to modify the tone once it has been initiated.

2. Relax, and vocalize, but this time intentionally do so at a level lower than in exercise (1).

3. Continue, going down the scale, until you have produced the lowest-pitched tone you are capable of vocalizing. It may help to think of a descending musical scale in going from your initial pitch level to your lowest. Do not strain for an abnormally low pitch. Stop at the level at which your voice becomes a low-pitched whisper.

4. Return to the initial pitch you produced in step (1). Now produce tones on an upward scale until you reach the highest-pitched falsetto. If you started vocalization at your natural pitch, you should be able to go up in pitch above twice the number of tones that you were able to descend below your initial level. If this is the situation, then you are probably initiating vocalization at or very close to your optimum or natural pitch.

An *alternate* technique for determining optimum pitch is through the matching of vocal and piano tones throughout the pitch range including the first low and first high falsetto tones.

1. Sing or chant from your lowest to your highest tone, matching each tone with a corresponding one on a well-tuned piano. If your own sense of pitch discrimination is not reliable, obtain the help of a friend with a reliable ear to establish your vocal range.

2. Repeat the singing or chanting several times so that you are certain that you have established your entire range. Your optimum or natural pitch is likely to be between one-fourth and one-third above the lowest tone you can produce.

3. Reproduce this tone until it is firmly fixed in your mind and you can initiate it without the help of the piano.

This approach should be repeated at different times during a day and on several different days. Pitch range may vary somewhat under conditions of fatigue or tension, but unless the variation is great, the optimum pitch level should not deviate by more than a single level.*

Habitual Pitch

In order to know whether there is any need to make a conscious effort to initiate voice at the optimum pitch level it is necessary to compare your habitual pitch with your optimum pitch. If the two are the same, or no more than a single pitch level (a half or a full tone) apart, then there is no need to think about your initial pitch. For most persons who have had no physical ailment or emotional trauma, the likelihood is that habitual pitch and optimum pitch are close enough so that no special concern is necessary. Just to be certain, however, all who are interested in producing voice according to their maximum capabilities might observe the suggestions which follow for determining habitual pitch and comparing it with optimum pitch.

Look over several easy prose passages and select one containing material which is neutral in affective (emotional) content and not

* Another approach for arriving at optimum pitch is through a technique of vocalizing while chewing. Dr. Froeschels, who is largely responsible for the discovery and popularization of the chewing technique for vocal therapy and vocal improvement, recommends the following as an approach: ". . . the patient is asked to chew as usual with closed lips, but without anything in his mouth, and to observe his tongue, which moves continually during the chewing. Immediately afterward he is asked to chew like a savage, that is, by opening the mouth, and with extensive movements of the lips and tongue. . . . If the chewing is done correctly, that is with vigorous movements of the lips and the tongue, a great variety of sounds escape the mouth. If uniform sounds, like *ham-ham-ham* are heard, the movements of the lips and tongue do not vary sufficiently." (E. Froeschels, "Hygiene of the Voice," *Archives of Otolaryngology,* August, 1943, 38:122–130.)

Our experience has been that persons who chew and vocalize in the manner described by Froeschels reflexively produce vocal tones at or close to their optimum pitch. For persons who have a poor sense of pitch discrimination and who are not excessively self-conscious, chewing may be used successfully as a technique for arriving at optimum pitch. It is not, however, a cure-all for all vocal ills.

particularly challenging in intellectual content. (Two such selections are provided at the end of this section on pages 92–93.) Be certain also that the selected passage includes no words that cause you uncertainty as to pronunciation. First read the selection aloud in as natural and conversational a manner as you can. On the second and third readings, when the thought content has been reduced to insignificance because of repetition, level off toward a monotone in pitch. You can accomplish this by intentionally avoiding inflectional changes. The final reading—fourth or fifth—will begin to sound like a chant. When this happens, you have probably arrived at a single level, or at least a narrow pitch range, at or close to your habitual pitch. At the conclusion of your chanted passage, vocalize a sustained *ah* at the same pitch level.

Locate the last level on a piano. Then say a series of *ah's*, matching your voice with the piano note. Count from one to ten on this level. Then say the alphabet on this level. If possible, have a companion listen to you to help you locate the level.

Compare your optimum pitch with your habitual pitch. Are the two nearly the same or no more than a tone or two apart? If they are, then you need not be further concerned about the matter of initial pitch. If not, then work to bring your habitual pitch closer to your optimum pitch. This accomplishment will pay large dividends if you are interested in good voice production. The most generous permissible margin of error between habitual and optimum pitch should not exceed two levels for persons with a narrow pitch range. This may be extended to one-third of an octave for individuals with a wide (two or more octaves) pitch range. In general, the closer habitual pitch is to optimum pitch, the better the voice is likely to be.

Reading Selections to Determine Habitual Pitch

1. A continent may be defined as the largest unit of land mass. The continents of the earth are North America, South America, Australia, Africa, Eurasia (Europe and Asia combined), and Antarctica. The combined continental surface areas constitute about 29 per cent of the total surface area of the earth. The northern hemisphere contains more land mass than the southern hemisphere. The continental masses properly include the elevated or exposed

areas above the sea level and the underwater shelves or ledges. The continental shelves slope from the exposed land surface into the depths of the oceans.

2. An index is a listing, almost always in alphabetical order, of the topics treated in a book or periodical. In most books the index is in the back. The purpose of a book index is to help the reader to locate the pages of subjects and names about which information is provided. The subject and the number or numbers of the pages on which the information is found is called the entry. A good indexer is able to anticipate where in the listing of topics a reader is likely to look for an item of information or a subject treated in the book. Some books have one index for proper names and another for other entries.

Widening the Pitch Range

In our discussion of optimum pitch we indicated that many persons tend to speak at the lower end of their pitch range. Although experimental evidence is not consistent, some studies have shown that effective speakers and male speakers considered to have good voices tend to use both greater variability and a wider range than do less effective speakers.* Better speakers, by and large, make greater use of the upper part of their pitch ranges, and their pitch ranges generally covered at least an octave and a half. Poor speakers, in contrast, tended to have pitch ranges limited to about half an octave.

Since optimum pitch is at the lower end of the pitch range, it follows that the direction for extending pitch range is likely to be up rather than down. With this in mind, the following exercises should be undertaken.

Exercises for Widening Pitch Range

1. Review the discussion of optimum pitch. Check your optimum pitch and your total pitch range.

2. Count from one through ten on your optimum pitch level. Now count to ten in a monotone three tones above your optimum pitch.

* See J. W. Black and W. E. Moore, *Speech*, McGraw-Hill Book Co., 1955, p. 56, and D. Lewis and J. Tiffin, "A Psychological Study of Individual Differences in Speaking Ability," *Archives of Speech*, 1934, pp. 43–60.

Raise the pitch level three more tones, and repeat the count. Finally, count to ten at the very top of your normal pitch range.

3. Say the sentence "I'm waiting for Bob Jones" on your optimum pitch. Practice the same sentence, initiating the first word on successively lower levels until you reach the lowest comfortable pitch level. Start again from your optimum pitch and now initiate the first word of the sentence on successively higher pitch levels until you have reached the top of your range.

4. Read the following sentences and paragraphs first in a manner natural or habitual for you and then intentionally extending the pitch range upward.

   a. Lincoln observed that force is all-conquering but its victories are short-lived.
   b. Our dreams are for the fulfillment of wishes. It is likely that a sleeping fox counts hens in his dreams.
   c. A wit once observed that though the race is not always to the quick, nor the battle to the strong, that nevertheless is the way to place your bets.
   d. A gentleman has been characterized as a man who can disagree without being disagreeable.
   e. Benjamin Franklin held that: "There are two ways of being happy: we may either diminish our wants or augment our means. Either will do, the result is the same. And it is for each man to decide for himself and do that which happens to be the easiest. . . ."
   f. Young men are fitter to invent than to judge; fitter for execution than for counsel; and fitter for new projects than for settled business.

                              FRANCIS BACON—*Of Youth and Age*

SPEECH MELODY (INTONATION)

Speaking and Singing

All of us, including those who are resigned to being classed among the nonsingers because of the violence we do to the melody of a song, use melody in our speech. The music of speech, however, is usually subtle, and the changes in pitch may not be as wide or as distinct as they are in singing. When speaking, our voices glide from sound to sound with an almost continuous change in pitch. In singing, changes in pitch are usually more clear-cut and usually take place in discrete steps equivalent to musical tones. Some of us, without intention, somehow manage to sing between the tones and our voices fall "flat" into the cracks between the piano keys. A few singers have earned a reputation by doing intentionally and under control what seems to have come naturally, accidentally, and inconsistently for others.

Intonation

Patterned vocal variation is an inherent feature of almost all spoken languages. In some, the changes in vocal tones are relatively slight while in others, such as Chinese, the changes are marked. Some languages, such as Norwegian, Swedish, and Lithuanian, have relatively fixed patterns of pitch changes. English pitch variation is relatively free. The melody of English speech is determined in part by conventions of sentence formation and in part by the mood and subjective responses of the speaker to the content of his speech and the over-all speech situation. Despite this highly individual determinant of American-English speech melody, there are several features that characterize the direction of inflectional changes (pitch changes that occur without interruption of phonation) for sounds of words. There are also characteristic pitch changes within word groups which constitute recognizable intonation patterns in our language.*

Downward or *falling inflections* (➘) are generally used to indicate the completion of a thought, and to give emphasis to an idea. The sample sentences that follow would end with falling inflections. The second sentence would probably have falling inflections on both italicized words.**

1. This is your *book*.
2. Of *course*, this is your *book*.

* See R-M. S. Heffner, *General Phonetics*, University of Wisconsin Press, 1949, pp. 216–223, for a review of basic tendencies relative to intonation patterns and alternate systems for their representations.
** In the examples to be presented the italicized words are those on which inflectional changes might be anticipated.

Command statements also end with falling inflections.

3. Come *here!*

A question that begins with an interrogative word—*when, where, who, why, how, whom*—for which an answer other than the single word "Yes" or "No" is anticipated, also ends with a falling inflection.

4. When did Tom *leave?*
5. Why did you read this *book?*

Upward or *rising inflections* (⟋) are generally used to suggest doubt, uncertainty, or incompleteness. It is also used for questions that call for a simple "Yes" or "No" answer. And we are likely to use rising inflections in statements that enumerate a series of items until the last item is stated. The last item would be spoken with a falling inflection.

6. It apparently didn't occur to *us* that this was your *book.*
7. Is this your *book?*
8. The robber stole Tom's *money,* his *jewelry,* his *shirts,* and his *ties.*

Circumflex Inflections

We would get into great difficulty if we attempted to illustrate how irony, innuendo, sarcasms, cynicism, skepticism, or surprise combined with disbelief or incredulity are expressed in pitch. These intellectual states and attitudes all have marked degrees of feeling. Most native Americans would probably employ some form of circumflex (down-up, up-down, or down-up-and-down) inflection to express them. If, for example, surprise and "I can't believe it" were to be expressed at the choice of a candidate through the use of the single word *Him!,* the inflection might be:

Him! ⟍⟋

A longer statement such as "Of all persons, to choose—him!" in which a related sentiment might be expressed relative to the same person might employ a series of circumflex inflections. The specific form of inflection is likely to be even more individualized than in the illustrations previously presented.

The examples presented below, and the generalizations we are about to make, might serve as guides for a speaker who has somehow not been able to get the tune of American-English speech. Once the basic tune is learned, the speaker should feel free to indulge in variations from the fundamental melodic theme or pattern.

1. Pitch change to some degree is almost continuous in normal conversational speech.

2. Major pitch changes occur at the end of phrases and sentences and on the most significant words within the phrase or sentence.

3. Falling or downward inflections are used when we make definite or positive assertions and when we wish to indicate the completion of a thought (examples 1, 2, and 3, pages 95–96). A falling inflection is also used on the final word of a question which begins with an interrogative word (examples 4 and 5).

4. A rising inflection is used to suggest incomplete or dependent thoughts and to express doubt or uncertainty. The rising inflection is also used in questions which may logically be answered by the words "Yes" or "No" (examples 6, 7, and 8).

5. The pitch level of the most important word within a phrase or unit of thought is likely to be at a different level from the other words of the unit. Most frequently, it will be higher in level, but occasionally the emphasized word may be uttered at a distinctively lower level than the other words of the unit.

6. The stressed syllable of a word is usually spoken on a higher pitch level than the unstressed syllable or syllables of the word.

The exercises that follow afford opportunity for application of the generalizations relative to inflectional changes and intonation patterns of American-English speech.

The first group of sentences would ordinarily end with falling inflections unless special meanings are read into them. For the present, avoid special meanings and read the sentences "straight" to indicate assertions and completed thoughts.

Exercises for Falling Inflections

1. I leave tonight.
2. The time is now.
3. This will do.

4. I've had enough.
5. I'm hungry.
6. Beware of the dog.

7. I'm glad I'm done.
8. The sun is setting.
9. Harry came alone.
10. You've heard the truth.
11. Come here!
12. It's time for bed.
13. That will be all!

14. That's a lie!
15. I know the way.
16. Give him the book.
17. Joe came alone.
18. Call me at eight.
19. That makes sense.
20. It's your turn.

Many of the items in the next group, if read straight, would normally employ falling inflections on the final words. If read to suggest doubt or uncertainty or to express an incomplete thought, rising inflections are employed. The questions ordinarily answerable by a "Yes" or "No" also end with rising inflections.

Exercises for Rising Inflections

1. I just don't know.
2. I guess that's so.
3. Well, I'll see.
4. That seems right.
5. Well, maybe.
6. You are going?

7. Do you like jam?
8. Can you come?
9. Have you seen Bill?
10. Is the pie good?
11. Is this yours?
12. Can you hold on?

All questions, we recall, do not end with rising inflections. Those which begin with interrogative words usually end with falling inflections when the questions are intended to elicit information. When a rising inflection is used for questions beginning with interrogative words, some special implication or meaning is intended other than the asking of information. Read the following sentences first with the expected falling inflection and then with a final rising inflection and note the change in meaning.

1. When will you come?
2. What day is this?
3. Where is my book?
4. Who came alone?
5. What is this?
6. Where did she go?

7. How long is the story?
8. Who knows the man?
9. What happened to you?
10. What are you doing?
11. What is this worth?
12. Why didn't Joe come?

As indicated in some of our earlier sample sentences, inflectional changes take place within sentences, normally on the last word of a phrase as well as at the end of a sentence. By and large, the nature of the inflectional change will be determined by the intended meaning and will be consistent with the generalizations previously listed relative to inflectional changes and intonation patterns.

Read the following sentences according to the indicated inflectional changes. What are the differences in implied meanings? *

1. Give me liberty, ⟋ or give me death. ⟍
2. Give me liberty, ⟍ or give me death. ⟋
3. Give me liberty, ⟍ or give me death. ⟍
4. While there is life ⟋ there is hope. ⟍
5. While there is life ⟍ there is hope. ⟍
6. Please give me the bread, ⟋ butter, ⟋ and jam. ⟍
7. Please give me the bread, ⟍ butter, ⟍ and jam. ⟍
8. Please give me the bread, ⟋ butter, ⟋ and jam. ⟋
9. She came, ⟋ he saw, ⟋ she conquered. ⟍
10. She came, ⟍ he saw, ⟍ she conquered. ⟋
11. She came, ⟍ he saw, ⟍ she conquered. ⟍

Exercises for Practice of Inflectional Changes

1. Say the word *yes* to indicate (a) certainty, (b) doubt, (c) indecision, (d) sarcasm.

2. Say the word *no* and, by changes of inflection, indicate the following:

a. "Definitely not."
b. "Well, maybe."
c. "I'm surprised to learn that."
d. "I'm annoyed to learn that."
e. "I'm pleased and surprised to learn that."

3. Say the sentence *I shall come* so that the following attitudes are implied.

a. Determination.
b. Pleasant agreement.
c. Surprise.
d. Annoyance.

* See G. Fairbanks, *Voice and Articulation Drillbook*, Harper & Brothers, 1940, pp. 184–188, for additional exercise materials on inflectional changes.

4. Say the sentence *He's a fine fellow* to bring out the following meanings.

  a. You admire the person about whom you're talking.
  b. You dislike the person.
  c. You are surprised at the newly discovered qualities of the person.

5. Speak the sentence *I like Bill* to bring out the following:

  a. A direct statement of fact. (You mean literally what the words say.)
  b. A contradiction of the literal meaning of the words. (You definitely do not like Bill.)
  c. Irritation and surprise that anyone could conceivably accuse you of liking Bill.
  d. Indecision as to your feelings about Bill.
  e. Specific indication that your liking is for Bill and not for anyone else who may be present.
  f. Your answer to the question "Who likes Bill?"
  g. An aggressive, emphatic answer to the question "Who could possibly care for a fellow like Bill?"

Avoidance of Monotony

In discussing the differences in pitch variation between singing and speaking, we pointed out that most pitch changes in song melody are discrete and take place in distinct steps. Each song syllable is likely to be maintained on a recognizable pitch level (note) longer than is likely to be the case in either conversational or public speech. Variation in speaking is almost continuous. Distinctive changes, however, should be noted when pitch is used for purposes of emphasis. For emphasis pitch change is likely to be on a higher rather than on a lower level than the preceding or following words. When the pitch change is to a lower level, the speaker must maintain or increase the volume of his voice to give the word or phrase the desired emphasis.

Repetition of pattern in singing constitutes melody. This is considered a desirable characteristic of classical song. In speaking, where verbal content rather than pitch pattern is usually important, repetition of pitch pattern should be avoided. In American and English speech subtleties of ideational content, we now appreciate, are expressed through pitch change. If pitch changes become patterned and repeated, shades of meaning cannot readily be communicated. Beyond this, pitch changes, if they can be anticipated, no longer command attention and tend to work against rather than for the maintenance of interest. For these reasons the effective speaker not only uses as wide a range of pitch as he can within his normal pitch range but is careful to avoid pitch patterning and its consequent monotony.

Pitch Variation in Content Characterized by Strong Feelings

Speech content characterized by strong feelings, which is more significant for the emotional than for the intellectual content, tends to use less pitch variation than most conversational speech. When we wish to establish a dominant mood, or to share a strong feeling with a listener, we begin to approximate the melody of song or the relatively sustained pitch of lyrical poetry. A passage from the Bible should not be read as one reads an item from the day's news. Neither should it be read with ministerial cadence and stereotyped intonations. It follows also, despite the tendency of some news commentators, that a news item should not be spoken as one should read a passage from the Bible.

In general, the pitch changes for an effective reading of poetry or emotional prose are less varied and longer sustained than for an effective reading of intellectual material. The exception is content of heightened feeling when the gay rather than the lofty is to be expressed. Then changes are likely to be more sweeping and to occur as often or more often than for predominantly intellectual material. Anger is also likely to be expressed with relatively wide pitch changes and in the upper pitch range. With these points in mind, the following passages should be read. Use pitch variation to emphasize changes in thought and feeling. Sober and solemn moods are probably best expressed through the use of relatively low, sustained pitch levels.

Exercises for Using Pitch Variation

1. Although many are given advice, only the wise, and those who usually least need it, are able to profit from it.

2. Addison observed: "There is nothing we receive with so much reluctance as advice. We look upon the man who gives it as offering an affront to our understanding, and treating us like children or idiots."

3. The deeper the sorrow, the fewer the words we have to describe it. The man who is sincerely sad cannot be articulate about it.

4. A goodly apple rotten at the heart:
   O, what a goodly outside falsehood hath!

WILLIAM SHAKESPEARE—The Merchant of Venice

5. In your reading of the following, level, sustained tones will help to establish the solemnity and reverence of your thought. Do not, however, fall into a patterned, unchanging reading.

> The Lord is my shepherd; I shall not want. He maketh me to lie down in green pastures: he leadeth me beside the still waters. He restoreth my soul: he leadeth me in the paths of righteousness for his name's sake. Yea, though I walk through the valley of the shadow of death, I will fear no evil: for thou art with me; thy rod and thy staff they comfort me.

Psalm XXIII

6. Let us therefore brace ourselves to our duties, and so bear ourselves that if the British Empire and its Commonwealth last for a thousand years, men will still say, "This was their finest hour."

WINSTON CHURCHILL, Speech, June 18, 1940

7. In the two following selections, contrast the use of a sustained, relatively low pitch for the Landor selection with the wide range of pitch called for in the light and gay verse of Leigh Hunt.

> a. I strove with none, for none was worth my strife,
>   Nature I loved, and next to Nature, Art;
> I warmed both hands before the fire of life,
>   It sinks, and I am ready to depart.

WALTER SAVAGE LANDOR
—On His Seventy-Fifth Birthday

b. Jenny kissed me when we met,
  Jumping from the chair she sat in;
Time, you thief, who love to get
  Sweets into your list, put that in:
Say I'm weary, say I'm sad,
  Say that health and wealth have missed me,
Say I'm growing old, but add
  Jenny kissed me.

LEIGH HUNT—Rondeau

8. Man's love is of man's life a thing apart,
  'Tis woman's whole existence; . . .

LORD BYRON—Don Juan

9. What is to come we know not. But we know
That what has been was good—was good to
  show,
Better to hide, and best of all to bear.
We are the masters of the days that were;
We have lived, we have loved, we have suf-
  fered . . . even so.

Shall we not take the ebb who had the flow?
Life was our friend. Now, if it be our foe—
Dear, though it spoil and break us!—need we
  care
  What is to come?

WILLIAM ERNEST HENLEY—What Is to Come?

10. His life was gentle, and the elements
  So mix'd in him that Nature might stand up
  And say to all the world, "This was a man!"

WILLIAM SHAKESPEARE—Julius Caesar

8 • Duration

Changes in duration, in the time given to the production of speech sounds and the time intervals between phrases, permit us to express feelings and to emphasize and subordinate meanings. On the emotional side, a markedly slow rate of utterance is associated with solemnity, depressed moods, and sadness and sorrow. A marked increase of rate is associated with happier states, with gaiety, and heightened feelings. The heightened feelings, however, need not always be pleasant. Anger is also expressed through an increased rate of utterance.

Changes in rate are associated with our physiological states and resultant muscular activity. We behave slowly when depressed and quickly when elated; we behave slowly when our thoughts are solemn and more quickly when our mood is gay or when we are excited. The muscles of our vocal and articulatory mechanism normally reflect these changes in our vocal tones and in our articulatory activity.

Changes in rate are, of course, correlated with changes in pitch and force. Heightened feelings are accompanied by increases in pitch level and force, depressed feelings by reduction in pitch level as well as decreased force.

Changes in duration, as indicated earlier, are achieved through either variation in rate of articulation or the use of pauses between groups of articulated sounds, or both. In general, content that is articulated slowly is considered more important than rapidly articulated content. If we listen to what is spoken slowly and are able to maintain attention while listening, we assume that what we have heard is more important than more quickly evoked content.

Some speech sounds—vowels and vowel-like consonants—lend themselves to a varied and controlled rate of articulation. Words such as *alone, rarely, home, gone, while* contain these sounds. They can be uttered quickly or slowly according to the will of the speaker. On the other hand, words such as *tip, step, quick,* and *get* are necessarily articulated rapidly. In lyric prose and poetry dominant moods can be established through language which incorporates slow sounds and rapid sounds. Compare, for example, the couplets:

>Alone, alone, all, all alone,
>Alone on a wide, wide sea!

with

>Jenny kissed me when we met,
>Jumping from the chair she sat in,

and the difference in mood becomes immediately apparent. The first couplet lends itself to a slow rate of articulation. But *Jenny* has to be articulated quickly or the result would be ludicrous.

Rate and Meaning

We must, of course, appreciate that when the rate of utterance is appreciably changed to be either relatively rapid or relatively slow, the most significant word within the phrase, or the most significant phrase within the sentence, is usually spoken more slowly than the rest of the phrase or sentence. Any sustained, unvarying rate may become monotonous. Nothing we say or read aloud of any considerable content should be uttered at the same rate, regardless of the feeling or mood.

The use of pause as a technique for varying rate is perhaps the best single indication of control and sophistication in speech. Both

Winston Churchill and Franklin Roosevelt made considerable use of lengthened and intentional pauses to create dramatic effects and to emphasize ideas. When a speaker pauses after a phrase, the listener must wait. While waiting, he tends to fill in the time gaps with the last bit of content he heard. The inner listener repetition of what the speaker has last said tends to emphasize the idea. A pause before and after a word or a phrase sets either off from the rest of the content and so becomes a technique for the vocal underlining of an idea.

A pause may also be used to indicate transition of thought in a larger context. This is the case when a speaker pauses after the evident completion of a thought. A short pause may separate sentences, a moderate pause may separate paragraphs, and a longer pause may prepare the listeners for a new line of thought.

Dramatic effects may be achieved by combining a pause with a rising inflection. If the phrase before the pause ends with an upward inflection, the result is the "suspension" of a thought. The thought is then completed in the content that follows. A similar effect may be achieved by pausing before and after a presented idea.

The speaker is obligated, when he uses an intentional pause, to satisfy the expectations of his listeners. If what comes after a pause is of no more significance than what some of our announcers of radio commercials present, the speaker has failed to meet his obligation and the listeners are likely to become distrusting.

We all use pauses to separate or group our phrases. In conversational speech such word groupings come naturally with the flow of thought. When our thoughts do not flow as freely as we might like, when we search for words to communicate our thoughts, we reveal it in our *unintentional pauses*. Under pressure of a large or formal audience, we may become fearful and anxious about pausing, and fill in the gaps with *uh uh*'s or their equivalent in nonverbal sounds. The speaker who is poised enough to wait, who pauses with intent and without fear, is one we tend to respect if what he has to say is worth the waiting and the listening. With these points in mind, the exercises that follow should be of help in the practice of some of the uses of duration for vocal variety and as a technique for revealing feeling and communicating thought.

Exercises for Practice of Controlled Rate

1. Read the following sentences so that full value is given to the italicized words. The sentences as a whole are to be spoken slowly and the italicized words more slowly than the others.

    a. The *air* was *still*, the sea was *calm*.
    b. *All* rivers *find* their *way* to the *sea*.
    c. In *solitude* we may be *least alone*.
    d. *Life's* but a *walking shadow*.
    e. *Where* are the snows of *yesteryear?*
    f. *Liberty* is one of the *few things* that *increases* as it is *shared*.
    g. *Tomorrow* will *come* as it *always has*.
    h. Man's *inhumanity* to *man* makes *countless* thousands *mourn*.
    i. Only through *memory* can we *recall* a *yesterday*.
    j. *Are* we *now* at a *time* when *knowledge* has *outrun wisdom?*

2. The next group of sentences should be spoken at a moderate rate but the italicized words somewhat more slowly for emphasis.

    a. *Mark Twain* held that *cauliflower* was *nothing* but *cabbage* with an *education*.
    b. Only a *rare* man can be *husband and hero* to his *own* wife.
    c. *Lawyers* soon *learn* that their *opinions* assume *value only* when they *exact* a fee.
    d. A *good listener* often achieves a *reputation* for being a good *conversationalist*.
    e. Coolidge held that *one with* the *law* constituted a majority.
    f. *Cynics* hold that a *majority* is *almost always wrong*.
    g. To *study mankind* begin with the *individual*.
    h. It might be said of *Thoreau* that he loved not *man* the *less* but *nature* the *more*.
    i. *Muscles*, like *iron*, wear out *faster* with *disuse* than with *use*.
    j. If we are *fortunate* we *understand* in our *mature years* what we *thought we learned* in our *youth*.

3. Read the following excerpts of verse at appropriate basic rates but with variation to emphasize the key words. The more serious or solemn the content, the slower the basic rate.

a. Come live with me, and be my Love,
   And we will all the pleasures prove
   That hills and valleys, dales and fields,
   Or woods or steepy mountain yields.
                          CHRISTOPHER MARLOWE
   —*The Passionate Shepherd to His Love*

b. Before mine eyes in opposition sits
   Grim Death, my son and foe.
                   JOHN MILTON—*Paradise Lost*

c. I chatter, chatter, as I flow
       To join the brimming river,
   For men may come and men may go,
       But I go on forever.
                     ALFRED, LORD TENNYSON
                          —*The Brook*

d. Oh, I am a cook and a captain bold
       And the mate of the *Nancy* brig,
   And a bo'sun tight, and a midshipmite
   And the crew of the Captain's gig.
                          W. S. GILBERT
              —*Yarn of the "Nancy Bell"*

e. 'Tis not the many oaths that
       makes the truth,
   But the plain single vow that
       is vow'd true.
                   WILLIAM SHAKESPEARE
       —*All's Well That Ends Well*

f. "The time has come," the Walrus said,
   "To talk of many things:

Of shoes—and ships—and sealing wax—
Of cabbages—and kings—
And why the sea is boiling hot—
And whether pigs have wings."
LEWIS CARROLL
—Through the Looking Glass

g. The Bird of Time has but a little way
To flutter—and the Bird is on the Wing.
OMAR KHAYYÁM—The Rubáiyát

4. Read the following passages, using intentional pauses to set off the significant thought groups. Punctuation may help, but occasionally it may be misleading. Determine the units of thought, and pause whether or not the material is punctuated. Indicate pauses by inserting the sign ‖ at the end of thought units at which you intend to pause. Underline the words that carry the essential meanings in each selection.

a. Nothing in life is so exhilarating as to be shot at without result.
WINSTON CHURCHILL—The Malakand Field Force

b. I can resist everything except temptation.
OSCAR WILDE—Lady Windermere's Fan

c. How sharper than a serpent's tooth it is
To have a thankless child!
WILLIAM SHAKESPEARE—King Lear

d. Know the true value of time; snatch, seize, and enjoy every moment of it. No idleness, no laziness, no procrastination: never put off till tomorrow what you can do today.
LORD CHESTERFIELD—Letters to His Son

e. We should have a great many fewer disputes in the world if words were taken for what they are, the signs of our ideas only, and not for things themselves.
JOHN LOCKE—Essay on Human Understanding

f. I remember my youth and the feeling that will never come
    back any more—the feeling that I could last forever, out-
    last the sea, the earth, and all men.

    JOSEPH CONRAD—*Youth*

g. All sorts of allowances are made for the illusions of youth;
    and none, or almost none, for the disenchantment of age.

    ROBERT LOUIS STEVENSON—*Virginibus Puerisque*

h. Samuel Johnson held that every man has a right to utter
    what he thinks truth, and every other man has a right to
    knock him down for it.

5. The passages that follow call for more deliberate pauses to
achieve emotional impact or to heighten and dramatize meaning. In
many instances these effects may be achieved by pauses before as
well as after the significant word or phrase.

a. These are the times that try men's souls. The Summer
    soldier and the sunshine patriot will, in this crisis, shrink
    from the service of their country, but he that stands it *now*
    deserves the love and thanks of man and woman. Tyranny,
    like Hell, is not easily conquered; yet we have this con-
    solation with us, that the harder the conflict the more
    glorious the triumph. What we obtain too cheaply we
    esteem too lightly; it is dearness only that gives everything
    its value. Heaven knows how to put a proper price upon its
    goods; and it would be strange indeed if so celestial an
    article as *freedom* should not be highly rated.

    THOMAS PAINE—*The Crisis*

b. The greatest thing a human soul ever does in the world
    is to *see* something, and tell what it *saw* in a plain way.
    Hundreds of people can talk for one who can think, but
    thousands can think for one who can see. To see clearly is
    poetry, prophecy, and religion, all in one.

    JOHN RUSKIN—*Modern Painters*

c. Hazlitt observed that Man is the only animal that laughs
    and weeps; for he is the only animal that is struck with the

difference between what things are, and what they ought to be.

d. There be three things which are too wonderful for me, yea four, which I know not: the way of an eagle in the air; the way of a serpent upon a rock; the way of a ship in the midst of the sea; and the way of a man with a maid.

Proverbs XXX: 18–19

e. This was the most unkindest cut of all;
For when the noble Caesar saw him stab,
Ingratitude, more strong than traitors' arms,
Quite vanquish'd him. Then burst his mighty heart;
    WILLIAM SHAKESPEARE—*Julius Caesar*

f. I speak not to disprove what Brutus spoke,
But here I am to speak what I do know.
You all did love him once, not without cause;
What cause withholds you then to mourn for him?
O judgment! thou art fled to brutish beasts,
And men have lost their reason. Bear with me;
My heart is in the coffin there with Caesar,
And I must pause, till it come back to me.
    WILLIAM SHAKESPEARE—*Julius Caesar*

g. Fear death?—to feel the fog in my throat,
    The mist in my face,
When the snows begin, and the blasts denote
    I am nearing the place,
The power of the night, the press of the storm,
    The post of the foe;
Where he stands, the Arch Fear in a visible form,
    Yet the strong man must go:
For the journey is done and the summit
    attained;
And the barriers fall.
Though a battle's to fight ere the
    guerdon be gained,

The reward of it all.
I was ever a fighter, so—one fight more
    The best and the last!
I would hate that death bandaged my eyes,
        and forebore,
    And bade me creep past.
No! let me taste the whole of it, fare
        like my peers.
    The heroes of old,
Bear the brunt, in a minute pay life's
        glad arrears,
    Of pain, darkness and cold.
For sudden, the worst turns the best to the brave,
    The black minute's at end,
And the elements' rage, the fiend-voices
        that rave,
    Shall dwindle, shall blend,
Shall change, shall become first a peace
        out of pain,
    Then a light, then thy breast,
O thou soul of my soul! I shall clasp
        thee again,
    And with God be the rest!

ROBERT BROWNING—*Prospice*

h. Mr. Chairman, Mr. Vice President, Mr. Chief Justice, Mr.
Speaker, members of my family and friends, my country-
men and the friends of my country wherever they may be.

We meet again, as upon a like moment four years ago,
and again you have witnessed my solemn oath of service
to you.

I, too, am a witness, today testifying in your name to the
principles and purposes to which we, as a people, are
pledged.

Before all else, we seek, upon our comman labor as a nation, the blessing of Almighty God. And the hopes in our
hearts fashion the deepest prayers of our whole people.

May we pursue the right—without self-righteousness.

May we know unity—without conformity.

May we grow in strength—without pride of self.

May we, in our dealings with all peoples of the earth, ever speak truth and serve justice.

And so shall America—in the sight of all men of goodwill —prove true to the honorable purposes that bind and rule us as a people in all this time of trial through which we pass.

DWIGHT D. EISENHOWER

—Second Inaugural Address, January 21, 1957

9 • Vocal Variety

Through the attributes of voice—pitch, quality, loudness, and duration—we tend to reveal our thoughts and feelings. The less inhibited we are, the more the element of feeling is expressed and conveyed through voice. When we were very young and not yet aware of and influenced by cultural pressures, our voices expressed our changes in feelings reflexively. As we grew older, cultural pressures exerted increasing control and we learned, almost always without awareness, of *how* we show feeling through voice. Even the manner of laughter was related to how people around us laughed. Our pitch ranges narrowed and began to conform to a pattern and to the linguistic code of our culture. The result was that by the time we were of school age, most of us spoke both the sounds and the melody (intonation) of the language or languages of our culture. We learned also that American-English speech has syllable stress within a word and word stress within a phrase. So we became able to emphasize ideas as we spoke. Our tendencies to talk at changing rates according to mood, to talk more rapidly under heightened feelings, more slowly in the absence of heightened feelings, and quite slowly when depressed, also became modified by cultural influences. Although cultural modifications direct us toward norms of

114

behavior, we still maintain our individuality. Sometimes we kick over the traces and our voices minimize the influences and effects of external pressures. Usually we manage to conform to a sufficient degree to sound considerably like the people around us while still sounding like ourselves.

With the possible exception of quality, each vocal attribute is capable of revealing thought as well as feeling. Within a phrase, the important word is likely to be spoken more loudly, more slowly, and at a different pitch from the other words.* These changes are paralleled for the phrase-sentence relationships, as well as for the sentence-paragraph, etc.

Through the use of vocal variety we are also able to capture attention and maintain listener interest. In brief, through voice we are able to reveal thought and feeling, to emphasize ideas, and to keep listeners attentive to our communicative efforts.

Quality

In our earlier discussions of quality we considered its relationship to resonance and to the avoidance of undesirable vocal aspects such as excessive nasality and breathiness. At this time we shall consider quality as it is related to feelings and moods and as an aspect of vocal variety.

Although modifications in vocal quality take place as a result of the behavior of our resonating cavities, except for those of us who tend to be either nasal or denasal, there is little that we normally should do consciously to bring about these changes. Normal changes in quality are related to feelings and moods, to the emotional rather than the intellectual aspects of our behavior. Unless we are dealing with a greatly inhibited individual, the feeling tone will be reflected and expressed in his vocal efforts. Usually, we have more difficulty in concealing our feelings than in revealing them. The speaker who does not strive to conceal his inner feelings, and yet does not make a point of putting them on display, will have no difficulty with quality changes. The normally responsive speaker who initiates tone properly and who uses an appropriate and flexible pitch range will do best with the quality which emerges reflexively and naturally.

* See M. D. Steer and J. Tiffin, "An Experimental Analysis of Emphasis," *Speech Monographs*, 1937, pp. 69–74, for basic research on this point.

In reading material written by another person, the speaker-reader will, of course, have to understand the feeling, mood, or emotion intended by the writer. With such an appreciation, appropriate initial quality and changes in quality should follow.

The exercises that follow have been chosen for their affective (feelings and emotions) rather than for their intellectual content. Assume, in reading them aloud, that you are more concerned with how the writer feels than with what he thinks. Determine the dominant mood and changes in mood and convey them through your voice.

Exercises for Vocal Quality

1. During the whole of a dull, dark, and resoundless day in the autumn of the year, when the clouds hung oppressively low in the heavens, I had been passing alone, on horseback, through a singularly dreary track of country, and at length found myself, as the shades of evening drew on, within view of the melancholy House of Usher. I know not how it was—but, with the first glimpse of the building, a sense of insufferable gloom pervaded my spirit.

EDGAR ALLAN POE—*The Fall of the House of Usher*

2. Home they brought her warrior dead:
   She nor swoon'd, nor utter'd cry:
   All her maidens, watching, said,
   "She must weep or she will die."

ALFRED, LORD TENNYSON
—*Home They Brought Her
Warrior Dead*

3. I am tired of tears and laughter,
   And men that laugh and weep;
   Of what may come hereafter
   For men that sow to reap:
   I am weary of days and hours,
   Blown buds of barren flowers,
   Desires and dreams and powers,
   And everything but sleep.

ALGERNON CHARLES SWINBURNE
—*The Garden of Proserpine*

4. She left the web, she left the loom,
   She made three paces thro' the room,
   She saw the water-lily bloom,
   She saw the helmet and the plume,
   She look'd down to Camelot.
      ALFRED, LORD TENNYSON
      —The Lady of Shalott

5. Gather ye rosebuds while ye may,
   Old time is still a-flying:
   And this same flower that smiles to-day,
   To-morrow will be dying.
      ROBERT HERRICK
      —To the Virgins, to Make Much of Time

6. Shall I, wasting in despair,
   Die because a woman's fair?
   Or make pale my cheeks with care
   'Cause another's rosy are?

   Be she fairer than the day,
   Or the flow'ry meads in May!
   If she think not well of me,
   What care I how fair she be?
      GEORGE WITHER
      —The Lover's Resolution

7. A flock of sheep that leisurely pass by,
   One after one; the sound of rain, and bees
   Murmuring; the fall of rivers, winds, and seas,
   Smooth fields, white sheets of water, and pure sky;
   I have thought of all by turns, and yet do lie
   Sleepless! and soon the small birds' melodies
   Must hear, first uttered from my orchard trees;
   And the first cuckoo's melancholy cry.
      WILLIAM WORDSWORTH—*To Sleep*

8. When I am dead, my dearest,
    Sing no sad songs for me;
  Plant thou no roses at my head,
    Nor shady cypress tree:
  Be the green grass above me
    With showers and dewdrops wet;
  And if thou wilt remember,
    And if thou wilt, forget.
                CHRISTINA ROSSETTI—*Song*

The materials that follow will afford the speaker "opportunities in depth" to employ his knowledge and his skill in the use of vocal variety. Be sure that you first read and understand the entire selection, and note the underlying, fundamental thought and mood as well as the nuances in feeling and thought. Experiment, using different techniques of emphasis—e.g., basic pitch change, force, or duration—and decide which of these is the most appropriate one to express the dominant meaning of each selection.

Review Selections

1. Language is not an abstract construction of the learned, or of dictionary makers, but is something arising out of work, needs, ties, joys, affections, tastes, of long generations of humanity, and has its bases broad and low, close to the ground.
                WALT WHITMAN—*Slang in America*

2. Yesterday, December 7, 1941—a date which will live in infamy —the United States of America was suddenly and deliberately attacked by naval and air forces of the Empire of Japan.

The United States was at peace with that nation and, at the solicitation of Japan, was still in conversation with its Government and its Emperor looking toward the maintenance of peace in the Pacific.

Indeed, one hour after Japanese air squadrons had commenced bombing Oahu, the Japanese Ambassador to the United States and his colleague delivered to the Secretary of State a formal reply to a recent American message. While this reply stated that it seemed useless to continue the existing diplomatic negotiations, it contained no threat or hint of war or armed attack.

It will be recorded that the distance of Hawaii from Japan makes it obvious that the attack was deliberately planned many days or even weeks ago. During the intervening time, the Japanese Government had deliberately sought to deceive the United States by false statements and expressions of hope for continued peace.

The attack yesterday on the Hawaiian Islands has caused severe damage to American naval and military forces. Very many American lives have been lost. In addition, American ships have been reported torpedoed on the high seas between San Francisco and Honolulu.

Yesterday the Japanese Government also launched an attack against Malaya.

Last night Japanese forces attacked Hong Kong.

Last night Japanese forces attacked Guam.

Last night Japanese forces attacked the Philippine Islands.

Last night the Japanese attacked Wake Island.

This morning the Japanese attacked Midway Island.

Japan has, therefore, undertaken a surprise offensive extending throughout the Pacific area. The facts of yesterday speak for themselves. The people of the United States have already formed their opinions and well understand the implications to the very life and safety of our nation.

As Commander-in-Chief of the Army and Navy I have directed that all measures be taken for our defense.

Always will we remember the character of the onslaught against us.

No matter how long it may take us to overcome this premeditated invasion, the American people in their righteous might will win through to absolute victory.

I believe I interpret the will of the Congress and of the people when I assert that we will not only defend ourselves to the uttermost but will make very certain that this form of treachery shall never endanger us again.

Hostilities exist. There is no blinking at the fact that our people, our territory and our interests are in grave danger.

With confidence in our armed forces—with the unbounding de-

termination of our people—we will gain the inevitable triumph—so
help us God.

FRANKLIN DELANO ROOSEVELT
—Address to Congress, December 8, 1941

3. O, who rides by night thro' the woodland so wild?
It is the fond father embracing his child;
And close the boy nestles within his loved arm,
To hold himself fast and to keep himself warm.

"O father, my father, see yonder," he says;
"My boy, upon what dost thou fearfully gaze?"
"O, 'tis the Erl-King with his crown and his shroud."
"No, my son, it is but a dark wreath of the cloud."

"O, come and go with me, thou loveliest child;
By many a gay sport shall thy time be beguiled;
My mother keeps for thee full many a fair toy,
And many a fine flower shall she pluck for my boy."

"O, father, my father, and did you not hear
The Erl-King whisper so low in my ear?"
"Be still, my heart's darling—my child, be at ease;
It was but the wild blast as it sung thro' the trees."

"O, wilt thou go with me, thou loveliest boy?
My daughter shall tend thee with care and with joy;
She shall bear thee so lightly thro' wet and thro' wild,
And press thee, and kiss thee and sing to my child."

"O father, my father, and saw you not plain,
The Erl-King's pale daughter glide past through the rain?"
"O yes, my loved treasure, I knew it full soon;
It was the gray willow that danced to the moon."

"O, come and go with me, no longer delay,
Or else, silly child, I will drag thee away."
"O father! O father! now, now keep your hold,
The Erl-King has seized me—his grasp is so cold!"

Sore trembled the father; he spurred thro' the wild,
Clasping close to his bosom his shuddering child;
He reaches his dwelling in doubt and in dread,
But, clasped to his bosom, the infant was dead!
SIR WALTER SCOTT—*The Erl King* (translation)

4. Home they brought her warrior dead;
　　She nor swoon'd, nor utter'd cry:
　All her maidens, watching, said,
　　"She must weep or she will die."

Then they praised him, soft and low,
　　Call'd him worthy to be loved,
　Truest friend and noblest foe;
　　Yet she neither spoke nor moved.

Stole a maiden from her place,
　　Lightly to the warrior stept,
　Took the face-cloth from the face;
　　Yet she neither moved nor wept.

Rose a nurse of ninety years,
　　Set his child upon her knee—
　Like summer tempest came her tears—
　　"Sweet my child, I live for thee."
　　　ALFRED, LORD TENNYSON
　　　—*Home They Brought Her*
　　　　　　Warrior Dead

5. How doth the little crocodile
　　Improve his shining tail,
　And pour the waters of the Nile
　　On every shining scale!

How cheerfully he seems to grin,
　　How neatly spreads his claws,
　And welcomes little fishes in
　　With gently smiling jaws.
　　LEWIS CARROLL—*The Crocodile*

6. As a matter of fact, although few things are spoken of with more fearful whisperings than this prospect of death, few have less influence on conduct under healthy circumstances. We have all heard of cities in South America built upon the side of fiery mountains, and how, even in this tremendous neighbourhood, the inhabitants are not a jot more impressed by the solemnity of mortal conditions than if they were delving gardens in the greenest corner of England. There are serenades and suppers and much gallantry among the myrtles overhead; and meanwhile the foundation shudders underfoot, the bowels of the mountain growl, and at any moment living ruin may leap sky-high into the moonlight, and tumble man and his merry-making in the dust. In the eyes of very young people, and very dull old ones, there is something indescribably reckless and desperate in such a picture. It seems not credible that respectable married people, with umbrellas, should find appetite for a bit of supper within quite a long distance of a fiery mountain; ordinary life begins to smell of high-handed debauch when it is carried on so close to a catastrophe; and even cheese and salad, it seems, could hardly be relished in such circumstances without something like a defiance of the Creator. It should be a place for nobody but hermits dwelling in prayer and maceration, or mere born-devils drowning care in a perpetual carouse.

ROBERT LOUIS STEVENSON—*Aes Triplex*

7. Like other tyrannies, the tyranny of the majority was at first, and is still vulgarly, held in dread, chiefly as operating through the acts of the public authorities. But reflecting persons perceived that when society is itself the tyrant—society collectively, over the separate individuals who compose it—its means of tyrannizing are not restricted to the acts which it may do by the hands of its political functionaries. Society can and does execute its own mandates: and if it issues wrong mandates instead of right, or any mandates at all in things with which it ought not to meddle, it practises a social tyranny more formidable than many kinds of political oppression, since, though not usually upheld by such extreme penalties, it leaves fewer means of escape, penetrating much more deeply into the details of life, and enslaving the soul itself. Protection, therefore, against the tyranny of the magistrate is not enough: there needs

protection also against the tyranny of the prevailing opinion and feeling; against the tendency of society to impose, by other means than civil penalties, its own ideas and practices as rules of conduct on those who dissent from them; to fetter the development, and, if possible, prevent the formation, of any individuality not in harmony with its ways, and compel all characters to fashion themselves upon the model of its own. There is a limit to the legitimate interference of collective opinion with individual independence; and to find that limit, and maintain it against encroachment, is as indispensable to a good condition of human affairs, as protection against political despotism.

JOHN STUART MILL—On Liberty

8. Suppose it were perfectly certain that the life and fortune of every one of us would, one day or other, depend upon his winning or losing a game at chess. Don't you think that we should all consider it to be a primary duty to learn at least the names and moves of the pieces; to have a notion of a gambit, and a keen eye for all the means of giving and getting out of check? Do you not think that we should look with a disapprobation amounting to scorn, upon the father who allowed his son, or the state which allowed its members, to grow up without knowing a pawn from a knight?

Yet it is a very plain and elementary truth that the life, the fortune, and the happiness of every one of us, and, more or less, of those who are connected with us, do depend upon our knowing something of the rules of a game infinitely more difficult and complicated than chess. It is a game which has been played for untold ages, every man and woman of us being one of the two players in a game of his or her own. The chess-board is the world, the pieces are the phenomena of the Universe, the rules of the game are what we call the laws of Nature. The player on the other side is hidden from us. We know that his play is always fair, just and patient. But also we know, to our cost, that he never overlooks a mistake, or makes the smallest allowance for ignorance. To the man who plays well, the highest stakes are paid, with that sort of overflowing generosity with which the strong shows delight in strength. And one who plays ill is checkmated—without haste, but without remorse.

My metaphor will remind some of you of the famous picture in which Retzsch has depicted Satan playing at chess with man for his soul. Substitute for the mocking fiend in that picture a calm, strong angel who is playing for love, as we say, and would rather lose than win—and I should accept it as an image of human life. Well, what I mean by Education is learning the rules of this mighty game. In other words, education is the instruction of the intellect in the laws of Nature, under which name I include not merely things and their forces, but men and their ways; and the fashioning of the affections and of the will into an earnest and loving desire to move in harmony with those laws. For me, education means neither more nor less than this. Anything which professes to call itself education must be tried by this standard, and if it fails to stand the test, I will not call it education, whatever be the force of authority, or of numbers, upon the other side.

THOMAS HENRY HUXLEY—*Essays*

9. Understand this clearly: You can teach a man to draw a straight line and to cut one; to strike a curved line and to carve it; and to copy and carve any number of given lines or forms, with admirable speed and perfect precision; and you find his work perfect of its kind: but if you ask him to think about any of those forms, to consider if he cannot find any better in his own head, he stops; his execution becomes hesitating; he thinks, and ten to one he thinks wrong; ten to one he makes a mistake in the first touch he gives to his work as a thinking being. But you have made a man of him for all that. He was only a machine before, an animated tool.

And observe you are put to stern choice in this matter. You must either make a tool of the creature, or a man of him. You cannot make both. Men were not intended to work with the accuracy of tools, to be precise and perfect in all their actions. If you will have that precision out of them, and make their fingers measure degrees like cog-wheels, and their arms strike curves like compasses, you must unhumanize them. All the energy of their spirits must be given to make cogs and compasses of themselves. . . . On the other hand, if you will make a man of the working creature, you cannot make a tool. Let him but begin to imagine, to think, to try to do anything worth doing; and the engine-turned precision is lost at once. Out come all his roughness, all his dullness, all his incapability; shame upon shame, failure upon failure, pause upon pause: but out comes the whole majesty of him also.

JOHN RUSKIN—*The Stones of Venice*

10. Way back in the dawn of history we have records of some of the thoughts and concepts of our early ancestors. The most intelligent, the most progressive, of those early men who crawled out of a cave to hunt a snake for dinner inscribed on the walls of his dismal home some of his concepts of society as he knew it. No doubt as he beat his hairy breast, with one foot clamped down on the prostrate neck of his conquered victim, he must have made the welkin so ring that Tarzan would be counted a baby in comparison. Then, with exultant glee, he crawled back into his cave to inscribe on dark and murky walls the pictures of his prowess—symbols of thought that still communicate concepts for us, even now.

As a man thus emerged from the bleak darkness of prehistoric void into the gray dawn of history he gradually, painfully, intermittently stumbled into an awareness of himself as an individual. Other individuals arose and forced their attentions upon him—and so a crude form of human society was born. Human beasts pitted against human beasts demanded that some kind of concerted action be instigated against such wanton fratricide.

Grunts, howls, and gesticulation commenced to take on specific meanings. A certain peculiar howl with proper leg and arm movements was followed by a punch in the nose—then that howl and gesture became the symbol of a threat that meant, unless heeded, a sore proboscis. A different kind of a grunt accompanied by a flashing grimace may well have meant, "Come on out, have grub worms and snails with the Mrs. and me today." So early man through rough symbols commenced to communicate thought.

I. G. MORRISON—"Behind the Symbol,"
Today's Speech IV, September, 1956.

SUMMARY

Vocal variety may be used to express feelings, to communicate meanings, to hold attention, and to make speaking and listening interesting. Any of the attributes of voice—pitch, quality, loudness, or duration—may be used toward these ends. Rarely is a single attribute used alone. Changes in pitch and force are frequently made together. Usually words spoken slowly are also spoken with increased force. The effective speaker achieves his effects by a combination of vocal factors but is able to control the factors according to the nature of what he has to say. The effective speaker is able to use a widened pitch range, appropriate inflection, modifications in vocal intensity, and changes in the tempo of his speech to indicate how he feels about his thoughts as he talks. Furthermore, he can use vocal variety as a means of pointing up essential ideas and subordinating less important ones.

Part Two · DICTION

10 • Introduction to Study of American-English Sounds

IMPROVEMENT OF DICTION

This part of the book has two related purposes. The first is to provide the reader with some fundamentals involved in the production of American-English speech sounds. The second is to provide specific information about the sounds of our language and practice materials for each of the sounds. Both purposes are intended to help the reader in his basic objective of becoming an effective speaker.

No attempt will be made to be prescriptive or to impose any one standard of diction as better or more desirable than another. We shall, however, work on the basic assumption that any manner or product of speech that attracts attention to itself rather than to the content of speech needs modification.

The sounds of speech, occasionally singly but usually in combination, constitute a symbol code which we use for oral and audible communication. We employ about forty distinctive sounds or *phonemes* in the symbol code of American-English speech. There are some variants in this code in different parts of this country. Major variants will be pointed out, but they are relatively few and almost never so great as to prevent ready communication between good speakers from widely separated parts of our country. Poor speakers may have difficulty in communicating in their own areas; their difficulties tend to increase as they try to make themselves understood when they travel at distances from home. For the most part, however, the good speaker from New Orleans, Louisiana, may need a little time to "tune in" to the speech of the Bostonian, the New Yorker, or the citizen from Chicago, but after a brief period all these citizens should be able to understand one another despite some regional differences in diction.

THE SOUNDS OF AMERICAN ENGLISH

Sound Representation

There are several ways of representing the sounds of our language. We can do so through spelling (orthographic representation) or through a system in which there is greater consistency between the visible symbol and the sound. It is obvious that a spoken language which has only twenty-six letter symbols and forty or more different sounds cannot have sufficient consistency between letter and sound to provide a reliable guide for articulation and pronunciation. Most of our dictionaries therefore employ a system of diacritical markings and symbols to help the reader appreciate how a word should be pronounced because of or despite of its spelling. Unfortunately, even the use of diacritical markings fails to provide a clear one-to-one relationship between sound and symbol. Still another system, more consistent than either of the others, employs selected symbols of the International Phonetic Alphabet (IPA). In the IPA system one symbol is used for each distinctively different sound. Our approach will emphasize the use of the last symbol code. We shall, however, indicate the Webster-Merriam dictionary equivalent of the IPA symbols. Through this approach, we hope that it will become possible for the reader: (1) to become aware of the sounds (phonemes) of our language, (2) to make distinctions according to the characteristics of the different sounds, and (3) to establish a visible basis to cue him on the manner of production for the individual sound, or for a series of sounds, in the contextual flow of speech.

The different sounds of American-English speech and their phonetic symbol and dictionary symbol representations follow.

THE COMMON PHONEMES OF AMERICAN ENGLISH

KEY WORD	DICTIONARY SYMBOL	IPA SYMBOL
	Consonants	
1. *p*at	p	[p]
2. *b*ee	b	[b]
3. *t*in	t	[t]
4. *d*en	d	[d]
5. *c*ook	k	[k]
6. *g*et	g	[g]
7. *f*ast	f	[f]
8. *v*an	v	[v]
9. *th*in	th	[θ]
10. *th*is	th	[ð]
11. *s*ea	s	[s]
12. *z*oo	z	[z]
13. *sh*e	sh	[ʃ]
14. trea*s*ure	zh	[ʒ]
15. *ch*ick	ch	[tʃ]
16. *j*ump	j	[dʒ]
17. *m*e	m	[m]
18. *n*o	n	[n]
19. si*ng*	ng	[ŋ]
20. *l*et	l	[l]
21. *r*un	r	[r]
22. *y*ell	y	[j]
23. *h*at	h	[h]
24. *w*on	w	[w]
25. *wh*at	hw	[ʍ] or [hw]
	Vowels	
26. f*ee*	ē	[i]
27. s*i*t	ĭ	[ɪ]
28. t*a*ke	ā	[e]
29. m*e*t	ĕ	[ɛ]
30. c*a*lm	ä	[ɑ]
31. t*a*sk	ă or à	[æ] or [a] depending upon regional or individual variations
32. c*a*t	ă	[æ]
33. h*o*t	ŏ or ä	[ɒ] or [ɑ] depending upon regional or individual variations
34. s*a*w	ô	[ɔ]
35. v*o*te	ō	[o] or [oʊ]
36. b*u*ll	o͝o	[ʊ]
37. t*oo*	o͞o	[u]

THE COMMON PHONEMES OF AMERICAN ENGLISH (*Continued*)

38. h*u*t	ŭ	[ʌ]
39. *a*bout	ă,ĕ,ĭ,ŏ,ŭ,à,ē	[ə]
40. upp*er*	ẽr	[ɚ]
		by most Americans and [ə] by many others
41. b*ir*d	ûr	[ɝ]
		by most Americans and [ɜ] by many others

Phonemic	*Diphthongs*	
42. ice	[ī]	[aɪ]
43. now	[ou]	[aʊ] or [ɑʊ]
44. boy	[oi]	[ɔɪ]

The Phoneme

Our study of the sounds of American-English speech will be approached through a consideration of the basic unit or sound family —the *phoneme*. Phonemes are distinctive phonetic (sound) elements of words. The phonetic elements are distinctive in that they constitute sound differences which enable us to distinguish between spoken words. For example, the word *sad* has three phonemes. If we change the first, we can distinguish between *sad* and *mad*; if we change the second, we can distinguish between *sad* and *sod*; if we change the last, we can distinguish between *sad* and *sap*.

A second aspect of the phoneme concept is variation. Speech sounds vary in production according to context. The [t] in *tell* is somewhat different from the [t] in *its* and *plate*. Despite the variations, however, they are essentially more alike than different, and we respond to all of these words as containing a [t]. These sound variations which do not affect our understanding of what we hear constitute the members of the phoneme or sound family. The individual variants are called *allophones*.

If our pronunciations and articulatory efforts do not show regard for possible phonemic differences, our listeners may become confused. If the vowel of *bad* begins to approximate the vowel of *bed* we may be misunderstood if we utter a sentence such as *This will be bad for you*. Similarly, if an [s] is produced so that it begins to suggest an [ʃ] (sh), we may not know whether something is for *sipping* or *shipping*.

Some of the difficulty foreign-born persons have in learning to speak English may be attributed to the fact that the phonemes in their native language are not always directly equivalent to ours. For example, we make a significant distinction between the vowels of words such as *heel* and *hill* and *seen* and *sin*. By way of television, radio, or movies, if not by direct experience, most of us know that many of our Mexican neighbors *think* with the vowel of *seen*. They may also have difficulty with the distinctions we make between *hail* and *hell*. We, of course, are not immune from these errors when we learn a foreign language. When speaking another language, we often produce vowels and some consonants of our closest equivalents and so manage to sound like a foreigner.

CLASSIFICATION OF SOUNDS

The sounds of our language may be classified in three large groups: consonants, vowels, and diphthongs. All are produced as a result of some modification of the outgoing breath by the organs of articulation.

Consonants are speech sounds which are produced by either a complete or partial obstruction or modification of the breath channel by the organs of articulation. Aside from voice, the sound characteristics of each consonant result from the manner of vibration of the breath stream. This is determined by the way in which the breath stream is (1) modified by the closures produced by articulatory activity, (2) released by the activity of the opening of the closure, or (3) modified but not completely obstructed (stopped) by the narrowing of the breath channel.

Vowels are produced by articulatory movements of the speech organs without obstruction or interference of the vibrating breath stream in its passage through the breath channel. We determine the characteristic features of the vowels of our language by modifying the size and shape of the mouth cavity and by changing the position of the tongue within the mouth.

Diphthongs are voiced glides which are uttered in a single breath impulse. Some diphthongs are blends of two vowels. Most, however, represent an instability or "breakdown" of what at one time in the history of our language was one vowel. Regardless of historical development, a diphthong may be defined as ". . . a syllabic element, which begins with one sound and shifts to another, and we understand this to exclude consideration of those brief building-up and dying-out stages which characterize every speech sound." *

Voice

All vowels and diphthongs, unless intentionally whispered, are produced with vocalization accompanying the articulatory activity. Consonants, however, may be produced with or without accompanying vocalization. Those which are produced with vocalization are known as *voiced* consonants, those produced without vocalization are referred to as *voiceless*.

Manner and Place of Articulation

In the individual descriptions of the consonant sounds which will be presented later, the manner and place of articulation will be considered for each sound. Some consonants will be described as *plosives*, others as either *fricatives, glides,* or *nasals*. We will anticipate some of the descriptions by defining a few terms at the present time.

Plosive or stop sounds are produced by a stopping of the breath stream. The plosive sounds are [p], [b], [t], [d], [k], and [g].

Fricatives are produced by a partial closure of the articulators. This action results in the creation of a constricted passage through which the stream of air must be forced. The partial closures may take place as a result of the grooving of the tongue or of having other organs of articulation come close together. The distinctively fricative sounds are [f], [v], [θ] (th), [ð] (th), [s], [z], [ʃ] (sh). and [ʒ] (zh). The sound [h] is produced with laryngeal constriction.

Nasal sounds are reinforced and emitted nasally. The three nasals are [m], [n], and [ŋ] (ng).

Glides are sounds which are produced with continuous rather than fixed articulatory positions. The glide consonants are [hw] or [ʌ], [w], [j] (y), and most varieties of [r].

Affricates are blends of two sounds, one a plosive and the other a

* R-M. S. Heffner, *General Phonetics,* University of Wisconsin Press, 1949, p. 112.

fricative. There are two affricates, [tʃ] (ch) as in *chum* and [dʒ] (dzh) as in *jam*.

The sound [l] is a *lateral* consonant. It is produced by the emission of vocalized breath at both sides of the tongue while the tip of the tongue is in contact with the gum ridge.

SOUNDS IN CONTEXT

Although our approach to the improvement of diction will begin with a descriptive analysis of the individual sounds of our language, speech does not consist of a series of individual sounds. Speech is a sequence or context of sounds. In context, individual sounds may be modified and produced differently from what they would be in isolation. If one were to speak as though our linguistic symbols were a series of sounds, he would be uttering phonetic nonsense. In context, differences in force and duration to emphasize meanings, differences according to the formality or informality of the speech situation, and differences according to the size of the listening group all make for modifications of individual sounds in the flow of speech. Some of these differences will be considered briefly.

ASSIMILATION

If asked for the pronunciation of the words *education, mature,* and *income,* many persons would carefully pronounce these words differently from their pronunciations in contextual speech. The word *education* may regularly be pronounced [ɛdjukeʃən] (edūkāshən) by some persons but most of us are likely to say [ɛdʒəkeʃən] (ejakāshən) in talking about "the education of our children" or in asserting that "education means—." When we change from the careful but less usual pronunciation of words such as *educate, income, handkerchief* or phrases such as *don't you* and *meet you* to the easier and more usual ones we are yielding to and demonstrating the effects of *assimilation in connected speech.*

Assimilation refers to the phonetic changes that take place when one sound is modified as the result of a neighboring sound or sounds in connected speech. Some of these changes become relatively fixed and so regularly influence the pronunciations of many words. Other assimilations depend upon particular contexts and so influence the articulation and pronunciation of words only in these contexts. Examples of each will be given in our brief discussions of some types of assimilative modifications.

Anticipatory Changes

Most assimilations reflect the influences of anticipatory changes. That is, the organs of articulation, in anticipation of a sound to follow, modify a preceding sound. The change tends to simplify or facilitate articulation. For example, in the word *congress,* the letter *n* is sounded as an [ŋ] (ng) in anticipation of the sound [g] that follows. It is easier to articulate [ŋg] than [n + g] simply because both the [ŋ] and the [g] are produced with the same parts of the tongue and the palate. For the same reason *income* is pronounced with an [ŋ] rather than an [n] followed by a [k]. Similarly, it is easier to say *this shoe* with a lengthened [ʃ] (sh) than with an [s] followed by an [ʃ]. The pronunciation of *this shoe,* incidentally, is an example of contextual, temporary assimilation.

Voicing

Changes produced in voicing by assimilation are perhaps best exemplified in words that end with a final *s* or *d*. In the words *liked, heaped, rasped, guessed* and *ropes, takes,* and *plates* the next to the last produced sound is a voiceless consonant. (The letter *e*, in each case, is silent.) As a result, the final *d* is pronounced as a [t] rather than [d] and the final *s* as an [s] rather than [z].

In words such as *passes, hedges, riches,* and *roses* the final *s* is produced as [z] because the next to the last sound is a vowel and is vocalized. Similarly, *grounded, breaded,* and *heeded* are each pronounced with a final [d]. In the words *begs, seems, togs,* and *roams* the final sound is voiced because of the influence of the preceding voiced consonant.

Other Assimilations

In some cases assimilations may result in the complete loss of one or more sounds which are replaced by a third sound. This happens in the assimilated pronunciation of *picture, nature,* and *feature,* where the sound [tʃ] (ch) is heard in the second syllable of each of the words.

STYLES OF SPEECH

In both manner and content speech is appropriate or inappropriate, correct or incorrect, according to circumstances and occasion. Despite possible differences in education, profession, and speaking ability, an individual's manner of communicating will or should vary according to the time, the place, and the speaking situation. The minister who feels the need to deliver a sermon to his family should do so differently from the way he would speak to his congregation in church. The minister should certainly not converse at home, with members of his family or with visiting members of his congregation, as he would talk to them from his pulpit. The lecturer speaking to a large audience on a formal occasion is likely to use more elevated language than the same speaker at his club, on a picnic, with friends, or at a home social gathering.

Informal speech employs many contractions. We use more *he's*, *don't's* and *I'm's* when speaking informally and intimately than when speaking formally. We do not, however, usually employ contracted forms when emphasis is intended. Public addresses, with the exception of the humorous after-dinner speech, are generally delivered formally unless, for special purposes (usually political), the speaker wants his listeners to feel that he is "one of the boys."

Pronunciation

We are aware that many words of our language have more than one acceptable pronunciation. Some pronunciations are current and therefore standard according to geographic areas. The Englishman and the American pronounce *laboratory* and *garage* with different syllable stress and with resultant differences in vowels. Our good, large dictionaries include, usually in order of frequency of usage, varying pronunciations of many words. They also indicate that many words have different meanings, and the more frequent meanings are presented. The authority of a dictionary in respect to pronunciations and meaning is succinctly summarized by Harrison Platt, Jr., in his preface to *The American College Dictionary*:

What . . . is the role of a dictionary in settling questions of pronunciation or meaning or grammar? It is *not* a legislating authority on good English. It attempts to record what usage at any time actually is. Insofar as possible, it points out divided usage. It indicates regional variations of pronunciation or meaning wherever practical. It points out meanings and uses peculiar to a trade, profession, or special activity. It suggests the levels on which certain words or usages are appropriate. A dictionary . . . based on a realistic sampling of usage, furnishes the information necessary for a sound judgment of what is good English in a given situation. To this extent the dictionary is an authority, and beyond this authority should not go.*

SPEECH STANDARDS

Pronunciation Variants

In going over the list of consonants and vowel sounds some observations may be made relative to minor differences in pronunciation among Americans.

Many of us do not distinguish between the [hw] in *what* and the [w] of *watt* but pronounce both the way we do the first sound of *will.*

There is considerable variation as to the pronunciation of the vowel of the word *ask.* Most Americans use the same vowel in the words *ask* and *hat;* others broaden the vowel in *ask* to that of the [ɑ] of *calm;* a smaller number of Americans use the vowel [a] which is phonetically between [æ] and [ɑ].

Most Americans use the same vowel in *hot* as they do in *calm.* A few, however, use a vowel intermediate between the vowel of *call* and the vowel of *calm.*

There is considerable variation in the production of the vowel of words such as *bird* and *heard.* Some use the vowel [ɝ] which has *r* coloring. Others include a clear-cut *r* preceded by a vowel much like the one in the word *bud.*

Paralleling the variations in the vowel of words such as *bird, heard, surf,* and *mirth* are those for the final sound of the words such as *after, supper,* and *thunder.* Most of us use the vowel [ɚ] which is much like the first sound of the word *above* with the addi-

---

* *The American College Dictionary,* New York, Harper & Brothers and Random House, 1948, p. xxxl.

tion of *r* coloring. Others add a clear-cut *r* sound after the same vowel, and a smaller number make no distinction between the first sound of the word *above* and the last sound of *after* and use [ə] for both.

To this short list of variants in American pronunciation, we might add another relative to the articulation of the *r* sound in words in which the spelling includes the letter *r*. We are in common agreement that an [r] sound is produced whenever a word contains an initial *r* in its spelling, as in *rug, rice, rain,* and *runs* and in words in which the *r* is preceded by a consonant and followed by a vowel as in *tree, grease,* and *prize*. The [r] is also pronounced in medial positions when it is followed by a vowel as in *forest* and *touring*. Practice differs, however, in words in which the *r* is medial in spelling and followed by a consonant as in *farm, card,* and *sharp* or final in the spelling as in *car, far,* and *soar*. These differences will be considered again in our more detailed consideration of the [r] sound.

Assimilations and Speech Standards

Most of the examples of assimilation given earlier are considered acceptable and in good standing by all except the most pedantic people. Some persons may prefer the unassimilated pronunciations of words such as *congress* and *income* and tax themselves to maintain the [n] rather than yield to economy in articulation and produce an [ŋ]. Not all assimilations, however, are acceptable even to our liberal dictionary editors. For example, the word *open,* despite temptation and frequent pronunciation by small children, should still be produced with a final [n] rather than an [m]. The word *gas* is still better pronounced with a final [s] than with a [z], though the second pronunciation is frequently given by persons not habitually careless in their speech.

Substandard Speech

Speech in general and pronunciation in particular are appropriate if they are consistent with the objectives of the speaker in his role of communicator of ideas. The listeners, the occasion, and the speaker as a personality are some of the factors which determine appropriateness. What is appropriate may be accepted as standard. Speech becomes substandard if the pronunciations are such that they violate the judgments and tastes of the listeners. We are likely to sense such violations if an official in high government office speaks to us as members of a large audience as he might to some of his intimate friends on a fishing trip. We might also sense some violation if a paid lecturer on the "Effects of Atomic Radiation" talked to us in the manner of a sports announcer.

Speech becomes distinctly substandard if it employs pronunciations which are not currently used by any persons whose backgrounds as speakers make their judgments as to linguistic usage worthy of respect. Even a liberal attitude as to pronunciation would not now justify the pronunciation of *asked* as [æst] (ăst) or of *ten* as [tin] (tĭn).

Pronunciations which reveal foreign language influence, such as the substitution of a sound which approximates the appropriate one in English, would also constitute substandard speech. The substitution of a [v] for a [w] in words such as *wife* and *went* or an [f] for a [v] in words such as *give* and *leave* are examples of substandard pronunciations frequently resulting from foreign language influence. Occasionally, they may reflect persistent foreign language influences in dialectal speech within this country.

The speaker who wishes to improve his speech, his articulation, and his pronunciation must be a good listener. He must listen with discrimination for what is best and current in the community in which he lives. He must listen to the educated and respected members of the community and use them as models but not imitate them slavishly. Above all, he should avoid trying to sound like somebody else, thus seeming to deny his individuality and his place of origin. This does not mean that he should maintain what may have been substandard in his background. It does mean that the man from New York should not consciously try to sound as though he were from Atlanta, Georgia, and that the speaker from Dallas, Texas, should not (it is extremely unlikely that he would wish to) try to sound like the Harvard-educated Bostonian. In time, if any of these speakers live long enough in an area, some of the flavor of the area's speech will naturally begin to appear. Careful listening is likely to translate itself into unconscious imitation of the speech of the immediate environment unless the speaker is negatively motivated toward the persons to whom he is listening.

11 • Individual Study of American-English Sounds: The Vowels

In our study of the sounds of American-English speech we shall maintain our objective of the improvement of diction. Some sounds have been found to be more troublesome—more frequently produced in a faulty manner—than others. These sounds will receive our major emphasis. They will be treated in more detail and a larger amount of practice-exercise material will be provided for them than for the sounds which cause little difficulty for the vast majority of speakers of American-English.

We shall begin our study with an analysis of the vowel sounds. Although differences in practice relative to the pronunciation of vowels are fairly wide in different parts of the country, most vowel sounds, because of their intensity and "open" manner of production, are comparatively easy to imitate. Pronunciation habits based upon regional practice may, however, result in the persistent use of one vowel in some words when most Americans use another. For example, there is considerable variation in the pronunciation of the vowel in the words *had, have, candy, bad* and *sad,* depending upon regional custom. There is also a fair amount of regional variation in the pronunciation of the vowels in words such as *word, bird, heard, dearth, earth, curdle,* and *merge.* There is also some variation in the choice of vowel for words such as *path, ask,* and *dance.* Some of the variations in practice in different parts of the country will be considered when the individual vowel sounds are discussed.

VOWEL PRODUCTION

All vowels share several characteristics: (1) They are all voiced sounds; (2) all are articulated in essentially the same manner in that they are continuant sounds without interruption and without restriction of the stream of breath; and (3) though lip activity is involved, the activity of the tongue makes the essential difference in the production of the different vowel sounds.

Vowel Classification

Vowels may be conveniently classified according to the part of the tongue most actively involved in the production of the sound. If you concentrate on the vowel sounds of the words *me* and *moo,* you

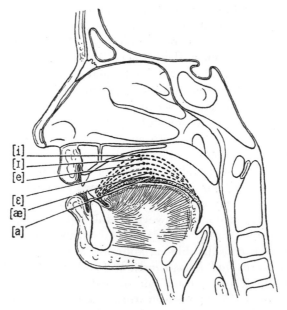

Fig. 10. Representative Tongue Positions for Front Vowels.

should be able to note that the blade of the tongue moves forward toward the hard palate for *me*. For *moo*, the back of the tongue moves toward the soft palate. Similar activity may be noted if you compare the vowels of *pet* and *paw*. For *pet*, the front of the tongue is most active. And for *paw* the back of the tongue is most active. For neither of the vowels, however, does the tongue move as high as for the vowels of *me* and *moo*. Comparable activity may be observed for all the other *front vowels* (those produced with the front or blade of the tongue most active) compared with the corresponding *back vowels* (those produced with the back of the tongue most active).

The approximate differences in tongue position for the front and back vowels are illustrated in Figs. 10 and 11.

Figure 12 illustrates the position of the tongue for the central vowels or mid-vowels (those produced with the middle of the tongue most active).

You may test these representative tongue positions with your own

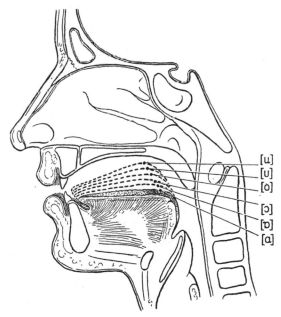

Fig. 11. Representative Tongue Positions for Back Vowels.

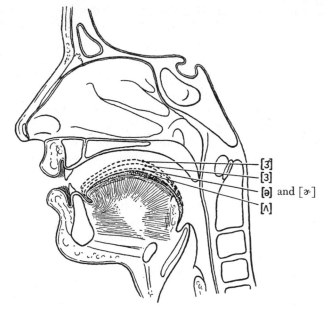

Fig. 12. Representative Tongue Positions for the Central or Mid-Vowels.

articulatory behavior relative to these vowels by incorporating them in the following key words.

Front	*Central*	*Back*
me		boot
mit		book
made	mirth	boat
met	*a*bove	bought
mat	mud	box
mask		balm

On the basis of the production of the key vowels, a twofold basis for classification becomes possible.

First, vowels differ in production according to *place of articulation*—and so may be classified as *front, mid-,* or *back* vowels according to the part of the tongue most actively involved.

Second, vowels differ as to *height-of-tongue* position. The vowel of *me* is a high front vowel; the vowel of *moon* is a high back vowel.

VOWELS OF AMERICAN-ENGLISH SPEECH

Front Vowels

	PHONETIC SYMBOL	DICTIONARY SYMBOL
meet	[i]	ē
milk	[ɪ]	ĭ
may	[e]	ā
men	[ɛ]	ĕ
mat	[æ]	ă
ask[a]	[a]	à

Mid-Vowels

	PHONETIC SYMBOL	DICTIONARY SYMBOL
mirth	[ɝ] or [ɜ˞]	ûr
about	[ə]	{ ȧ, ĕ, ĭ, ŏ / ŭ, à, ē }
mud	[ʌ]	ŭ

Back Vowels

	PHONETIC SYMBOL	DICTIONARY SYMBOL
boon	[u]	o͞o
book	[ʊ]	o͝o
boat	[o]	ō
ball	[ɔ]	ô
bog	[ɒ]	ŏ
balm	[ɑ]	ä

[a] When the speaker compromises between the vowels of *mat* and of *balm*. This vowel is intermediate in placement as well as in sound between [æ] and [ɑ].

145

The vowel of *mask* is a low front vowel; that of *balm* is a low back vowel.

A *third basis* for the classification of vowels is *muscle tension*. If we compare the vowel of *peek* with that of *pick*, we should feel that the tongue is more tense for the vowel of *peek* than it is for the one in *pick*. Similarly, the vowel of *boat* is produced with the tongue somewhat more tense than in the production of the vowel of *book*. Tension may also be felt in the muscles behind the chin.

Before we go into our more detailed discussion of the individual sounds of our language, we might review briefly some features of vowel production. All vowels, unless intentionally whispered, are voiced, continuant sounds. When produced as isolated sounds, the tongue tip is usually placed behind the lower gum ridge. The vowel sounds are differentiated as a result of activity of the blade, the middle or the back of the tongue elevated to different positions (heights) within the mouth cavity. Some vowels are produced with muscle tension as an additional characteristic. The articulatory aspects which characterize the production of each of the vowels will now be considered.

INDIVIDUAL CONSIDERATION OF
THE VOWELS OF AMERICAN ENGLISH
THE FRONT VOWELS

[i] (ē) As in *See*

An examination of the front-vowel diagram will reveal that [i] is produced with the blade of the tongue arched high in the front of the mouth. It is produced with a considerable degree of tongue tension and a lesser degree of lip tension. When [i] is produced as an isolated sound, the lip position approximates a tight-lipped grin. Tension should also be present in the muscle bulge behind the chin.

Muscle tension is necessary to produce a clear [i] and to distinguish it from the vowel [ɪ] (ĭ) which is a more relaxed sound.

The sound [i] has many different English spellings. The most frequent include *e, ee, ea, ei, i*, and *ie* as in *be, see, each, receipt, ski*, and *believe*.

Practice Materials

Initial

even	eager	equal	ego
ether	eel	eaves	Easter
east	eat	ease	edict

Medial

breathe	feast	conceive	machine
breed	meat	please	crease
please	sweet	breeze	team
heat	yield	intrigue	achieve

Final

agree	pea	tree	sea
glee	flee	ski	spree
esprit	key	bee	lea
tee	she	we	knee

Sentences

1. Eva likes green peas.
2. Because she was indiscreet the policeman did not yield to Eve's appeal.
3. Pass the sweet meats, please.
4. A team without *esprit de corps* is not well esteemed.
5. The breeze made the heat bearable.
6. The edict included the area East of Eden.
7. Edith was fond of eating eels.
8. The geese flew over Lake Erie.
9. Was Eve the first to speak in the Garden of Eden or did Adam precede Eve?
10. We are a unique species because many of us seem to live to eat rather than to eat to live.
11. In his eerie dream he could see the sheep leaping unceasingly over the green field.
12. If we esteem freedom we must speak our beliefs.
13. Stephen Steel observed with some feeling that he viewed a woman as not quite complete if she lacked an air of conceit.

[ɪ] (ĭ) As in *Bit*

The vowel [ɪ] differs from [i] in two respects; [ɪ] is produced with a tongue position somewhat lowered than [i] and *without articulatory tension.*

The lip position for [ɪ] is approximately a relaxed smile in contrast with the tight-lipped grin for [i]. The difference in tension and lip may be observed by placing your hand behind your chin and looking in the mirror as you change from the word *heat* to *hit.*

The most frequent spelling for [ɪ] is the letter *i* as in *sit, wit, fit,* and *lit*; other spellings include *u, ui,* and *e* as in *busy, build,* and *English.*

Some speakers use the vowel [ɪ] for the final *y* in words such as *busy, city, petty.* Other speakers are likely to use a vowel somewhere between [i] and [ɪ]. Still others may use a vowel closer to [i] than to [ɪ].*

Practice Materials

Determine your own practice by testing yourself with the following lists of words.

sea	city	sit
pea	pity	pit
key	kitty	kit
me	meaty	mit
cheese	cheesy	chit
see	seedy	sit

Practice Materials

Initial

ill	it	ingot	infer
imp	is	Italy	intake
ink	itch	indicate	ignore
Indian	inch	inn	insert
into	imply	ignorant	image

* C. K. Thomas in his *Handbook of Speech Improvement,* Ronald Press, 1956, p. 102, observes that "whenever English [i] is prolonged it is characterized by a gradually increasing muscular tension which can be symbolized by [ɪi]." Thomas would use the symbols [ɪi] in the words of our above list.

Medial

business	tryst	strip	flick
differ	women	shrimp	whisk
fill	wishes	shrill	hymn
quick	drip	grill	quilt
wilt	mince	lick	think
eclipse	instill	bib	admit
addict	crib	simple	spin

Sentences

1. Jim Wilson made a business trip to Italy.
2. In traffic it is better to be quick than wishful.
3. Women who are intelligent are also adaptive.
4. Impressions may be made indelible without India ink.
5. Isabel's voice was thin and shrill.
6. Irrigation has helped to make arid land fertile.
7. The physicist whistled as he split his atom.
8. One can be witty and yet stick to simple thinking.
9. Grilled shrimp is Matilda's special dish.
10. Phil is partial to mince pie and ginger cake.

For persons who have difficulty in distinguishing between the tense vowel [i] and the relaxed [ɪ] the following material should be of help. Place your hand behind your chin and feel the tension for the vowel in the first word of each pair. The second word, in contrast, should have a relaxed chin.

seat	sit	leak	lick
beat	bit	sheep	ship
meat	mit	sleep	slip
heat	hit	peach	pitch
greet	grit	leap	lip
cheap	chip	green	grin
peep	pip	heap	hip
fleet	flit	peak	pick
reed	rid	greed	grid
feel	fill	heel	hill

In the following sentences the first italicized word has the tense vowel [i]; the second has the relaxed vowel [ɪ].

Sentences
1. Her *green* mouth made us *grin.*
2. Do not *eat it* now.
3. Mary's high *heels* made it difficult for her to climb up the *hill.*
4. The *sheep* were *shipped* by train.
5. The *beets* were cut into *bits.*
6. *Steel* is *still* scarce.
7. The *eel* made us *ill.*

[e] (ā) As in *Mate*

Most Americans are more likely to produce the vowel [e] as part of the diphthong [eɪ] than as a pure vowel. Whether produced as part of a diphthong or as a pure sound [e] is a tense, front, mid-high vowel (see front-vowel diagram, page 142).

Some speakers use the diphthongal form more or less regularly in a stressed syllable and the pure vowel form in an unstressed syllable. However, there are no words in our language which would be distinguished in meaning from one another on the basis of the use of a pure vowel [e] or the diphthongal form [eɪ]. We do not recommend the cultivation of either form for the sake of consistency. We do, however, recommend that excessive prolongation of the diphthong to a triphthong [eɪə] be avoided.

The vowel [e] or the diphthong [eɪ] is most frequently represented in spelling by the letter *a* as in *date, mate,* and *hate*; other frequent spellings include *ay, ai, ey,* and *ei* as in *say, mail, they,* and *vein.*

Practice Materials

Initial

ace	angel	eight	ate
ail	April	ape	ache
age	aim	aviator	aid

Medial

bail	place	grate	station
deign	plate	lace	caged
date	rate	chaste	strafe
sake	flake	awake	failure

Final

shay	delay	bay	ray
pay	hay	neigh	portray
day	may	betray	fray
way	they	play	display

Note whether you distinguish between the vowel and diphthong forms in the following sentences. Careful listening may help you to decide that sentence context may make a difference.

Sentences
1. Amy was fond of baking angel food cake.
2. Sadie wore a long cape around the nape of her neck.
3. The cape was of an ancient Asian type.
4. Texas is a state of mind as well as a state of the United States.
5. May's picture was painted during her visit in Maine.
6. Grace married an aviation ace named Hale.
7. The cake was stale to no one's dismay.
8. The almost naked sheep grazed over the plain.
9. Jay fell asleep near the bale of hay.
10. The stack of hay was taken away.
11. Days pass in haste when a debt is waiting to be repaid.
12. Mamie gazed in dismay at the antics of the zany caged animal.

Avoid excessive prolongation of the diphthong [ei] in the following sentences.

1. Do not *fail* to find the *trail*.
2. A punished dog may drag his *tail*.
3. *May* looked *faint* at the sight of the wounded *quail*.
4. He set *sail* to avoid going to *jail*.

[ɛ] (ĕ) As in *Help*

The vowel [ɛ] differs from [e] in that the former is produced with a slightly lower front tongue position and *without articulatory tension*.

The most frequent spelling for the vowel [ɛ] is the single letter *e*; other spellings include *a* as in *any*, *ay* as in *says*, *ai* as in *said*, and *ea* as in *bread*.

Practice Materials

In the lists of words for initial and medial [ɛ] avoid any tendency to prolong the vowel into the diphthong [ɛə].

Initial

ebb	empty	enter	engine
end	any	energy	exit
echo	elf	elk	elder
egg	elbow	edge	effort
etch	edible	entry	extra

Medial

beckon	said	jest	center
lend	gem	wren	theft
guess	thread	deaf	health
pleasant	meant	check	pensive
self	tent	ready	settler

Sentences

1. Ethel held that you lose your friends if you permit them to be in debt.
2. The hen was set until her nest of eggs was hatched.
3. Ed's elder brother was deaf.
4. Ezra could not always check his pent-up energies.
5. Though she entered an empty room, Esther kept her elbows sharp.
6. Not all students are inept who fret at a test.
7. The bell sounded its knell at ebb tide.
8. Fred could only guess at what the gesture meant.
9. Birds of a feather are not all hens.
10. The dog was inept at picking up the scent.

Be certain that clear distinctions are made for the italicized words in the sentences that follow.

1. The *pen* was placed next to the *pin*.
2. Is a *setting* hen also a *sitting* hen?
3. You can *get* your mail at the *gate*.

[æ] (ă) **As in** *Bat*

[æ] is a low front vowel. It is almost always produced with a lax tongue; occasionally some contexts call for a slightly tense tongue but emphatic tension should be avoided. The tongue is lower in position and the mouth wider open for [æ] than it is for [ε] (see front-vowel diagram, page 142.

The letter *a* as in *mash, pack, rack,* and *sack* is the most frequent spelling representation for the vowel [æ].

In some parts of the United States the vowel blend [εə] tends to be substituted for the vowel [æ]. In much of the United States a vowel closer to [ε] than to [æ] is heard in words in which the vowel is followed by the sound [r] as in *marry, parry,* and *Harry.*

Practice Materials

Determine your own practice for the following words in which the vowel [æ] is an acceptable pronunciation. Doubts, if they exist, should be determined by usage of respected speakers in your community.

cap	shall	had	bag
can	carry	fact	tapped
cast	parrot	fancy	plant
back	drank	ham	shall

Initial

angle	antler	act	add
apple	anchor	alkaline	aster
atom	agonize	ample	Alice
angry	abduct	annual	Alps

Medial

crack	lacking	jagged	hack
stack	slapped	ragged	wax
mash	flax	flagging	hatched
pack	bagged	wrapped	satin

Sentences

1. Calvin carried his bride from the carriage into the house.
2. Alice planted three rows of asters.
3. The pack had ample room for a dozen apples.
4. The Swiss Alps have many jagged peaks.
5. Jam and pancakes make a snack for a boy and a meal for a man.
6. Thaddeus fancied himself a man of action.
7. Alan went to California to enhance his acting career.
8. A good match is preceded by a good catch.
9. The cab's wheels sank deep into the sand.
10. Hatless and ragged, his spirits never flagged.
11. A hammer rather than an ax should be used for a tack.
12. The jam sandwiches were wrapped in wax sacks.

In the following sentences be careful to avoid excessive tension or nasality for the vowels of the italicized words. Keep your jaw and tongue relaxed.

1. The *ban* on *canned ham* was dropped.
2. *Nan ran* a mile after *Ann.*
3. Alfred had *random* thoughts when he *napped.*
4. *Angus planned* to raise *cattle.*

[a] (à)

We are intentionally excluding a key word for the vowel [a] because most Americans do not use this sound as a pure vowel but use it only as the first element of the diphthong [aɪ] as in *I, my,* and *ice.* The pure vowel [a] is used by a minority of American speakers, most of whom probably reside in the New England area. These speakers would use the vowel in words such as *ask, grass,* and *mask.*

In regard to tongue position the vowel [a] is a compromise between the front vowel [æ] and the low back vowel [ɑ] (ä), as in *calm.*

There is, of course, no objection to cultivating the vowel [a] if there is some cultural reason for doing so. We would suggest, however, that the cultivation of this vowel be accompanied by some degree of consistency and that the speaker avoid fluctuating between [a] in *dance, craft,* and *mask* and [æ] for *France, laugh,* and *ask.*

Practice Materials

Determine your practice in the use of the vowel [æ] or [a] for the following materials. Consistency of vowel pronunciation is recommended but not prescribed.

ask	task	advance	dance
grass	calf	craft	demand
mask	laugh	France	bath

Sentences
1. The birds took their bath in the moist grass.
2. We attended a dance wearing masks.
3. The craft took off for France.
4. The cowboy's task was to rope the calf.

THE BACK VOWELS

[a] (ä) As in *Calm*

The first of the back vowels we shall study is [a]. The back vowels, we recall, are those which are produced with the back of the tongue most active (see Fig. 11, page 143). In changing from the low front vowel [æ] to the back vowel [a] the tongue arching is moved from the front to the back of the tongue.

The vowel [a] is produced with the tongue in about as low a position as it is likely to assume without applying direct external pressure to the flat of the tongue. [a] is a low, back, lax vowel. The mouth is open wide and the lips are unrounded.

In spelling, the [a] is most frequently represented by the letters *a* and *o*. In words such as *ah, alms, charm, psalm,* and *balm,* the sound [a] is consistently heard throughout the United States. In the words *hot, cot, cog, ox,* and *stock,* there is less consistency in pronunciation. Many speakers will use the [a] vowel, but others will use a variant with lip rounding [ɒ] which is absent for [a].

Practice Materials

Initial

ah	argue	arbor	ardent
alms	arch	army	almond
armor	artful	ark	archives

Medial

calm	hearten	qualify	balmy
cargo	guard	sergeant	carved
dart	partner	hearth	swamped
harbor	farthing	sparse	scarred
discharge	qualm	embark	Antarctic

Sentences

1. The barber set to sea when the night was calm and the air was balmy.
2. The ship's cargo was thrown into the harbor.
3. Noah's ark had a varied cargo.
4. The recruit's awkwardness disheartened the drill sergeant.
5. Fathers do not always behave like guardian angels.
6. The shah enjoyed his bazaar.
7. Martha was an ardent bargain hunter.
8. The calm waters were well charted.
9. The army embarked for the Arctic.
10. Varnish may cover up considerable tarnish.

Most speakers use the vowel [ɑ] for the following words with *o* spellings. Others modify the sound by some lip rounding and so produce a sound which is or approximates [ɒ] (ŏ).

Determine your tendency by looking at your mouth in a mirror as you practice with the following materials.

odd	option	cot	otter
olive	cog	job	fodder
occupy	frog	rob	lock
ox	hot	hod	respond
got	golf	pot	top

Sentences

1. Olive had to exercise her odd option.
2. An ox may fear a frog.
3. The hod was used to carry the bricks aloft.
4. The stock enjoyed the fodder.
5. The otter did not enjoy the hot weather.
6. We were too shocked to respond after we were robbed.
7. A stop watch cannot take much shock.

[ɒ] (ŏ)

As we noted earlier, the vowel [ɒ] is used by some Americans in words in which the vowel [ɑ] is used by others. The vowel [ɒ] is also used as a variant for the vowel [ɔ] (ô) as in *dog* and *cough.*

In manner of production and in acoustic impression, [ɒ] is somewhere between [ɔ] and [ɑ]. The vowel [ɒ] is low and lax and is produced with slight rounding of the lips.

No list can be given of words for which the vowel [ɒ] is con, sistently used throughout the United States, or even in any major area within the United States. Though not confined to eastern New England, the sound [ɒ] is more likely to be heard there than elsewhere.

The vowel [ɒ] may be heard in words in which the spelling includes the letter *o* followed by the consonants [f], [θ] (th), or [s]. It is not, however, limited to these spellings.

Practice Materials

In the practice materials which follow determine what your pronunciation is for the key words and compare your pronunciation with that of the respected members of your community. First, however, you may wish to review the word list and sentences for the vowels [ɑ] or [ɒ] on page 156.

cough	aloft	across	broth
loss	coffee	moss	soft
office	froth	costly	scoff
glossy	tossed	offer	frost

Sentences
1. The frosty weather made Ross cough.
2. Coffee has become a costly drink.
3. A moth should not scoff at the flame.
4. Who is the boss in your office?
5. I prefer a clear broth to a drink with froth.

Additional opportunity for practice will be furnished after our consideration of the vowel [ɔ] (ô) which follows immediately.

[ɔ] (ô) As in *Author*

[ɔ] is a low, back vowel produced with definite lip rounding. The tongue is slightly higher for [ɔ] than it is for [ɑ] and [ɒ] (see back-vowel diagram, page 143).

The most frequent spellings for [ɔ] include *a* as in *call, aw* as in *awful,* au as in *taught,* ou as in *bought,* and the letter *o* as in *horse.*

In many words, including some of those used as examples in the previous paragraph, the vowel [ɑ], and less frequently [ɒ], may be heard instead of [ɔ]. Some of the variations are more or less uniform according to geographic regions; others seem to be more individualized according to speaker choice.

Practice Materials

If you are not certain of your own pronunciation habits, practice before a mirror will help to distinguish the [ɔ] from the [ɑ] pronunciations. If you wish to establish a clear distinction make certain that your lips are rounded for [ɔ]; for [ɑ] the lips are unrounded and the tongue is lax.

In the list that follows, the words of the first two columns are most likely to be pronounced with the vowel [ɔ]; the words of the other columns are likely to be pronounced with [ɑ] or [ɒ]. The vowel [ɔ] may, however, be used for any of the words.

hall	hawk	song	frog
ball	sawing	wrong	torrid
ought	call	soft	orange
taught	flawless	lost	foreign
wall	chalk	off	porridge
August	awesome	cost	forest
auto	claws	coffin	horrible

The words in the following list are most likely to be pronounced with the vowel [ɔ] rather than either of the other back vowels we have studied.

author	calked	orphan	stall
awkward	yawn	north	organ
tall	falter	halt	thorn
nought	ordeal	shawl	horse

horn	fourth	reform	snort
corn	born	morbid	scorned
fortune	mourning	normal	storm

Sentences for [ɔ]

1. The horse went through a painful ordeal because of the thorns in his leg.
2. The yawl was calked to prevent leaking.
3. Because he did not know his parents, the orphan felt morbid.
4. It is normal for an adolescent to be awkward.
5. The author's autobiography told how he was reformed.
6. Paul's widow wore a black shawl to show that she was in mourning.
7. Autoists should blow their horns only as a signal of warning.
8. A tall man may feel forlorn in a country of dwarfs.
9. Norman's jaw became set and taut when he heard his wife's fourth snort.
10. Saul caught a long fly ball in the hot August sun.

[o] (ō) As in *Mode*

[o] is a mid-high, rounded back vowel. (See back-vowel diagram, page 143.) The tongue position is higher for [o] than for the vowel [ɔ]. The vowel [o] is only infrequently used as a pure sound. In most contexts, this sound is lengthened into the diphthong [ou].

The most frequent spellings of the vowel [o] or the diphthong [ou] are the letters *o, oe, oa,* and *ow* as in *no, foe, boat,* and *grow.*

There is no special value in working to maintain a distinction between the vowel [o] and the diphthong variant [ou]. Phonetic context will generally determine whether the vowel or diphthong will be used. There is value in avoiding excessive prolongation so that a triphthong ending with a weak vowel [ə] is produced and a word such as *hold* [hold] becomes [houəld].

Practice Materials

Initial

oat	obey	odor	Oklahoma
opal	old	ocean	only
oak	oaf	own	over
ode	opaque	Ohio	open

Medial

boast	scold	frozen	flowing
boat	grope	moaned	choked
bones	coma	slowly	stone
loan	folder	soldier	whole
poker	mode	joker	gloat

Final

woe	low	dough	Joe
foe	snow	bureau	hoe
stow	borrow	know	crow
flow	yellow	tow	below

Sentences

1. Joe was full of woe because he could not make good his boast.
2. The boat sailed slowly with the flowing river.
3. Broken bones followed the poker game.
4. O'Brien gave his love a yellow gold choker.
5. "So long" may be words of sorrow.
6. The joker is a good card to hold in the game of poker.
7. In winter snow falls in Ohio and Oklahoma.
8. O'Reily broke his toe with a hoe.
9. Poe's poetry often borrowed the sorrows of tomorrow for today.
10. Few can blow the oboe except to make woeful sounds.

[ʊ] (o͞o) As in *Book* and [u] (o͞o) As in *Pool*

[ʊ] is a high, back, lip-rounded vowel. The tongue is lax and in a higher position than for the vowel [o].

The spellings for [ʊ] include *u* as in *pull, full,* and *put, oo* as in *book* and *cook, ou* as in *could* and *would,* and *o* as in *wolf.*

In many words of native English origin, especially those spelled with *oo,* practice varies as to the use of [ʊ] or the vowel [u] (o͞o). For comparative purposes, therefore, we shall need to describe the vowel [u].

[u] (o͞o) is characterized by more lip rounding than any of the other vowels in American-English speech. [u] is the highest of the back vowels (see back-vowel diagram, page 143, and compare [ʊ]

and[u]). The tongue is tense in contrast with the lax tongue for [ʊ].

The most frequent spellings for [u] are *oo* as in *school, fool, ooze,* and *choose; o* as in *do; u* as in *dupe;* and *ou* as in *coup* and *soup.*

The distinction between [u] and [u] may be brought out by comparing the pronunciation of the following pairs of words.

[u]	[ʊ]	[u]	[ʊ]
pool	pull	too	took
shoe	should	shoot	shook
boot	book	wooed	would
fool	full	cooed	could

Determine your pronunciation of the words below. If your tongue is tense and your lips rounded, you are using the vowel phoneme [u]; if your tongue feels relaxed and your lips not so distinctively rounded, then you are probably using the vowel phoneme [ʊ]. Do not be surprised that you are not entirely consistent in vowel usage for the words that follow. Many Americans vary according to the individual word. Make certain, however, that your pronunciation is distinctly either [u] or [ʊ].

roof	hoop
room	hooves
broom	root

Practice Materials

The material which follows immediately is for practice with the vowel [ʊ]. Note its regular occurrence as a medial sound.

bush	cook	crooked	mistook
could	wolf	pudding	neighborhood
hood	should	wooden	pulpit
good	bull	woolen	sugar
put	bosom	Brooklyn	understood
stood	bushel	would	pullet
rook	bulletin	forsook	cookies

Sentences

1. The wolf ate the uncooked pullet.
2. The pudding needed more sugar.

3. The crook was a footpad from Brooklyn.
4. Many brooks run a crooked course.
5. Brooks delivered his talk from the pulpit.
6. The bull calf forsook his mother for the shade of the bush.
7. A hail of bullets stopped the crook who had stolen the hooked woolen rug.
8. The cooky batter was mixed with a wooden stick.
9. Our neighborhood bulletin board is made of wood.
10. A wooden pulley was used to lift the goods from the Lynbrook loft.
11. Who forsook this good woman?

The material below is for practice with the vowel [u].

boost	rude	truant	grew
coo	loon	druid	boom
ooze	brood	blooming	recluse
food	whose	toothless	shrew
group	choose	accrue	threw
true	through	ado	cue
swoon	spoon	brew	view
troops	tool	zoo	rue
move	rumor	buffoon	blue
booth	luminate	soup	plume

Sentences
1. Who threw the shrew into the zoo?
2. The toothless witch stewed an evil brew.
3. Troops on the move need large amounts of food.
4. We had a splendid view of the blooming flowers.
5. A rumor started a new boom in uranium mining tools.
6. The truthful do not need to be ruthless.
7. The rumors grew as the time flew.
8. Few can continue to be truants from thought.
9. The Ubangi bride had a sparse trousseau.
10. Stuart was a truant from school.

Many [u] words are preceded by the sound [j] (y) as in *you,* *youth, use, muse,* and *hue.* In some of these words, the spelling *y* suggests the sound [j], but in others the spelling is not a guide to the pronunciation. The following list contains some of the more frequent [ju] words.

use	usual	feud	hew
you	utilize	cue	accuse
youth	mule	mute	huge
usury	hue	imbue	humor
unique	pupil	review	pew
eulogy	amuse	few	humid

Sentences
1. Few youths enjoy humid weather.
2. Our usury laws need review.
3. The mule carried a huge load.
4. Eulogies are not intended to be amusing.
5. The unique feud began over a ewe.

There is considerable regional and individual variation as to the use of [ju] or [u] for some words. Tendencies exist on historical bases and may influence local and individual pronunciations. In general, our advice is to follow the pronunciations of persons in your community whose speech is deserving of respect. Do not strain for consistency for groups of words. Instead, work for consistency in the acceptable pronunciation of individual words.

Sentences for [ʊ] *and* [u]
1. The prudent butcher was accused of having crooked scales.
2. Groups of everblooming bushes grew in the garden.
3. Some who pretend to be buffoons are too shrewd to be fools.
4. Tuesday we will say our adieus and leave for the kangaroo country.
5. The Sioux Indian knew that something was askew.
6. Too few brides choose pewter for their trousseaus.
7. Few pupils review enough to be imbued with what they are taught.
8. She looked as if she could ride either a broom or a mule.
9. The blue plume belonged to Lucy.
10. Matthew blew the tuba better than he could the flute.

Selection

The crest and crowning of all good,
Life's final star, is Brotherhood.
EDWIN MARKHAM—*Brotherhood*

CENTRAL VOWELS

The *central vowels* are those which are made with the middle of
the tongue arched toward the palate. The central vowels include
[ɝ] (ûr), [ɜ] (ûr), [ɚ] (ər), [ə] (ə), and [ʌ] (ŭ) (see central-
vowel diagram, page 144).

[ɝ] (ûr) or [ɜ] As in *Bird, Curl,* and *World*

Most Americans use the vowel [ɝ] in the key words indicated
above and in the accented syllable of words such as *avert, guerdon,
journal,* and *unfurl.* Some phoneticians consider the [ɝ] to be essentially a variety of the [r] sound and suggest that the articulation of
the sound can best be acquired by lengthening the initial [r] of
words such as *rose, red,* and *rim.* Such an [r] might be produced
with the tongue as a whole slightly retracted and the middle of the
tongue raised toward the soft palate. We may think of the sound [ɝ]
as a vowel blended with the vowelized consonant [r]. The lips are
unrounded for the production of [ɝ].

Speakers who generally do not use the [r] sound except when the
letter *r* is immediately followed by a vowel are likely also to use [ɜ]
rather than [ɝ] in the key words given in the preceding paragraph.
The sound [ɜ] is produced with a slightly lower tongue position,
with lips unrounded, and without the [r] coloring of [ɝ].

The use of [ɝ] or [ɜ] is largely a matter of regional practice.
In the list of words which follows, most Americans would use [ɝ].
Many speakers in New England, New York City, and in the southern
coastal states, however, use [ɜ]. Individual speakers who have been
influenced by British speech or who were trained for the stage with
eastern or British "standard" diction might also use [ɜ] regardless of
where they live.

We may note that the spelling of words in which [ɝ] or [ɜ] is
used usually includes the letters *ur, or, ir,* or *ear.* The word *colonel*
is one of the few exceptions in which the spelling does not include
the letter *r.*

Some speakers substitute the diphthongal blend [ɜɪ] for the vowel [ɜ]. The word *bird* may then become [bɜɪd] and *girl* may become [gɜɪl]. This diphthongal variant seems acceptable to many speakers in the South.

Practice Materials

Initial

earth	urchin	ermine	irksome
earn	irked	earnest	erg
err	urban	earl	urn
early	erstwhile	urge	Ernest

Medial

certain	sermon	determine	preserve
curl	terse	concern	rehearse
first	dirt	swirl	spurn
guerdon	third	excursion	curd
hurt	bird	person	unfurl
mirth	word	avert	burden
skirt	curve	heard	shirk
swerve	surface	lurk	adjourn

Final

her	fur	occur	cur
err	stir	refer	demur
blur	infer	defer	burr
deter	were	spur	inter

Sentences

1. The customer was terse but the merchant far from taciturn.
2. Myrtle needed little urging to marry Earl.
3. A bird in the hand is worth a good deal on earth.
4. Ernest did not bestir himself to avert the falling urn.
5. The colonel's third lady was a well-preserved person.
6. The curtain fell and the rehearsal was adjourned.
7. Merton was disturbingly discursive throughout the excursion.
8. Though hurt, he unfurled the guerdon for all to observe.
9. "Early to rise" has a happier ending for the bird than for the worm.

10. Bertha could toss her curls to produce the effects of a sermon.
11. Few girls need to be urged to wear ermine.
12. Urban life has unheard-of burdens.

[ɚ] [ər] or (ĕr) and [ə] As in the Unstressed Syllables of *Ever* and *Other*

The vowel [ɚ] is the unstressed "equivalent" of [ɝ]. In words such as *earner* and *murmur* the first syllable vowels are stressed and so are pronounced as [ɝ] by most American speakers. The second, unstressed, syllable is pronounced [ɚ] by the same speakers—the majority of Americans who habitually pronounce medial or final *r's* whenever the letter occurs in the spelling of the word.

[ɚ] is a lax, unrounded, mid-vowel. It has a lower tongue position than [ɝ]. Because of its occurrence in the unstressed position, [ɚ] is less intense and shorter in duration than its stressed counterpart.

[ə] is a mid-vowel produced with a lax tongue and unrounded lips in a position slightly lower than [ɜ] (see Fig. 12, page 144).

[ə] is probably the most frequently used vowel in our language. This is so for the following reasons:

1. It is the most frequently used vowel in unstressed syllables regardless of the spelling of the vowel. Some examples of the varied spellings are indicated in the italicized letters of the following: *a*lone, sof*a*, foc*u*s, lab*e*l, prec*iou*s.

2. In addition to its occurrence in unstressed syllables of polysyllabic words, [ə] is also the most frequently used vowel when prepositions, articles, conjunctions, and auxiliary verbs are unstressed in sentence context. For example, in the sentence, "I of*ten* find it diffic*u*lt *to* believe *the* man," each italicized word or syllable may appropriately be pronounced with the vowel [ə].

3. The vowel [ə] also replaces [r] in words such as *hear, dare,* and *cure* for those speakers who do not pronounce final *r's,* or *r's* in general unless they are immediately followed by vowels. These, of course, are the same speakers from New England, New York City, and parts of the South who use [ɜ] rather than [ɝ] in stressed syllables.

Practice Materials

Check the pronunciation in your community and decide whethei you prefer [ɚ] or [ə] for the unstressed syllables of the following words.

baker	either	bettei	alter
copper	treasure	other	feather
drummer	brother	humor	weather
driver	poster	mirror	murmur
wander	yonder	squander	hinder

Sentences
1. Baker's brother was a drummer.
2. The driver kept murmuring about the weather.
3. The treasure was either gold or copper.
4. We wandered off to yonder orchard.
5. Robert was a man of good humor.
6. A good mirror does not alter your features.

Note the occurrence of the "weak" vowel [ə] in the unstressed syllables of the words in the list and in the sentences that follow.

above	annoy	tuba	American
about	agree	soda	urban
allow	anoint	data	surgeon
appoint	Texas	Canada	precious
avoid	assist	circus	stirrup

Sentences
1. The American spoke with a Texas drawl.
2. A tuba may be annoying to hear alone.
3. Canada is north or above the United States.
4. Vienna is a city in Austria.
5. Ella was fond of azaleas.
6. Bacon and eggs make a good breakfast.
7. Are you aware of how often the vowel [ə] is used in American speech?
8. Eva and Ella had vanilla sodas.
9. The Russian avoided the open forum.
10. The Cuban was most gracious in his admissions.

[ʌ] (ŭ) As in *Cup*

[ʌ] is produced with a relatively relaxed tongue arched a little bit toward the middle or back of the palate. If it is produced with middle of the tongue arching, it is a mid-vowel. Many persons, how-

ever, produce the sound with back tongue arching as a back vowel
rather than a mid-vowel. Either way, the mouth is open fairly wide
without lip rounding. The tongue should be arched higher for [ʌ]
than for [ɑ] so that a clear distinction is made between these vowels
and between words such as *sup* and *sop, suck* and *sock,* and *nut*
and *not.*

The vowel [ʌ] is represented by several letters in spelling, including *u* as in *cup, ou* as in *double,* and *o* as in *done.*

Except for the tendency of some speakers to produce an [ɑ] instead of a [ʌ], the vowel causes little difficulty. For those persons
who may be inclined to make the [ɑ] substitution, it might be of
help to know that [ʌ] is the vowel the American Indian is alleged
to make when he grunts "Ugh."

Practice Materials

The first set of exercises should help to establish the distinction
between [ʌ] and [ɑ]. Be certain to raise your tongue slightly higher
for [ʌ] than for [ɑ]. The mouth is somewhat more open for [ɑ]
than for [ʌ]. Note that [ʌ] appears only in stressed syllables.

[ʌ]	[ɑ]	[ʌ]	[ɑ]
come	calm	gut	got
done	don	color	collar
sup	sop	chuck	chock
suck	sock	wonder	wander
nut	not	bubble	bobble
duck	dock	putt	pot

In the sentences that follow the first italicized word contains the
vowel [ʌ], the second the vowel [ɑ].

Sentences
1. *Come* and be *calm.*
2. The *ducks* were left at the *dock.*
3. What *color* was her *collar*?
4. The crook had no *luck* in picking the *lock.*
5. We were *done* with *Don.*
6. The *cup* was made of *copper.*
7. The cuckoo *clucked* as it came out of the *clock.*

Additional Practice Materials

Initial

up	other	udder	upward
under	onion	utter	ulcer
us	ugly	uncle	ultra
upper	usher	oven	ultimate

Medial

blood	lunge	asunder	mud
blunder	mumble	assumption	much
brother	mutton	begun	rugged
bud	once	benumb	stuck
cub	rubber	instruct	tuck
club	supper	lump	won
done	punish	hungry	thunder
cuff	rough	enough	thumb
love	monkey	honey	funny
buck	bubble	trouble	rubble

Sentences
1. The night is done; get up and greet the new day's sun.
2. Thunder tore the bridge asunder.
3. Twins have been defined as double trouble.
4. Customs get some of us in a rut.
5. We had too much for supper.
6. Blood on his cuff brought about his arrest and punishment.
7. Love speaks with honeyed words.
8. We stumbled our way along the rugged ruts.
9. The assumption was that a monkey caused the trouble.
10. Butler likes to lunch at his club.

Selection
When Duncan told Gustav that "well begun is half done," Gustav mumbled, "But not begun may be more fun." Duncan, who was a rugged fellow, was about to cuff Gustav for his ugly answer but kept the peace instead by uttering some honeyed words.

12 • Diphthongs

Diphthongs are vocalic glides which are uttered in a single breath impulse within a single syllable. A superficial analysis of a diphthong, as well as a literal interpretation of the term, suggests that a diphthong is a combination of two sounds. Actually, a diphthong is a continuous change of sound from the first element to the second. The first phonetic symbol of a diphthong really represents the approximate initial sound, and the second element represents the approximate final sound. Thus, the diphthong [ɔɪ] (oi) is initiated with the sound [ɔ]. The organs of articulation are then modified to produce a continuous change of sound until the diphthong is completed with what approximates the vowel [ɪ].

We shall consider three American-English phonemic diphthongs. Each represents a distinctive sound unit and each serves as a basis by which we distinguish between spoken words without depending upon context. The phonemic diphthongs are [aɪ] (i) as in *I* and *my;* [ɔɪ] (oi) as in *boy* and *toy;* and [ɑʊ] (ou) as in *house* and *out.*

Earlier, in our study of the individual vowel sounds, nonphonemic variants of the vowels [e] and [o] were considered. Another group of sounds which might be considered diphthongal variants are the sound combinations of persons who do not pronounce final *r*'s. This group of sounds include [ɪə], [ʊə], [ɔə], and [ɛə] as pronunciations for words such as *dear, poor, core,* and *care.*

[aɪ] (ī) As in *Ice* and *Nice*

The diphthong [aɪ] is initiated with a raising of the tongue in the front part of the mouth. It ends, as indicated, with the vowel [ɪ].

The most frequent spellings for [aɪ] are *i* at the beginning and middle of words and *y* as the final letter of words as in *ice, spice, entice, my,* and *cry.*

Practice Materials

aisle	ripe	riot	invite
ice	diagram	aspire	remind
item	drive	beguile	requite
idle	height	design	unsightly
eyes	mine	devise	aside
iron	ride	bribe	butterfly
island	thigh	kind	spy
I'll	twice	strive	try
I'm	slide	rhyme	buy
idea	why	time	pie

Sentences

1. The bride had a beguiling smile as she walked down the aisle.
2. The spy tried to bribe the designer of the island bridge.
3. The sun is high in the sky in June and July.
4. I am frequently reminded by girls that they are composed of sugar and spice and allied things reputed to be nice.
5. Time and tide reach a height and slide away.
6. Her bright-eyed glances caused mild riots.
7. No tiger got his stripes by striving for or buying them.
8. There are always times to try men's lives and test the heights to which they aspire.

Selections

1. Gather ye rosebuds while ye may,
   Old Time is still a-flying:

And this same flower that smiles to-day
To-morrow will be dying.

ROBERT HERRICK
—*To the Virgins,*
to Make Much of Time

2. She walks in beauty, like the night
     Of cloudless climes and starry skies;
     And all that's best of dark and bright
     Meet in her aspect and her eyes:
     Thus mellow'd to that tender light
     Which heaven to gaudy day denies.

LORD BYRON
—*She Walks in Beauty*

3. There was an old woman who swallowed a fly,
     I don't know why she swallowed a fly.
     Poor old woman, she'll probably die.

     Now this same woman, she swallowed a spider,
     Imagine a spider way down inside 'er.
     But she swallowed the spider to catch the fly,
     Poor old woman, she'll probably die.

The Old Woman Who
Swallowed a Fly—Ballad

[aʊ] (ou) or [ɑʊ] As in *Now* and *How*

Whether the speaker produces the diphthong [aʊ] or [ɑʊ] in the indicated key word depends phonetically on whether the front or back of the tongue is elevated in the first part of the blend. It is likely that his articulatory habit is determined by what he hears in his community. Both pronunciations are used by cultured and educated speakers throughout the United States.

The tendency to substitute the vowel [æ] for the first element of the diphthong is one we recommend avoiding or correcting. We also recommend avoiding or correcting the triple vowel combinations [æaʊ] or [æɑʊ] for either [aʊ] or [ɑʊ].

The most frequent spellings for the diphthong are *ou* as in *out, house,* and *mouse* and *ow* as in *cow, how,* and *brow.*

Practice Materials

ounce	proud	allow	mouth
out	shout	bow	stout
owl	town	brow	tower
count	about	cow	lounge
doubt	announce	how	mount
gown	trounce	now	south
frown	astound	plough	hound
ground	rebound	thou	flower
outline	carouse	impound	shower
our	abound	endow	flout

Sentences

1. The count dismounted and bounded into the tower.
2. The town dog-catcher had to impound the hound.
3. Our farmer friend was proud of his cow because she could frown and look profound.
4. We could not allow the scoundrel his wish to see his hangman in a shroud.
5. Showers moistened the ground and freshened the flowers.
6. Our house in town looks over a mound to the south.
7. A place to carouse is often someone else's house.

Selections

1. When clouds appear like rocks and towers,
    The earth's refreshed by frequent showers.
    Old Weather Rhyme

2. He never sold the truth to serve the hour,
    Nor paltered with Eternal God for power.
    ALFRED, LORD TENNYSON
    —Ode on the Death of
    The Duke of Wellington

3. Clouds permit us to project our thoughts, our feelings, and our imaginative powers. When our moods are mournful, clouds may

look like shrouds. When we are more outgoing, clouds may suggest
animate beings. We may fancy ourselves soaring through space on a
wild, winged horse; we may see a gentle cow, a blinking owl, or a
towering giraffe. Clouds can be turned around and about according to our inner needs and forces as well as by the outer powers of
the winds.

[ɔɪ] (oi) As in *Boy, Soil,* and *Noise*

The diphthong [ɔɪ] is appropriately produced by beginning with
the back, rounded vowel [ɔ] and ending with the front vowel [ɪ].
The most frequent spellings include *oi* and *oy* as in *oil, boil, toy,*
and *boy.*

Some speakers tend to substitute [ɜɪ] for [ɔɪ]. This tendency is
generally considered substandard and we recommend that it be
avoided or corrected. Another tendency to be avoided is the substitution of [oɪ] for [ɔɪ].

Practice Materials

oil	join	employ	anoint
oyster	broil	decoy	rejoice
ointment	toil	enjoy	void
choice	coil	poison	cloy
joy	soil	adjoin	spoils
boy	annoy	foyer	poignant
poise	noise	point	recoil

Sentences

1. Avoid a voice that makes you coy or a manner that seems
to cloy.
2. Oysters were a favorite dish with the royal family.
3. The noise was annoying and spoiled the boy's poise.
4. Men of the soil may enjoy their toil.
5. Are the spoils of battle ever worth the toil of battling?
6. The broiler was boiled and enjoyed by the hungry boys.
7. Roy, when still a small boy, began to collect coins.
8. Doyle took great joy in his work as a piano hoister.
9. Joyce employed an ointment to soothe Boyd's burns.
10. Lloyd had as his slogan "Joy to the honest toiler!"

Selection
> 1. Friend, ahoy! Farewell! Farewell!
>   Grief unto grief, joy unto joy,
>   Greeting and help the echoes tell
>   Faint, but eternal—Friend, ahoy!
>   HELEN H. JACKSON
>   *—Verses, Friend, Ahoy!*

[ɛə] As in *There*

The nonphonemic diphthong [ɛə] is used instead of the more frequently heard [ɛr] or [ɛɚ] * by persons who omit *r*'s in their pronunciations except before vowels. It is heard in such words as *air, their, fair, care, dare, chair,* and *pear.*

[ɛə] is also heard as a not entirely approved substitution for the vowels [æ] and [a] in words *such as ask, last, class,* and *bath.*

Speakers who generally pronounce their *r*'s when they occur in the spelling are likely to use the combination [ɛr] or [ɛɚ] rather than [ɛə] in the words that follow.

Practice Materials

air	lair	compare	repair
bear	fair	declare	unaware
care	their	chair	heirloom
dare	wear	forbear	heiress
flair	affair	prepare	impair
hair	beware	welfare	despair

Sentences
1. Because he was unwary the bear was caught in his own lair.
2. Girls seem often to be in despair about things to wear.
3. The heiress would not declare her heirlooms.
4. The mare won a prize at the country fair.
5. Who broke the chair beyond repair?

Selections
> 1. I could lie down like a tired child,
>   And weep away the life of care
>   Which I have borne, and yet must bear.
>   PERCY BYSSHE SHELLEY—*Dejection*

* [ɛr] and [ɛɚ] are alternative transcriptions for the same diphthong.

2. Had I but plenty of money, money enough and to spare,
   The house for me, no doubt, were a house in a city square;
   Ah, such a life, such a life, as one leads at the window there!
       ROBERT BROWNING—*Up at the Villa—Down in the City*

[ɔə] and [oə]

The diphthongs [ɔə] and [oə] are used by persons who are inclined to omit the [r] from their pronunciations except before vowels. Practice in regard to [ɔə] and [ɔr] or [oə] and [or] varies along the following lines.*

In words such as *horse, lord, accord,* and *north* usage is fairly uniform throughout the United States. The pronunciation is [ɔr] for most Americans and [ɔə] in the "*r*-dropping" sections of the country.

Usage varies between [o] and [ɔ] pronunciations for the words *board, mourning, course,* and *more.* These words are pronounced with either [o] or [or] by most American speakers. In the New York City area these words are pronounced with [ɔ] by "native" speakers. Thus, except for the New York City area, most Americans make distinctions between the words *horse* and *hoarse, for* and *four,* and *cord* and *cored.* The sound [ɔ] is more likely to be used for the first word of these pairs and the [o] for the second.

Practice Materials

Determine your own practice by comparing the pronunciation of the following pairs of words.

border	boarder
horse	hoarse
morning	mourning
war	wore

Sentences
1. Guns were stored in the fort.
2. Each pull on his oars brought him closer to the shore.
3. Four hours of riding on his horse brought him to the border.
4. The lion roared because he wanted more food.
5. The owner of the resort inn was noted for being in accord with forty different points of view.

* The transcriptions [ɔɚ] and [oɚ] are alternatives for [ɔr] and [or].

Selections
1. Cruel Remorse! where Youth and Pleasure sport,
   And thoughtless Folly keeps her court,—
   ANNA L. BARABAULD—*Ode to Remorse*

2. Come in the evening, or come in the morning,
   Come when you're looked for, or come without warning,
   Kisses and welcome you'll find here before you,
   And the oftener you come here the more I'll adore you.
   THOMAS O. DAVIS—*The Welcome*

[ɪə] As in *Dear*

The diphthong [ɪə], as noted earlier, is used by persons who omit medial and final [r] sounds from the pronunciation of such words as *dear, fear, hear, beard, cheerful,* and *earful.* Throughout most of the United States, all of these words are more frequently pronounced with the combinations [ɪr] or [ɪə·] rather than with the diphthong [ɪə].

Practice Materials

Determine your own pronunciation for the following words and compare them with the pronunciation of respected speakers in your community.

beard	pier	gear	piercing
beer	cheer	queer	seared
dear	arrear	cheerful	fierce
fear	mere	earful	spear
hear	drear	fearful	bier

Sentences
1. To the unbearded, persons who wear beards may seem queer.
2. The sere leaves gave the trees a dreary appearance.
3. "Crying in one's beer" is not considered a cheerful act.
4. For some an earful of what's tearful may make up for life's sad arrears.
5. A fierce fire destroyed the pier.

Selections

1.   But at my back I always hear
Time's wingèd chariot hurrying near;
                ANDREW MARVELL
        —*To His Coy Mistress*

2. Damn with faint praise, assent with civil leer,
And without sneering, teach the rest to sneer;
            ALEXANDER POPE—*Prologue to Satires*

3. It is unfortunate that children do not know that they are supposed to be cheerful and fearless. Adults who should know better have poetically asked the years to flow backward so that they could be relieved of the weariness of toil and of tears. These adults have forgotten their own yesteryears. Childhood is a time of fears. However dear children are to us, we cannot secure them against tears and fears of the known and the unknown. Children become weary waiting for years to pass. They are probably as cheerful, and as fearful, as the adults with whom they live.

[ʊə] As in *Poor*

The diphthong [ʊə] is likely to be used by speakers who are inclined to pronounce [r] only in contexts in which the letter *r* is immediately followed by a vowel. These speakers would probably use [ʊə] rather than [ʊr] or [ʊɚ] in words such as *poor, sure,* and *tour.*

Practice Materials

Determine your own pronunciation for the words that follow and compare each with what is current in your community.

poor	lured	assure	fury
sure	moor	jury	endure
tour	boor	ensure	alluring

Sentences
1. There is little that is alluring about a boor.
2. Some of life's allure is derived from the few matters about which we can be sure.

3. If you're poor, it is unlikely that you can afford to tour among the Moors.

4. The members of the jury had to control their feelings of fury to ensure their arriving at an enduring verdict.

Selection

1. Hope! of all ills that men endure,
   The only cheap and universal cure.
   ABRAHAM COWLEY
   —*The Mistress*

13. Consonants: The Lip (Bilabial) Sounds

Consonants, we recall, are speech sounds produced as a result of modification of the outgoing breath stream by the organs of articulation. The form of modification produces the characteristics peculiar to the various consonants. Unlike vowels, which are all voiced sounds unless the speaker is intentionally whispering, some consonants are appropriately voiced and others are appropriately voiceless.

The description and manner of production of each of the consonant sounds will be considered individually. Precautions to be observed and pitfalls to be avoided will be indicated for those sounds which many American-English speaking adults find difficult.

The Favored Articulatory Contact

Many languages seem to have a favored place of articulatory contact. In French, Spanish, and Italian many sounds are produced by contact between the tongue tip and the upper teeth. In German the point of contact is a bit lower. In American-English, the favored contact area is the upper gum ridge. At this point, by contact with the tongue tip, the sounds [t], [d], [l], and [n] are articulated. A fraction of an inch behind the gum ridge, articulatory placements are made for the sounds [s], [z], [ʃ] (sh), [ʒ] (zh), [tʃ] (ch), [dʒ] (j), and for one of the varieties of [r].

Because of the proximity of articulatory positions for the American-English sounds and those much like them in Spanish, French, Italian, and German, the tendency to carry over foreign language speech habits is understandable. We should also be able to appreciate the need for special precautions and considerable practice to overcome these foreign language influences. A good beginning in correcting such influences, and in establishing awareness of the favored place of American-English articulation, is to study the diagram of Fig. 13.

The consonant sounds will be presented approximately according to place of major articulatory activity proceeding from the front to the back of the mouth (see chart, page 182). This order of presen-

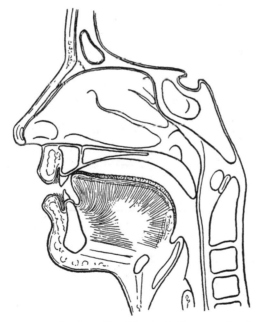

Fig. 13. Diagram Indicating the "Favored Contact Area" for American-English Consonants. The upper gum ridge is the contact point for [t], [d], and [l]. Essentially the same tongue tip and gum ridge contact is made for [n].

PRODUCTION OF CONSONANTS IN AMERICAN-ENGLISH SPEECH

Articulators Used

Manner of Articulation	LIPS (BILABIAL)	LIP-TEETH (LABIO-DENTAL)	TONGUE-TEETH (LINGUA-DENTAL)	TONGUE TIP GUM (LINGUA-ALVEOLAR)	TONGUE AND HARD OR SOFT PALATE	LARYNX (GLOTTAL)
Voiceless stops	p			t	k	
Voiced stops	b			d	g	
Voiceless fricatives	hw	f	θ (th)	s, ʃ (sh)		h
Voiced fricatives		v	ð (th)	z, ʒ (zh)		
Nasals (all voiced)	m			n	ŋ (ng)	
Lateral				l		
Glides (vowel-like consonants)	w			r*	j (y), r**	

* The tongue tip in many instances is curled away from the gum ridge toward the center of the hard palate.

** In combinations such as k or g followed by r, the r sound may be produced in this position.

tation is not to be interpreted as necessarily the most desirable or the prescribed one to be followed. We believe that the specific order of consonant study should be determined by the instructional needs of the students or the philosophy of the teacher. An individual student, aware of his own limitations in diction, or striving for improvement in a given direction, might well begin with the sound, or one of the sounds, requiring attention. An instructor might determine the order of consonant study based on a screening of his group of students. The sound most in need of improvement for the largest number of students in his class may then be selected as the one with which to begin. If the instructor believes that it is better to teach a relatively difficult sound by contrasting it with another easier sound for the student, then this may become the proper initial sound to be studied. An instructor who has many students coming from a given speech region and who, on the basis of his experience, is able to anticipate frequent consonant difficulties, may choose to begin his improvement program in the light of his anticipations. He will soon learn whether the students are living up to his expectations or whether his own program for his particular group of students is in need of modification. Such an approach will afford the individual student and the class as a whole the greatest amount of instructional time and opportunity for work on common problems and for frequent review during the course of a term.

[p] As in *Pea, Soap, Separate,* and *Spy*

[p] and [b] are bilabial, closed lip, stop consonants. These sounds are produced as a result of lip-closing action that momentarily stops the flow of breath. Both of these sounds require a raised soft palate * so that after the lip action, the sound produced is emitted orally rather than nasally.

The sound [p] in initial or stressed positions, as in *pea* and *plate,* requires considerable breath pressure. The lips must be tightly compressed to permit the production of a vigorous [p]. The separation of the lips in anticipation of the next sound should be accompanied

---

* All but three American-English sounds are normally produced with an elevated soft palate. Except for the three nasal consonants [n], [m], and [ŋ] (ng), the reader should assume that the directions for the production of a sound include the one to *elevate the soft palate.*

by a noticeable puff of breath. In other positions there is considerably less breath pressure and less vigorous lip action. In final positions, [p] may not be exploded. In all positions, [p] is a voiceless sound. In an initial [p] followed by a vowel, a distinct puff of breath should accompany the completion of the sound.

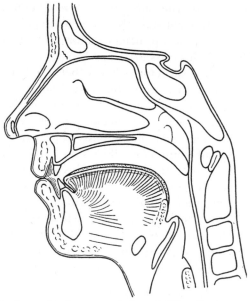

Fig. 14. Articulatory Positions for [p] *and* [b]. *The lips are tightly compressed and the soft palate is raised.*

Practice Materials

Initial

pay	peck	pout	pawn
pat	peel	pike	port
pen	pool	pine	pork
pan	park	pouch	pause
pack	poor	powder	pile
pitch	purr	pole	peak
pit	pert	poke	pull
pin	pail	pie	push
pinch	pace	put	poise
peg	page	pun	point

When a medial [p] is followed by a stressed vowel, a distinct puff of air should accompany the completion of the [p]. In combinations preceded by an [s], however, the aspirate quality is considerably reduced.

Medial (stressed positions)

appeal	rapport	apart	rupee
appease	repair	repay	turnpike
repeat	repartee	upon	repugnant
repeal	apex	apology	umpire
unpin	report	deport	suppose
repaid	repatriate	opiate	epistle
repent	rapier	supine	epitome
repel	oppose	superior	opaque
repast	appoint	superb	opinion

For a medial [p] in unstressed positions lip activity is less vigorous and there is less accompanying breath puff in anticipation of the sound following the [p].

Medial (*unstressed positions*)

aped	stupor	rapier	napping
happy	sweeping	steeple	chopping
carpet	champion	taper	clapped
typify	grapple	stepping	flippant
tipped	hoping	clipping	wrapper

[pl] and [pr] Blends

plea	plume	plight	place
please	Pluto	pliant	play
plenty	plot	plow	pleasure
plate	plum	applaud	plural
plain	plug	aplomb	plunder
plan	pluck	plausible	plunge
preen	prune	price	spread
pray	reprove	pride	sprite
prick	proof	proud	sprawl
press	prawn	prow	sprain
prank	prod	praise	spree
prattle	prolix	approve	prized

Sentences

1. Peter was fond of drinking out of paper cups.
2. Paul's pride made him aspire to the championship.
3. The press publicity resulted in a probe of the public funds.
4. Some of the Alps are perpetually capped with snow.
5. Polly was pleased with her plaid apron.
6. Neither perch nor carp is popular in Paris.
7. Pat was a prodigy at painting and sculpting.
8. A pig with an apple in his mouth is beyond help.
9. The plundering of the ships was blamed on a plot by harpies.
10. Maple syrup with pancakes is pleasant for breakfast.
11. Products become worth what their purchasers will pay for them.
12. The poorest persons are those who have no patience.

Selection

> Now when a doctor's patients are perplexed,
> A consultation comes in order next—
> You know what that is? In a certain place
> Meet certain doctors to discuss a case
> And other matters, such as weather, crops,
> Potatoes, pumpkins, lager-beer, and hops.
>
> OLIVER WENDELL HOLMES
—*Rip Van Winkle, M.D.*

[b] As in *Bean, Rabid,* and *Robe*

[b] is a voiced, lip-stop consonant produced with less lip and breath pressure than [p]. Lip activity should be precise so that there is a clear-cut stop and release action for the [b] even though it is less vigorous than for the [p].

By way of review, [b] is articulated with (1) a firm closing of the lips, (2) a compression of air behind the lips, and (3) a sudden parting of the lips to release the *vocalized sound.* Final [b] may be articulated without the explosive or release phase.

Practice Materials

Make certain that you show a clear distinction between [p] and [b] in the following words and sentences.

pea	bee	purr	burr
pit	bit	pun	bun
pate	bait	prude	brood
pet	bet	pole	bowl
pat	bat	pall	ball
pound	bound	pike	bike

Sentences

1. The sweet peas invited the bee.
2. Pat swung his baseball bat.
3. The pit was a bit deep.
4. He took pride in his new bride.
5. The announcement of the sad news caused a pall to fall over the ball.

Initial

bean	boon	burn	broom
bill	bull	bud	bruise
bale	boor	breach	brought
beg	boat	bring	brain
back	ball	bread	brine
bask	bog	brass	brown
busy	bulk	bleed	bloom
bunch	burrow	blink	blue
base	bird	black	block
blame	burst	breath	blurt

Medial

about	table	somebody	disturbing
abate	feeble	habit	rubber
abbey	stable	noble	ribbon
abet	number	tumble	tribute
abhor	lumber	fumble	robust

Final

rib	tube	disturb	curb
crab	nub	cube	jibe
web	rub	hob	daub
stab	robe	sob	cob
dab	lobe	rob	mob

Sentences
1. Bill is fond of brown berries.
2. Ben abhorred boasting.
3. Bacon and beans were a habit with Bess.
4. Beulah played a brass tuba.
5. Somebody permitted the black horse to break out of the stable.
6. Few buds bloom in February.
7. The barn was swept with a bulky broom.
8. Lobsters and crabs were brought in on the old boat.
9. Bricks and boards are building materials.
10. Bob hit the ball for a three-base hit.

Selections

1. But far on the deep there are billows
   That never shall break on the beach.
   A. J. RYAN—*Song of the Mystic*

2. These are the days when birds come back,
   A very few, a bird or two,
   To take a backward look.
   EMILY DICKINSON—*Nature*

[m] As in *Me, Summer,* and *Plum*

[m] is one of the three nasal, continuant consonants. As such, it is produced with a lowered soft palate, nasal cavity reinforcement, and nasal emission. [m] is articulated with the lips in relaxed contact and the teeth slightly parted. Vocal fold vibration is a necessary accompaniment for the [m] as well as for the other two nasal sounds. As indicated in Fig. 15, the tongue usually lies at the bottom of the mouth in the production of the [m].

The sound [m] is usually represented by the single letter *m*. Occasionally, the *m* is followed or preceded by a "silent" letter as in *lamb* and *dumb, psalm* and *calm*. The sound is found in initial, medial, and final positions. Unless hurried, slurred, or produced with the lips too tight, the [m] is a relatively easy sound to produce. As suggested in our discussion on nasal reinforcement (see pages 77–80, the [m] lends fullness and roundness to the voice. The mate-

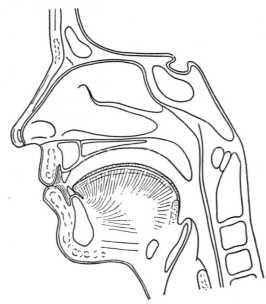

Fig. 15 Articulatory Positions for [m]. *Note lip-contact and lowered soft palate.*

rial and exercises for [m] in the section on voice should now be reviewed.

Practice Materials

Initial

me	main	most	mirth
meek	mend	mode	murky
meal	met	mote	murder
mean	mess	motive	mud
meat	man	motor	moist
middle	map	mourn	mouth
milk	mash	mortar	mount
mist	mask	mauve	mouse
make	mass	mock	my
mate	match	month	might
mail	mood	mob	mine
made	moon	monk	mile

Medial

demean	ember	foaming	human
seemly	emanate	reformed	humor
seams	embank	informing	grimy
dreaming	embassy	armor	slimy
remit	embattle	termed	smile
permit	cement	termite	smite
simple	amnesty	terms	smother
Amy	smooth	grumble	smock
emblem	emote	stumble	smirk
empty	bemoan	umbrella	smolder

Final

beam	game	groom	worm
seem	gem	tomb	term
team	stem	tome	drum
theme	phlegm	comb	hum
dream	lamb	dome	I'm
dim	ham	home	dime
trim	tam	form	climb
slim	sham	dorm	grime
aim	slam	calm	crime
same	doom	farm	prime
tame	room	alarm	column
blame	broom	bomb	autumn

In final, unstressed position, the final [m] may sometimes have syllabic value. What is your pronunciation for the words that follow?

chasm	schism	spasm	bedlam
bottom	rhythm	theism	bosom
prism	atom	truism	column

In the material below, work for a light, sustained [m]. At first eaggerate the length of the [m] and avoid carrying over nasal quality to proximate nonnasal sounds.

Sentences

1. Moss covered the bottom of the elms in the dismal forest.
2. Amy mourned for memories that might have been.

3. Termites undermined the grimy house.

4. Mamie grumbled because she stumbled over her umbrella.

5. Jim was phlegmatic about matters which made most men storm.

6. Mending and making neat seams were Amanda's prime ways of staying calm.

7. The monk remained in good humor as he informed his friends about the tomb.

8. Mortar, a material used for masonry, is made by mixing lime or cement with sand.

9. Motivated men can remove mountains.

10. Mary, broom in hand, was in no mood to be stymied by a mouse in either animal or human form.

11. Man is mighty in his ability to transform molehills into mountains.

12. Morton dreamed that no mound was too high for him to climb, or chasm too wide for him to jump.

13. Emerson held that each mind has its own method.

14. Too many men have empires in their minds to permit the humble to remain calm.

15. Many monuments to men in time need their own memorials.

16. The moon may look on many men, but a man has but one moon.

17. Remembrance, and repentance, often come together in the morning.

Selections

1. Hawthorne, in his *Mosses from an Old Manse,* observed that "An unhappy gentleman, resolving to wed nothing short of perfection, keeps his heart and hand till both get so old and withered that no tolerable woman will accept him."

2. Thackeray advised young men: "Remember, it's as easy to marry a rich woman as a poor woman."

3. Go! you may call it madness, folly;
   You shall not chase my gloom away!

There's such a charm in melancholy,
I would not, if I could, be gay.
SAMUEL ROGERS—*To*—

4. In his *Maxims* Nietzsche remarked, "Many a man fails to become a thinker for the sole reason that his memory is too good."

5. And frame you mind to mirth and merriment,
Which bars a thousand harms and lengthens life.
WILLIAM SHAKESPEARE—*Taming of the Shrew*

6. O wild and wondrous midnight,
There is a might in thee
To make the charmed body
Almost like spirit be,
And give it some faint glimpses
Of immortality!
JAMES RUSSELL LOWELL
—*Midnight*

7. We are the music-makers,
And we are the dreamers of dreams,
Wandering by lone sea-breakers,
And sitting by desolate streams;
World-losers and world-forsakers,
On whom the pale moon gleams:
Yet we are the movers and shakers
Of the world for ever, it seems.
A. W. E. O'SHAUGHNESSY—*Ode*

8. He left a Corsair's name to other times,
Linked with one virtue, and a thousand crimes.
LORD BYRON—*The Corsair*

The Bilabial Glide Consonants: [ʍ] or [hw] (hw) As in *What* and *When* and [w] As in *Will* and *Wit*

The consonants [ʍ or hw] and [w] are *glide sounds*. Such sounds are produced with the organs of articulation in movement from an

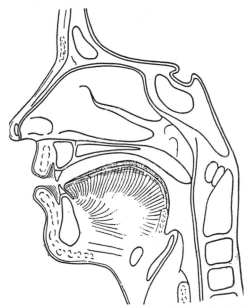

Fig. 16. Initial Articulatory Position for Glide Sounds [ʍ] *and* [w]. *Note that the back of the tongue is raised.*

initial, determinate position to a final position determined by the sound which immediately follows. The sound [ʍ] or [hw] is voiceless; [w] is voiced. Both are initiated with the lips rounded in a close, pursed position as for the vowel [u]. The tongue is raised in back toward the soft palate. Study Fig. 16 for the initial position for the lip glide sounds. Note that the lips do not touch the teeth, as they necessarily do for the sounds [f] and [v]. The palate is raised for the bilabial glide sounds, and the sounds are emitted orally.

[ʍ] (hw) occurs in words spelled with *wh* initially or medially. Many speakers, however, use the voiced [w] rather than the (ʍ) in words such as *why, what,* and *when.* The [ʍ] also occurs in contexts following a [t], [s], or [k] as in *twine, swim,* and *quit.*

Practice Materials

To determine whether you use a [hw] or [w], place your hand in front of the mouth for the trial words *what* and *where.* The [hw]

should begin with a definite stream of unvocalized breath. In contrast, [w] is vocalized and there is no obvious stream of breath.*
The word pairs which follow should help to make the distinction between the two sounds.

[hw]	[w]	[hw]	[w]
whither	wither	while	wile
where	wear	white	wight
wheel	weal	whether	weather
whet	wet	whacks	wax
what	watt	whirled	world
which	witch	whine	wine
when	wen	Whig	wig
whirred	word	whish	wish
whale	wail	whist	wist
whey	way	whoa	woe

Initial [hw]

wheat	whistle	wharf	whiting
wheedle	whelp	whimper	whittle
wheeze	whence	whimsy	whipsaw
whiff	whirl	whiskey	whang
whim	whistling	whiffle	wheal
whip	whop	whinny	whetstone
whisper	whorl	whisker	whelp

Medial [hw]

pinwheel	somewhat	meanwhile	millwheel
anywhere	awhile	bobwhite	buckwheat
nowhere	somewhere	freewheeling	erstwhile

Sentences

1. Do you prefer the song of the bobwhite or the whippoorwill?
2. What was the whispering about?
3. Where did the whaling ship go?
4. Despite his wheezing, his appetite was whetted by the sight of the food.

* Test for vocalization by placing your index finger over the thyroid cartilage as you prolong the initial sound. Vibration will be felt if the sound is [w].

5. The bewhiskered sailor stood at the wheel of his ship.
6. Farmer White had a bumper crop of wheat.
7. Whitman exercised his whims when playing whist.
8. The cargo was unloaded somewhere on the wharf.
9. Whiting and whale meat were served for dinner.
10. Watts whistled and whittled as he worked the mill wheel.

Initial [w]

we	web	woe	wonder
weak	well	won't	wise
weep	went	war	wire
weed	west	warn	wind
wield	wag	wasp	wound
wink	wax	watch	wow
wind	wool	were	worn
wane	wolf	work	worship
waste	woo	worse	wither
wave	womb	won	witness

Medial [w] (*note that the spelling may be* u *and* o *as well as* w)

biweekly	await	inward	unworthy
unwieldy	reweigh	unwavering	rewed
dwindle	away	awoke	earthworm
unwitting	awake	unworn	reworked
unwary	bewail	rewarned	anyone
unwept	byway	onward	everyone
unwelcome	unwilling	reweave	everyway
unwise	unworldly	reward	rewash
dwell	unwanted	unwind	Cromwell
unwell	unwonted	reweb	earthenware

Sentences
1. Norway has many natural wonders.
2. Kingsley wrote that "Men must work, and women must weep."
3. We walked through the quagmire to earn a reward.
4. The flame waxed and waned and dwindled into nothingness.

5. On awaking, Watson wanted the market quotations for the stocks over which he often wailed.

6. William West was fond of walking in the quiet of the evening.

7. Wendie tripped over a twig and twisted her ankle.

8. The Welsh soldiers were in a quandary as to how best to march in the wide quod.

9. In a twinkling of an eye everyone was deceived by the quick-working magician.

10. The woods were alive with quail and quacking birds.

Selections

1. I'll walk where my own nature would be leading—
   It vexes me to choose another guide—
   Where the grey flocks in ferny glens are feeding,
   Where the wild wind blows on the mountain-side.

   EMILY BRONTË—*Often Rebuked*

2. Women have, commonly, a very positive moral sense; that which they will, is right; that which they reject is wrong; and their will, in most cases, ends by settling the moral.

   HENRY B. ADAMS—*The Education of Henry Adams*

3. Wave may not foam nor wild wind sweep
   Where rest not England's dead.

   FELICIA HEMANS—*England's Dead*

4. The old hound wags his shaggy tail,
   And I know what he would say:
   It's over the hills we'll bound old hound,
   Over the hills, and away.

   GEORGE MEREDITH—*Over the Hills*

[w] and [v]

Some persons, probably because of foreign language influence, tend to confuse the bilabial [w] with the labio-dental (lip-teeth) [v]. The following word pairs should help to establish the distinction between these two sounds. Observe the lip action in a mirror and make certain that there is no contact of the teeth and lips for the [w].

Practice Materials

wane	vein	wend	vend
wary	vary	worse	verse
west	vest	wine	vine
weld	veld	wiper	viper
wiser	visor	wow	vow
went	vent	wile	vile

Sentences

1. It is wise not to get caught in a vise.
2. Wine is made from the fruit of the vine.
3. The man from the West was fond of his red vest.
4. As the vain writer grew older, his ability was on the wane and his verse became worse.
5. To vend his various wares he had to wend his weary way and be wary of wily customers along the wayside.
6. The knight looked wiser behind his visor.

14 • The Lip-Teeth Sounds

[f] As in *Feel, Fun, Afraid,* and *Enough*

[f] is a voiceless, fricative, lip-teeth (labio-dental) consonant. It is made by pressing the lower lip against the upper teeth and forcing a stream of breath between the narrow spaces of the upper teeth or between the lower lip and upper teeth. The soft palate is raised to prevent nasal emission of breath.

In spelling, the sound is most frequently represented by the letter *f*. Other spellings include *ph* as in *phrase* and *gh* as in *rough*. The sound occurs in initial, medial, and final positions.

Practice Materials

Initial

feet	fact	far	fight
feast	fast	farm	fowl
fill	fool	fog	pheasant
fig	food	first	foil
fickle	full	fuss	foist
fade	phone	fun	foible
fate	phobia	fudge	fume
fed	fall	fire	few
fez	force	file	feud
fell	fought	fine	feel

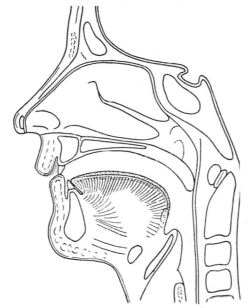

Fig. 17. Articulatory Position for [f] and [v].

Medial

coffee	defect	afford	afar
enfeeble	after	effort	stuffing
effete	aft	soften	rifle
sphere	raft	affirm	trifle
efficient	raffle	refurbish	stifle
sphinx	laughed	unfurl	sapphire
swift	refuse	roughen	refute
chafed	effuse	shuffle	prophet
effect	careful	sofa	reference
defend	barefoot	loafer	breakfast

Final

beef	skiff	chafe	half
chief	cliff	deaf	staff
reef	whiff	chef	graph
belief	stiff	chaff	enough
thief	strafe	laugh	tough
tiff	safe	calf	golf

Sentences

1. Despite Frank's rough ways, he was careful not to offend.
2. Fred felt proud to unfurl the flag.
3. After the fog lifted, the planes took off for far places.
4. Coffee is a favorite breakfast drink.
5. Fred and his father are fond of golf.
6. "Fair, fat, and forty" is fraught with folly.
7. Rudolph went to a physician for his sniffles.
8. The roast pheasant was served on a chafing dish.
9. The thief came to grief over the theft of the sapphire.
10. Farnum had a phobia of fire.

Selections

1. As Tammie glowr'd, amaz'd and curious,
   The mirth and fun grew fast and furious;
   ROBERT BURNS—*Tam o' Shanter*

2. Time stoops to no man's lure;
   And love, grown faint and fretful,
   With lips but half regretful
   Sighs, and with eyes forgetful
   Weeps that no loves endure.
   ALGERNON CHARLES SWINBURNE
   —The Garden of Prosperine

3. A faithful friend is a strong defence: and he that hath found such an one hath found a treasure.

Ecclesiasticus

4. Here rests his head upon the lap of Earth
   A Youth to Fortune and to Fame unknown.
   Fair Science frown'd not on his humble birth,
   And Melancholy mark'd him for her own.
   THOMAS GRAY
   —Elegy in a Country Churchyard

[v] As in *Vote, Believe,* and *Grieve*

[v] is the voiced counterpart of [f]. It is, of course, produced like the [f] except that [v] is voiced and as such requires less breath pressure than the [f].

Except for the *f* in *of*, [v] is spelled as it is sounded.

[v] causes little or no difficulty to American-English speakers. Some foreign-born speakers may have difficulty because they confuse the [v] and [w]. (See pages 196–197.)

Practice Materials

Initial

Venus	valley	vault	visit
veal	van	vaunt	vile
venal	value	varnish	vinc
veer	vend	varlet	vital
vigor	very	verse	vulgar
vim	vary	virtue	vulture
victor	voodoo	vernal	volume
vein	vogue	voice	volunteer
vale	vote	void	Volga
vapor	voracious	vice	vowel

Medial

evening	paved	proven	reverse
Eva	shaved	grooved	nervous
even	revel	hooves	convert
believing	event	roving	jovial
given	prevent	clover	revile
livid	having	Dover	trivial
evil	gavel	marvcl	avoid
devil	travel	carving	invite
raving	ravel	starving	lover
staved	avid	avert	cover

Final

deceive	delve	mauve	dive
receive	shelve	starve	strive
heave	have	carve	alive
sleeve	salve	nerve	hive
give	move	curve	naïve
live	groove	swerve	resolve
gave	prove	glove	revolve
knave	rove	above	twelve
slave	stove	shove	love
stave	strove	dove	trove

Sentences

1. Victor would not volunteer to test the voodoo.
2. Eve, an avid traveler, began her voyage from Dover.
3. The devil, for his evil purposes, can be a scrivener as well as a quoter of scriptures.
4. It is naïve to approach a beehive without covering.
5. Jovial conversation accompanied the carving of the turkey.
6. Some have tried to improve the figure of Venus with drapes, but very few have tried gloves.
7. Twelve Javanese were found roving through the valley.
8. The banging of the gavel put a stop to the verbalizations of the convention.
9. The thieves found it of value to cultivate a Harvard accent.
10. It took nerve as well as verve to keep the revels alive.

Selections

1. Ever let the fancy roam,
   Pleasure never is at home!

   .   .   .   .

   Where's the eye, however blue,
   Doth not weary? Where's the face
   One would meet in every place?
   Where's the voice, however soft,
   One would hear so very oft?
   JOHN KEATS—*Fancy*

2. For a man can lose neither the past nor the future; for how can one take from him that which is not his? So remember these two points: first, that each thing is of like form from everlasting and comes round again in its cycle, and that it signifies not whether a man shall look upon the same things for a hundred years or two hundred, or for an infinity of time; second, that the longest lived and the shortest lived man, when they come to die, lose one and the same thing.

   MARCUS AURELIUS—*Meditations*

3. All is ephemeral,—fame and the famous as well.
   MARCUS AURELIUS—*Meditations*

15 • The Tongue-Teeth Sounds

[θ] (th) As in *Thin*, *Thank*, and *Theory*

The [θ] is a voiceless fricative. It is produced by placing the tip of the tongue lightly against the back of the upper teeth or slightly between the teeth. Air is forced through the place of contact to produce the characteristic fricative quality. In spelling, the sound is represented by the letters *th*. [θ] may occur initially, medially, or finally.

[θ] tends to be a somewhat troublesome sound for many speakers. Native-born Americans exposed to substandard speech influences may substitute a [t] for the initial [θ] so that words such as *thin* and *three* are pronounced as though they were *tin* and *tree*. Foreign-born speakers who do not have the [θ] in their native language tend to substitute their nearest approximation for it. Frequent substitutions include a dentalized [s] and a dentalized [t]. A comparison of Figs. 18 and 19 (p. 211) for the [θ] and [t] and practice with the material that immediately follows should help to establish the distinctions between [θ] and [t] and [θ] and [s].

Practice Materials

Distinguish between [θ] and [t]:

| thank | tank | theme | team |
| thin | tin | thought | taught |

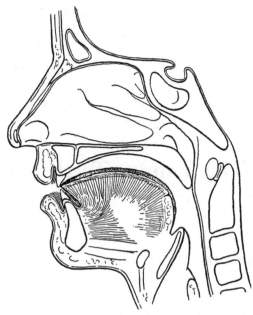

Fig. 18. Representative Articulatory Positions for [θ] and [ð] as Post-dental sounds.

through	true	deaths	debts
thread	tread	ether	eater
thrill	trill	sheaths	sheets
thick	tick	forth	fort
thrips	trips	bath	bat
thorn	torn	oath	oat
faithful	fateful	ruthless	rootless
myths	mitts	tooth	toot

Distinguish between [θ] and [s]:

theme	seem	thought	sought
think	sink	thumb	sum
thick	sick	thigh	sigh
thing	sing	thin	sin
thank	sank	kith	kiss
thaw	saw	myth	miss

faith	face	moth	moss
truth	truce	bath	bass
mouth	mouse	math	mass
worth	worse	fourth	force

Sentences

1. We needed a thin sheet of tin.
2. Beth's dress was torn by the rose thorn.
3. The team had fair play as its theme.
4. The infantry went forth to capture the fort.
5. Persons who are ruthless may find themselves rootless.
6. We heard the story through and believed it to be true.
7. You may improve your thought if you are willing to be taught.
8. When the truth was made known a truce was declared.
9. The mouse held a bit of cheese in his mouth.
10. A child's face may shine with faith.

Initial

three	through	thud	thousand
thesis	throe	thunder	thymus
theme	throat	thump	theory
thimble	throne	third	threat
thicken	thrall	Thursday	throttle
theft	thought	thirst	thrust
thalamus	thwart	thirteen	thicket
thank	thaw	thigh	theology
thrash	throb	thyroid	thermostat
Thrace	throng	thrive	Theodore

Medial

ether	pathos	enthusiasm	lengthen
breathy	pathetic	author	strengthen
anything	bathtub	orthodox	earthy
nothing	wrathful	orthopod	forthright
healthy	ruthless	slothful	toothless
wealthy	truthful	mirthful	atheist

stealthy	ethyl	toothache	method
rethread	birthday	mythical	lethargy
deathly	earthquake	synthetic	panther
youthful	hawthorn	arithmetic	Cathay

Final

wreath	booth	month	hearth
beneath	uncouth	mouth	sleuth
myth	both	warmth	troth
pith	oath	south	froth
kith	fourth	growth	length
faith	north	eighth	fifth
death	moth	ninth	breath
zenith	cloth	path	truth
wrath	dearth	mammoth	Ruth
stealth	earth	worth	Beth

Sentences

1. A famous author of many birthdays held that youth is wasted on those too young to know what it means to be youthful.

2. It is not kind to think that a boy likes filth merely because he prefers not to take a bath.

3. The Fourth of July is celebrated both in the North and the South of the United States.

4. Rewards are better than threats in therapy.

5. The earthquake in Cathay was recorded on Thursday, the fifth of June.

6. A toothache held the atheist in throe.

7. Theodore's thirst was satisfied with his third drink.

8. Beth had to learn the difference between being truthful and ruthless.

9. Faith may be strengthened when we face death.

10. The panther crept stealthily through the thicket.

Selections

1. The youthful Keats was the author of many famous lines. Among the best known are the following from *Endymion* and *Ode on a Grecian Urn*:

A thing of beauty is a joy forever:
Its loveliness increases; it will never
Pass into nothingness.

"Beauty is truth, truth beauty,"—that is all
Ye know on earth, and all ye need to know.

2. In *My Lost Youth* Henry Wadsworth Longfellow, often called the poet of the hearth, wrote:

A boy's will is the wind's will,
And the thoughts of youth are long, long thoughts.

3. In his *Resignation* Longfellow wrote of death. Perhaps most famous are the lines:

There is no Death! What seems so is transition;
    This life of mortal breath
Is but a suburb of the life elysian,
    Whose portal we call Death.

4. Thomas Moore is probably best known to us for his tender song themes. He was also the author of the following prophetic and almost wrathful verse taken from his poem *Lulla Rookh*:

And from the lips of Truth one mighty breath
Shall like a whirlwind scatter in its breeze
That whole dark pile of human mockeries:—
Then shall the reign of mind commence on earth,
And starting fresh as from a second birth,
Man in the sunshine of the world's new spring
Shall walk transparent like some holy thing!

[ð] As in *That* and *Those*

[ð] is the voiced counterpart of [θ]. It is represented by the letters *th* and may occur initially, medially, or finally as in *these, bathing,* and *wreathe.* The [ð] is produced with light tongue-tip contact either behind the upper teeth or between the cutting edges of the teeth. Air is forced through the place of contact while the vocal folds are in vibration.

There is no certain way of determining whether a particular word should be pronounced with a [θ] or a [ð]. We may note a tendency, in initial positions at least, for words which are stressed and significant in a sentence, such as nouns, verbs, and adjectives, to be pronounced with the voiceless [θ]. Pronouns, articles, and conjunctions, which are more likely to be unstressed and weak in sentence context, tend to be pronounced with a [ð]. Because of this, the [ð] tends to occur more often than the [θ] in our speech.

Persons who are inclined to substitute a [t] for a [θ] are also likely to substitute a [d] for a [ð]. The first set of practice materials should help to establish a clear distinction between the [d] and [ð]. (See page 218 for description of [d].)

Practice Materials

Distinguish between [ð] and [d]:

thee	dee	their	dare
they	day	thence	dense
then	den	lather	ladder
than	Dan	lathe	laid
though	dough	loathe	load
those	doze	seethe	seed
thy	dye	other	udder
thine	dine	worthy	wordy

Initial

these	than	the	thine
this	those	thus	them
then	though	thy	therefore
they	there	that	therein

Medial

either	weather	although	mother
neither	feather	loathing	bother
heathen	lather	brother	logarithm
leather	rather	father	further

Final

breathe	soothe	scythe	swathe
bathe	scathe	writhe	teethe
wreathe	blithe	tithe	with

Sentences

1. The weather man was not bothered by his forecasts.
2. Father bought brother a leather belt.
3. The infant writhed in pain because he was teething.
4. A heathen is sometimes defined as one who does not bother with clothes.
5. Mother is fond of wearing a feather in her hat.
6. The family gathered with blithe spirits.
7. Little brother considered it a bother to bathe.
8. The heather withered in the field.
9. The farmer used a scythe to cut his northern acre.
10. The engineer had a leather bound book of logarithms.

Selections

1. Like the diet prescribed by doctors, which neither restores the strength of the patient nor allows him to succumb, so these doles that you are now distributing neither suffice to ensure your safety nor allow you to renounce them and try something else.

DEMOSTHENES—*Third Olynthiac*

2. In many ways the saying "Know thyself" is not well said. It were more practical to say "Know other people."

MENANDER—*Thrasyleon*

3. Worth makes the man, and want of it the fellow;
   The rest is all but leather or prunella.

ALEXANDER POPE—*Epistle IV*

4. With too much quickness ever to be taught;
   With too much thinking to have common thought.

ALEXANDER POPE—*Moral Essays*

16 · The Tongue-Tip to Gum-Ridge and the Postdental Sounds

[t] As in *Ton*

We shall begin our study of the tongue-tip to gum-ridge consonants with the [t] as in *tea, ton,* and *too.* It is our belief that if the contact point and manner of articulation for [t] are mastered, the speaker will have an excellent point of reference for the production of other American-English alveolar speech sounds.

To produce the [t] as in *ton* or as an isolated sound, the tongue is raised so that the tongue tip comes into contact with the upper gum ridge (see Fig. 19). The soft palate is raised to prevent nasal emission of breath. The sides of the tongue near the tip are in contact with the upper molars. The tongue, tense and extended, is held in this position for a fraction of a second. Then, quickly and as completely as possible, the tongue is retracted with a resultant slight "explosion" of air at the tongue tip. This should be felt as a puff of breath if you hold your hand in front of your mouth.

The [t] as just described occurs whenever the sound appears in a stressed syllable and is immediately followed by a vowel. The [t] in such contexts is a lingua-alveolar (gum ridge), stop-plosive consonant. In producing this [t] the following cautions should be observed:

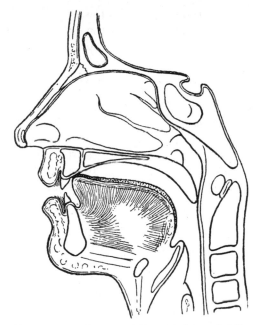

Fig. 19. Articulatory Position for [t] *and* [d].

1. Make certain that the tongue tip is in contact with the gum ridge and *not the upper teeth*. The contact, when broken, should be quick and complete.

2. Do not permit the tongue to slide so that contact is made between the front surface of the tongue and the gum. If this happens, a [ts] blend is likely to be produced.

Practice Materials

Establish the contact position for the stressed [t] by practice with the material that follows. Repeat each of the words of the list at least three times.

Initial

tea	take	too	tole
tee	ten	tube	talk
tip	tell	took	taught
tell	tag	tomb	tog
tape	tap	toe	top

turn	type	town	tone
Turk	time	tower	team
tub	tide	toy	teach
ton	tile	toil	tease
tie	tire	towel	tool

Phrases

1. take your time
2. tip to toe
3. ten and ten
4. twenty and two
5. tap the top
6. the town tower
7. talk and toil
8. took the type
9. ten times
10. turn the tube
11. take a tub
12. tie the tog

Medial (*followed by a vowel*)

attend	interne	Utopia	partake
atone	iterate	Utah	pitied
attack	deter	intake	rotate
attempt	detect	eternal	stale
attach	until	retool	steam
attain	utensil	retook	stay

Sentences

1. Tom played a tuba.
2. Ted's toe was taped.
3. Tell Tillie the time.
4. Tea was served for two.
5. The tower was attacked and attained.
6. Time and tide are eternal.
7. Tuesday was made tag day.
8. Utah was named for the Ute Indians.
9. The interne was born in Turkey.
10. The detective turned behind the tower.

Final *

eat	bat	note	cut
it	boot	bought	hut
ate	foot	blot	hurt

* A final [t] is exploded when it is followed by a vowel in the next word within the same phrase, as in *the cat is here*. Most persons do not explode the final [t] at the end of a sentence as in *I'll come at eight*.

might	emit	right	nought
out	flout	might	suit
quoit	incite	sought	root

Sentences

1. We will eat at eight.
2. Football is a favorite American sport.
3. Nat was hurt by the bat.
4. Mint and fruit juice make for a pleasant drink.
5. The boat was lost in the mist.
6. A boot is not good unless it can fit the foot.
7. Most boys like to eat things that are sweet.
8. The note was brought by a servant who wore a blue suit.
9. The quoit contest was won by the Ute.
10. A blot will seldom set things right.

[t] As in *Safety*

The sound [t] in an unstressed syllable followed by a vowel is produced in a less vigorous manner than when it occurs in a stressed syllable. The contact between tongue tip and gum ridge is not held as long as for a stressed [t] and there is less breath puff following the breaking of the contact. Avoid assimilating the unstressed [t] either in the direction of substituting a [d] for it or omitting the sound entirely.

Practice Materials

The words that follow provide practice for the unstressed [t].

city	latter	utter	tempted
plenty	faulty	bitter	twenty
better	mountain	fifty	written

Practice in discriminating between the unstressed [t] and [d] in the following pairs of words:

latter	ladder	wetting	wedding
betting	bedding	written	ridden
heated	heeded	butting	budding
bitter	bidder	tenting	tending
rating	raiding	contented	contended
shutter	shudder	writer	rider

The following words provide practice for [t] followed by a vowel or in the final position.

tell	waste	fateful	bit
ten	last	inter	flat
till	quite	contain	flute
time	after	rotary	hoot
told	comet	twine	root
tab	lout	twist	tote
tangle	between	twig	wart
toll	return	palliate	what
at	continue	unity	flirt
boat	atone	beet	wheat

Sentences

1. Ten and ten and two count up to twenty-two.
2. Tom Tucker will have to be told to wait for tomorrow.
3. Ted, please put the cat and the light out before you take off.
4. The tidings of the times portended that temptation was to be avoided.
5. On my trip out West I sat next to a taciturn gentleman from eastern Texas.
6. The stars twinkled in the Oriental sky.
7. Thomas learned that it was easier to incite than to settle a riot.
8. Thompson could not take being twitted though he was adept at taunting others.
9. We had to wait for twelve minutes between the acts of the play.
10. Too few try to find out if it is for them for whom the bells toll.

Selections

1. Temptation can be many different things to different men. It has been a time-honored subject for the poet, the moralist, the dramatist, and the timeless philosopher. Some views of temptation will be presented in the quotations that follow.

    a. "I can resist everything except temptation," Oscar Wilde had one of his characters protest.

b. In contrast, the ever optimistic Browning asserts in his *The Ring and the Book*:

Why comes temptation but for man to meet
And master and make crouch beneath his foot,
And so be pedestaled in triumph?

c. Finally, for the moment at least, we have the terse statement of the British humorist and poet Douglas Jerrold who, in his *The Catspaw* contends: Honest bread is very well— it's the butter that makes the temptation.

2. That great mystery of Time, were there no other; the illimitable silent, never-resting thing called Time, rolling, rushing on, swift, silent, like an all-embracing ocean tide, on which we and all the Universe swim like exhalations, like apparitions which *are,* and then are *not:* this is forever very literally a miracle; a thing to strike us dumb,—for we have no word to speak about it.

THOMAS CARLYLE—*Heroes and Hero Worship*

3. Night's candles are burnt out,
and jocund day
Stands tiptoe on the misty
mountain-tops.

WILLIAM SHAKESPEARE
—*Romeo and Juliet*

Other Varieties of [t].

As we indicated earlier, the consonant [t] varies somewhat in manner of production and acoustic end result according to speech context. Some of the more frequent variations will be considered.

[t] **followed by** [θ] (th) **or** [ð] (th) **As in** *Right Things* **and** *At The.* In combinations such as *at the, hit that, light things,* and *eighth,* the [t] is produced by contact between the tongue tip and the upper teeth rather than at the gum ridge. The dentalized [t] in these combinations is produced as a result of the assimilative influence of the next sound [θ] or [ð] which is articulated dentally.

This variety of [t] is least likely to be produced defectively by persons with foreign language backgrounds. It is the variety most likely to be produced habitually by speakers whose English speech is influenced by French, Spanish, Italian, or German.

Practice Materials

eighth time	sweet thoughts
hit the ball	right thinking
swat the fly	bright theories
light the lamp	slight theme

Sentences
1. Bright theories make for right thoughts.
2. Tom struck out the eighth time at bat.
3. Tess could not bear to swat the fly.
4. The poet thought in slight themes.

[t] Followed by [l] or [n] As in *Little* and *Button*. When the [t] sound is immediately followed by an [l] or [n] it is not necessary to remove the tongue tip from the gum ridge to complete the sound. Instead, the sides of the front part of the tongue break contact with the side teeth to permit a *lateral* escape or explosion of breath. When the [t] is followed by [l] as in *little, battle, settle, kettle,* and *mortal,* the breath of the explosion is emitted orally.

In words in which the [t] is followed by [n], as in *written, button, cotton,* and *rotten,* the tongue position is maintained in going from the [t] to the [n]. When the velum is lowered for the [n] a nasal rather than an oral explosion takes place. If you place your hand just below the nostrils, you should be able to feel a nasally emitted puff of air.

There is a marked tendency to substitute a throat or glottal (laryngeal) click sound for the [t] when it is followed by [l] or [n]. This substitution, in American speech, is generally considered substandard. You may check your tendency for glottal substitution by placing your hand at the larynx while speaking the list of words and sentences that follow. If you feel a click, it is likely that you are using a glottal catch sound instead of the [t]. To avoid this tendency, pay special attention to the prescribed manner of articulation for the [t] in [tl] and [tn] combinations.

Practice Materials

little	mortal	bitten	rotten
battle	glottal	button	batten
kettle	brittle	cotton	written
bottle	scuttle	mountain	fatten
metal	fettle	eaten	gotten

Sentences

1. Little by little Morton drained the contents of the bottle.
2. Cattle men were sometimes mortal enemies of mutton raisers.
3. Matilda's cotton dress had a row of bright red buttons.
4. The sailors were ordered to batten down their hatches so that their ship would not be scuttled.
5. Well-written words can be immortal.
6. The land at the foot of the mountain was too rugged for growing cotton.
7. The cattle were fattened before they were taken to the market.
8. Ill-gotten gains may be brittle and ephemeral.

[t] Followed by [s] and Preceded and Followed by [s] As in Pets and Posts. In contexts in which the [t] is immediately followed by an [s], the tip of the tongue is permitted to slide forward in anticipation of the [s]. Care should be taken not to omit the [t] entirely, especially in combinations in which the [t] is medial between two [s] sounds. The fine articulatory movements required for the [sts] combination increase the tendency for the omission of the [t].

Practice Materials

Practice with the words and sentences that follow should help to focus attention on the precise articulation required for [ts] and [sts].

pets	pots	insists	pests
lots	flights	breasts	ghosts
gates	paints	posts	resists
facts	mists	rests	persists

Sentences

1. The last acts of plays should be the playwright's best.
2. Painted pots were placed next to the fence posts.
3. Gray mists stopped the planes' flights.
4. The hard facts of life may interfere with the attainments of the heart's desires.

[d] As in *Done, Ado,* and *Glad*

The consonant [d] in *done* is articulated in essentially the same manner as the [t] in *ton* except that the [d] is voiced. The [d], like the [t], is a variable sound. The varieties of [d] parallel those for [t]. Faults in articulation also parallel those for [t], the chief one being the tendency for dental articulation. A second tendency to be avoided is the substitution of a [t] for a [d] in words in which the final [d] should be voiced. This fault may be especially noted in the speech of German-born persons or in the speech of persons for whom German was and perhaps continues to be a strong influence. The probable reason for this is that the final [d] does not occur in German.

Practice Materials

The first set of materials should help to establish a clear distinction between [t] and [d]. Make certain that the [t] is voiceless and the [d] is voiced.

Distinguish between initial [t] and [d]:

teem	deem	tune	dune
tip	dip	tomb	doom
tail	dale	toe	doe
ten	den	taunt	daunt
tan	Dan	tot	dot
time	dime	town	down

Distinguish between final [t] and [d]:

seat	seed	brute	brood
bit	bid	note	node
ate	aid	nought	gnawed
late	laid	not	nod

bat	bad	cart	card
set	said	stunt	stunned
cat	cad	hurt	heard

Initial

deep	duel	dark	dear
din	dough	dirt	dean
day	dote	dearth	dream
debt	dawn	dub	drip
dance	dock	dike	drain
dew	dog	doubt	draw

Phrases

1. dance till dawn
2. day by day
3. dark and dreary
4. din at daybreak
5. dry desert
6. dog at the dock
7. dearth of dough
8. dim doubts
9. daily dozen
10. duel in the dew

Medial

admit	fading	bedlam	hinder
ardent	hidden	candor	needed
oddly	eddy	splendor	indoor

Final

add	amid	said	spade
crowd	old	lead	code
rude	bald	heed	abode
hoard	fraud	reed	node
heed	curd	rod	aloud

Sentences

1. Undaunted by earlier failures, a dozen determined ladies began a ten-day diet.

2. Dan claimed that frequently he could not distinguish between candor and rudeness.

3. As the day was dying, a deep red colored the mountain top.

4. The dog's barking at dawn warned Duncan and helped him to foil a dastardly plot.

5. Daybreak is held to be a good time for duels.

6. Dig deep into your dreams and you may discover your true desires.

7. The disillusioned peddler sold his medals for a dollar a dozen.

8. London is a city of dense fog and bright traders.

9. The drug made Dick's head droop as he dropped off to sleep.

10. Matilda married her admiral in the garden.

Selections

1. When Adam was created,
   He dwelt in Eden's shade,
   As Moses has related,
   Before a bride was made;
   Ten thousand times ten thousand
   Things wheelèd all around,
   Before a bride was formèd
   Or yet a mate was found.

   GEORGE PULLEN JACKSON
   —"Wedlock," *Spirituals of the
   Southern Uplands*

2. The day is done, and the darkness
   Falls from the wings of Night
   As a feather is wafted downward
   From an eagle in his flight.

   .   .   .   .

   And the night shall be filled with music,
   And the cares that infest the day
   Shall fold their tents, like the Arabs
   And as silently steal away.

   HENRY WADSWORTH LONGFELLOW
   —*The Day Is Done*

3. No living man can send me to the shades
   Before my time; no man of woman born,
   Coward or brave, can shun his destiny.

   HOMER—*Iliad*

4. In Islington there was a man,
   Of whom the world might say,
   That still a godly race he ran,—
   Whene'er he went to pray.

And in that town a dog was found,
   As many dogs there be,
Both mongrel, puppy, whelp, and hound,
   And curs of low degree.

This dog and man at first were friends;
   But when a pique began,
The dog, to gain some private ends,
   Went mad and bit the man.

. . . . .
The wound it seem'd both sore and sad
   To every Christian eye;
And while they swore the dog was mad,
   They swore the man would die.

But soon a wonder came to light,
   That showed the rogues they lied;
The man recover'd of the bite,
   The dog it was that died.

OLIVER GOLDSMITH
*—An Elegy on the Death
of a Mad Dog*

[s] As in Sea, Asleep, Icy, Best, and Less

The consonant [s] is a high-frequency, voiceless, tongue-tip fricative which requires careful and precise articulatory action for its production. The adjustments involve the following:

1. The tongue is raised so that the sides are pressed firmly against the inner surfaces of the upper molars.
2. The tongue is slightly grooved along the midline. Air is forced down along this groove.
3. The tip of the tongue is placed about a quarter of an inch behind the upper teeth. The tongue tip is almost in position for a [t]. (Persons

not able to attain this adjustment will probably find it easier to place the tongue tip close to the lower gum ridge.)

4. The teeth are brought in line, with a very narrow space between the rows of teeth.

5. The breath stream is directed along the groove of the tongue toward the cutting edges of the teeth.

6. The soft palate is raised to prevent nasal emission of the sound.

Use a mirror to see the articulatory adjustments for the [s]. The recommended articulatory position is represented in Fig. 20.

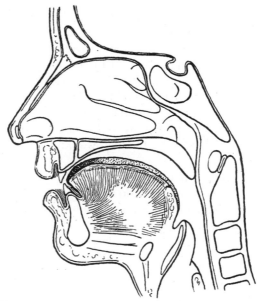

Fig. 20. Articulatory Adjustments for [s] *and* [z].

In producing the [s], exercise special care to avoid having the tongue tip touch either the upper teeth or the gum ridge. Neither should you permit the tongue tip to slide down so as to protrude between the rows of teeth. The first articulatory error will result in the production of a [ts] blend or in a lateral sound resembling a voiceless [l]. The second fault will result in the production of an infantile lisp resembling a voiceless (th) [θ].

Persons who habitually produce [t] and [d] sounds with dental rather than gum-ridge contacts are likely to lower the tongue tip for the production of [s]. The result, in most instances, is the production of a dull, low-pitched sibilant.

In some instances, the articulatory adjustments just described do not help to produce the desired result of a high-frequency, sibilant sound. Occasionally, the person, possibly because of his unusual mouth structure, must make individual adjustments to arrive at the same acoustic end result. With some articulatory adjustments, a low-pitched sound may be the best that the individual can achieve. Most persons, however, regardless of articulatory mechanism, can learn to produce an [s] that acoustically resembles the high-pitched fricative described above.

Apart from the manner of articulation, the sound [s] in American-English speech may present some difficulty for the foreign-born speaker because of the varied spelling representations for the sound. The most frequent representation is the letter *s*; other representations include the *ss* as in *less, sc* as in *scene, c* as in *race*, and *x* as in *hoax*. The foreign-born speaker of English may be forgiven his failure to know when to produce the sound [s] if we realize the many ways the letter *s* may be pronounced. In addition to the [s] we have [ʒ] (zh) as in *treasure*, [ʃ] (sh) as in *sure*, and [z] as in *his*. To add to the consternation of the foreign-born speaker, we also have the "silent" *s* as in *island* and *aisle*.

Practice Materials

Because of the frequency of the [s] in American-English speech, we recommend that a considerable amount of attention be given to this sound. Practice first to produce the sound in isolation until a clear, high-frequency sibilant can be articulated at will. Then incorporate the sound in nonsense syllables. The advantage of nonsense syllable practice in the early stages of establishing or correcting a sound lies in the avoidance of habits of articulation that may be faulty. Suggested nonsense syllable combinations follow.

seef	sif	sef	saf	sek
sah	sof	soo	sook	sawp
sut	sug	sul	sool	sipe

ahsah	ahsaw	eesaw	aysaw
ohso	ohsoo	ooso	oosoo

Initial *

see	sew	suck	circuit
seat	soak	seal	cease
say	saw	sale	citric
sane	sought	ceiling	cinch
sin	sog	sigh	scenic
sit	sop	cite	scent
set	song	civil	sceptre
sell	sock	cider	science
sat	sir	cigar	scion
sag	certain	cinder	screen
sue	soil	cipher	screw
soot	sun	circle	scratch

Medial

asleep	boost	essay	tracing
mist	rooster	icy	trousseau
hasten	boast	pressing	bracer
pest	bossy	blessing	hoist
last	twosome	history	peaceful

Finial

crease	loops	choice	loss
leaps	loose	voice	dross
miss	dose	terse	hiss
kiss	horse	verse	hex
pace	Norse	curse	fix
race	bus	fuss	tricks
bets	truss	mouse	cheeks
debts	puss	house	plates
pass	worse	dress	waits
caps	hearse	niece	fleets
farce	entice	boss	keeps

* Additional word lists will be provided for [s] blends. Some of the words of the early lists may again be used when the frequent [s] blends are presented.

[s] Preceded and Followed by Vowel

deceive	casing	assume	gusset
acetic	assay	twosome	russet
precede	resale	isobar	assign
acid	assemble	isolate	nicety
assimilate	assent	isotype	oscillate
asymmetry	asset	assault	ossify
aseptic	brassy	assort	ascend
essay	glassy	asunder	assail
lacing	messy	assert	asylum

Sentences
1. Six horses started in the race.
2. The slim lass wore a silken dress.
3. Miss Sweet fussed about the squeaking mouse.
4. Clever verse is often terse.
5. Sam had a choice of a dose of medicine or a glass of cider.
6. The wrecked sloop was a sorry loss.
7. Steve's debts began as racing bets.
8. The Scots were enticed by the farce.
9. "Puss in Boots" is a story for small children.
10. Some cynics say that there is no such person as a good boss.

If the [s] sound cannot be mastered directly, it may be of help to begin with a [t] and to work initially for a [ts] blend. This is especially helpful for persons who have no difficulty with the [t] but do have some with the [s]. The words that follow should be useful for this approach.

heats	mats	yachts	riots
beats	cats	divots	hurts
bits	hoots	blots	nights
gets	notes	ruts	blights
debts	floats	hurts	weights
hits	thoughts	flights	quoits

[θ] (th) and [s]

Some speakers must exercise caution not to confuse the voiceless [θ] (th) with the [s]. The [θ] is properly produced with the tip of the tongue in contact with the back of the upper teeth or slightly protruded between the teeth. This contact is to be avoided for the [s].

Practice Materials

The following pairs of words should help to establish the difference between articulatory positions and acoustic results.

theme	seem	thaw	saw
thick	sick	thuds	suds
thank	sank	thought	sought
thigh	sigh	thong	song
thumb	sum	third	surd
Thane	sane	thunder	sunder
path	pass	worth	worse
bath	bass	kith	kiss
truth	truce	myth	miss
math	mass	Beth	Bess

Make certain that the distinction between the [θ] and the [s] is made clear in the following material.

Sentences

1. We saw the snow thaw.
2. The violent Thane did not look sane.
3. He needed his thumb to add the sum.
4. We heard him sigh when he hurt his thigh.
5. The third sound in *after* is a surd.
6. The sky was cracked asunder by the thunder.
7. The miss maintained the myth that only kin and not kith could kiss her.
8. Although he did not catch the bass, he had an early morning bath in the stream.
9. A truce was established when the truth was made known.
10. The path went over a mountain pass.
11. We have heard it argued that whether from kith or from kin, a gentle kiss is not a sin.

Frequent [s] Blends

Initial [sk]

scheme	scalp	score	sky
skiff	scab	scorch	scare
skin	scan	scorn	scallop
skill	scandal	skirt	scamp
skip	scant	scar	skewer
skit	scatter	Scot	sketch
schedule	school	skull	sceptic
scale	schooner	skunk	squire
skate	scold	scout	squid
scathe	scone	scour	squeal

Medial [sk]

risking	discount	Alaska	Ruskin
discuss	ensconce	basket	landscape
asking	Muskogee	escape	musket

Final [sk]

brisk	whisk	bask	task
disk	desk	flask	tusk
frisk	musk	mask	rusk

Initial [st]

steam	stay	sterile	stark
steel	stain	stirrup	start
steep	station	stew	starve
steer	stealth	stole	style
stiff	step	stone	store
still	stem	stove	stork
stick	stigma	stack	stock
sting	stool	stamp	stop
stint	stout	stub	storm
steady	stoop	stunt	story

Medial [st]

Easter	roster	wasteful	basting
feasting	mastiff	coaster	toasted
blister	tasty	costly	castor
master	blasted	frosted	castaway
monster	aster	musty	punster

Final [st]

beast	mist	past	host
east	best	roast	cost
least	rest	post	frost
priest	pest	roost	lost
yeast	guest	just	first
fist	cast	rust	nursed
list	last	toast	oust
kissed	mast	most	Faust

Initial [skr]

scream	script	scrap	scrawl
screech	scrutiny	scramble	scrub
screen	scribble	scroll	scribe
scrivener	scrape	scruple	scrabble

Medial [skr]

discredit	miscreant	descry	unscrew
discreet	proscribe	describe	prescribe
discriminate	discretion	enscribe	inscrutable

Initial [str]

streak	strain	straw	strut
stream	strength	strong	stripe
strip	strap	strop	strive
stricken	strew	struck	strident
string	stroke	struggle	striate
stray	stroll	strike	structure

Medial [str]

restrict	instruct	upstream	distrust
construe	restraint	district	distress
constrain	unstrung	destroy	distrophy
constrict	hamstring	distraught	frustrate
construct	enstrange	distract	prostrate

Initial [sm]

smear	smack	smart	smug
smithy	smooth	smolder	smudge
smitten	smote	smother	smile
smell	small	smirk	smite
smelter	smock	Smyrna	smirch

Initial [sw]

Sweden	swing	swoon	swan
sweep	sway	swoop	swamp
sweet	sweat	swollen	swallow
swig	swelter	swarm	swine
swim	swear	swirl	swipe
swivel	swag	swap	swindle

Initial [sn]

sneak	snap	snare	snatch
sneer	snoop	snort	snipe
sniff	snow	snub	snicker
snip	snob	snuff	snug
snail	snarl	snake	snore

Final [ns]

wince	fence	glance	romance
pence	quince	lance	prance
hence	mince	manse	enhance

Medial [ns]

answer	balancing	instead	punster
dancer	instant	install	bouncing
Frances	instill	ensnare	winsome

Initial [sp]

speed	span	spore	spun
speak	sparrow	sparse	spunk
spill	spat	spark	spy
spin	spew	spare	spike
speck	spool	Sparta	spine
spell	spook	spirit	spout
spade	spoof	spur	spoke
Spain	Spode	spurt	spoil
spent	spawn	sponge	spider

Final and Medial [sp]

lisp	crisp	despondent	despoil
asp	grasp	despair	despot
clasp	rasp	desperate	respect
hasp	cusp	aspire	respond
wasp	grasping	despise	respite
wisp	resplendent	bicuspid	perspire

Practice Materials

Sentences

1. Scones are thin cakes liked by the Scots.
2. The schooner brought in a catch of scallops.
3. Prescott, the village squire, scorned all scandal.
4. Brisk winds are a constant feature in parts of Alaska.
5. A score of hunters risked their lives to obtain six elephant tusks.
6. Despite the skipper's skill in handling his skiff, it was upset in the heavy sea.
7. A squid is a species of cuttlefish.
8. The ship's mast could not be seen through the mist.
9. The master of the house offered his guest yeast cakes and sweet wine.
10. Schoolmasters are not fond of deciphering their students' scrawled notes.
11. Stewart used his full strength with each ax stroke.
12. Stephen had to constrain himself from strutting when he strolled with Selma.

13. Strident tones are a strain to listen to as well as to produce.
14. One straw too many can cause even the strong to struggle.
15. The scrivener was asked to enscribe the scroll.
16. A snoring swain is not likely to make his escort swoon.
17. The taste of the bitter quince made the Swede wince.
18. The mastiff snarled at the snake which was ensnared in the skillfully set trap.
19. Frances balanced books on her head to enhance her appearance and win approving glances.
20. Sponges are sea animals which live in colonies attached to rocks.

[sts] and [sks]

The combinations [sts] and [sks] are somewhat difficult because of the quick and precise tongue action needed in their production.

Practice Materials

The following word lists and sentences should be useful as practice materials.

feasts	lasts	hosts	jousts
lists	roosts	ghosts	rusts
pastes	frosts	twists	blasts
pests	costs	bursts	toasts
rests	boasts	firsts	infests
asks	husks	risks	frisks
basks	desks	tasks	casks
masks	flasks	discs	whisks

Sentences
1. The insect pests spoiled the outdoor feasts.
2. Two blasts signaled that the jousts were about to begin.
3. Ghosts do not bother with boasts.
4. Six gun bursts were heard along the coasts.
5. Good hosts seem not to be concerned about costs.
6. Risks are involved in many tasks.
7. Three discs and two flasks were on the small desks.

Additional Practice Materials for [s]
in Various Contexts

Sentences

1. Genius without a striving for work may be a waste of intelligence.
2. Signs on the highways offer advice to passing motorists.
3. Satire cannot always be distinguished from farce.
4. The moon cast a silvery light over a serene sea.
5. Some persons scoff at mystics; others seem superstitious about their beliefs.
6. Scrupulous golfers keep honest scores and replace all divots.
7. Ghosts are said to stay in desolate places.
8. Plates, forks, and spoons constitute table settings.
9. Jurists must be objective about all aspects of arguments.
10. A beast, when asleep, may be a peaceful animal.

Selections

1. On top of old smoky
   All covered in snow,
   I lost my true lover
   By courtin' too slow.
   Old Smoky
   —An American
   Folk Song

2. Among the many interests of the most versatile of American geniuses, Benjamin Franklin, was spelling reform. Franklin was an astute student of our language and a strong advocate that our spelling be modified. In 1768 the genius Franklin wrote "A Scheme for a New Spelling Alphabet and Reformed Mode of Spelling." It was published in an unfinished state in 1779 as part of his *Political, Miscellaneous, and Philosophical Pieces.* Franklin stimulated Noah Webster, who accepted many of his suggestions and recommendations for changing British to American spellings. In a sense, Franklin anticipated the science and study of phonetics. His analysis of sounds was surprisingly accurate. One of the factors that stimulated Franklin in his study of sounds and spelling reform was his

observations about the inadequacies of and inconsistencies in English letters as representations of the sounds of our spoken language. Franklin's scheme for spelling reform would have had each sound consistently represented by the same letter. Silent and unnecessary letters were to be dropped. Despite the fact that Franklin did not complete his study and his work, his analysis as to the formation of the sounds of our language is still considered to be essentially accurate and phonetically correct.

3. H. L. Mencken, the so-called sage of Baltimore, enjoyed having people think of him as an acidic and outrageous person. He sometimes earned this right by sentences such as: "Philosophy consists very largely of one philosopher arguing that all others are jackasses."

[z] As in *Zoo, Cousin, Azalea,* and *Buzz*

Except for accompanying vocalization for the [z], the sound is produced like the [s]. [z] may be described as a lingua-alveolar voiced fricative. Generally it is produced with somewhat less tongue muscle tension than is necessary for the [s].

The spellings for [z] are varied and include *z* as in *zero, s* as in *rose* and *nasal,* and *zz* as in *buzz.*

Persons who have difficulty with the articulation of the [s] are also likely to find the [z] troublesome. Vocalization, however, may conceal some of the acoustic faults that become apparent when an [s] is defectively produced. If your best [s] is articulated with the tongue tip behind the lower teeth rather than behind the upper gum ridge, the same adjustment should be made for the [z].

Practice Materials

Initial

zebra	zest	zircon	zeal
zee	zephyr	Zouave	Zeno
Zeeland	Zachary	Zurich	zone
zinc	zoo	zither	zip
zinnia	Zeus	zyme	zoology
zany	zoom	zealous	zounds
zenith	zodiac	Zion	Zoe

Medial

teasing	spasm	designate	design
pleasing	plasma	nozzle	desire
blizzard	music	cousin	enzyme
lazy	using	dozen	raising
daisy	dozing	used	noisy
pleasant	causing	desert	reason
resin	buzzer	deserve	appeasing
hazard	poser	preserve	resign

Final

ease	whose	because	toys
please	choose	repose	annoys
tease	doze	crows	boys
his	woes	yearns	ties
fizz	hose	spurns	replies
raise	grows	burns	dyes
maize	goads	buzz	rhymes
days	claws	eaves	wise
has	flaws	cows	surmise
lads	calls	brouse	symbols

Sentences

1. A good zoo should be open in all seasons.
2. To live zestfully is one of man's objectives.
3. His habit was to dose off when others became aroused by their emotions.
4. Symbols are man's way of communicating and preserving ideas.
5. Zachary presented zircons to his best girls.
6. Snows make the mountains near Zurich pleasant views.
7. The Mormons converted the desert into green pastures.
8. Girls and boys soon learn that words can tease or please.
9. Zinnias bloom late in the summer season, but daisies are early flowers.
10. The blizzard caused the travelers hours of delay in their journeys.

[dz]

Persons who have difficulty with the articulatory position for [z] might find it helpful to begin with [d] and to "move" from [d] to [z]. Be sure that you start with a tongue tip to gum ridge contact for the [d] and then retract the tongue tip slightly for the [z]. Practice with the following:

weeds	cads	chords	cards
beads	lads	fords	rods
lids	moods	hoards	brides
bids	foods	birds	chides
maids	toads	herds	tides
raids	loads	builds	grounds

[z] Blends

Many of the words of the practice lists for medial and final [z] contained blends of [z] preceded by an [m], [b], [v], [n], [l], or [d]. The word lists and materials that follow feature these combinations.

Practice Materials

Final [mz]

beams	gems	brooms	alms
creams	frames	combs	calms
reams	names	domes	charms
teams	crams	homes	harms
rims	lambs	storms	qualms
whims	booms	forms	alarms
hems	tombs	norms	farms
stems	chums	climbs	germs
clams	crumbs	chimes	firms
hams	numbs	dimes	terms

Final [bz]

Thebes	webs	dabs	tubes
cribs	ebbs	stabs	absorbs
fibs	jabs	tabs	cobs
nibs	cabs	cubes	nobs

robs	lobes	hubs	disturbs
swabs	jobs	nubs	herbs
squabs	robes	stubs	verbs

Final [vz]

believes	delves	wharves	shoves
deceives	shelves	carves	drives
eaves	elves	starves	hives
thieves	calves	curves	knives
gives	halves	nerves	strives
lives	grooves	serves	thrives
braves	moves	swerves	wives
knaves	proves	doves	leaves
staves	roves	gloves	weaves
waves	stoves	loves	saves

Final [nz]

beans	stains	ruins	darns
screens	remains	fawns	burns
bins	dens	mourns	turns
fins	glens	dawns	spurns
grins	bans	groans	guns
brains	clans	owns	runs
trains	loons	stones	tons
lanes	boons	barns	gowns
refrains	tunes	earns	clowns
mines	signs	coins	joins

Final [lz]

deals	gales	coals	boils
keels	jails	doles	coils
wheels	nails	foals	spoils
hills	bales	moles	tiles
tills	duels	goals	miles
frills	fools	falls	wiles
mills	spools	appalls	jowls
stills	tools	stalls	cowls
gills	pulls	lolls	towels
wills	bulls	hobbles	owls

Final [dz]

beads	heads	goads	birds
bleeds	weds	loads	herds
creeds	cads	frauds	curds
deeds	lads	swords	words
weeds	goods	towards	abides
bids	hoods	hods	hides
rids	foods	nods	chides
aids	moods	pods	abounds
fades	broods	floods	hounds
wades	intrudes	buds	rounds

Sentences

1. On many farms ears of corn are stored in cribs.
2. Some persons still wear charms as protection against germs.
3. Bees store their honey in the combs of their hives.
4. Dimes are American coins.
5. The storm's fury left many homes in ruins.
6. Hams are frequently sold in halves.
7. The thieves insisted that the theft of the gems was an expression of their whims.
8. The cads were imprisoned for their frauds.
9. Pistols and swords were favorite weapons for duels.
10. Squabs are young pigeons.
11. Piles of overseas goods were stored on the wharves.
12. Not all Indian braves wore feathers on their heads.
13. Trucks and trains carry the farmer's goods to cities and towns.
14. Many wives share jobs with their husbands.
15. Prunes are varieties of plums.

[z] and [s]

Some persons with a foreign language background have difficulty in distinguishing between the [z] and the [s]. If the element of voice is not distinctive, then both phonetic and semantic differences may be broken down in word pairs such as *price* and *prize; race* and *raise;* and *zoo* and *sue.*

Practice Materials

Practice with the word pairs and the sentences that follow to make certain that the [z] is clearly voiced and that the [s] is voiceless.

zee	see	lose	loose
zeal	seal	prize	price
zip	sip	doze	dose
zinc	sink	pads	pats
zoo	sue	sends	cents
zone	sown	bids	bits
peas	peace	codes	coats
rays	race	kids	kits
maize	mace	beds	bets

Sentences
1. A seal eats fish with considerable zeal.
2. The bids ran high for the bits of gems.
3. The prize was won at a large price.
4. We went to see the Zuyder Zee.
5. Zinc was used to line the sink.
6. Sister Sue enjoyed her trip to the zoo.
7. The codes were found in the pockets of the coats.
8. The maize was pounded with a mace.
9. Grace disliked to graze her cattle.
10. The racer was given a razor as a prize.

Selections
1. In his *An Unsocial Socialist*, George Bernard Shaw argues that, "A day's work is a day's work, neither more nor less, and the man who does it needs a day's sustenance, a night's repose, and due leisure whether he be a painter or ploughman."
2. Speaking of himself in his *Sixteen Self Sketches*, Shaw said, "I always astonish strangers by my amiability, because, as no human being could possibly be so disagreeable as they expect me to be, I have only to be commonly civil to seem quite charming."
3. Possibly to justify his own ways and manners, Shaw insisted

that, ". . . it is necessary for the welfare of society that genius should be privileged to utter sedition, to blaspheme, and to outrage good tastes, . . . and generally to scandalize one's uncles." There are some others who insist with equal strength and vehemence that the ends served by genius can be sought and attained without the incidental and often self-conscious display of selfishness and surly manners.

> 4. There is some soul of goodness in things evil,
>   Would men observingly distil it out;
>   For our bad neighbor makes us early stirrers,
>   Which is both healthful and good husbandry.
>   Besides, they arc our outward consciences,
>   And preachers to us all, admonishing
>   That we should dress us fairly for our end.
>   Thus may we gather honey from the weed,
>   And make a moral of the devil himself.
>   WILLIAM SHAKESPEARE—*Henry V*

> 5. There is a silence where hath been no sound,
>   There is a silence where no sound may be,
>   In the cold grave—under the deep, deep sea,
>   Or in wide desert where no life is found,
>   Which hath been mute, and still must sleep profound;
>   THOMAS HOOD—*Silence*

> 6. Here a star, and there a star,
>   Some lose their way,
>   Here a mist, and there a mist:
>   Afterwards—day!
>   EMILY DICKINSON—*Life*

> 7. Terms ill defined, and forms misunderstood,
>   And customs, when their reasons are unknown,
>   Have stirred up many zealous souls
>   To fight against imaginary giants.
>   MARTIN F. TUPPER—*Of Tolerance*

8. Poets heap virtues, painters gems, at will
   And show their zeal, and hide their
   want of skill.
   ALEXANDER POPE—*Moral Essays*

9. . . . a sorrow's crown of sorrow is remembering
   happier things.
   ALFRED, LORD TENNYSON—*Locksley Hall*

10. Persuasive Speech, and more persuasive sighs,
    Silence that spoke, and eloquence of eyes.
    HOMER—*Iliad*

11. Blessed is the man who having nothing to say, abstains from giving us wordy evidence of the fact.
    GEORGE ELIOT—*Impressions of Theophrastus Such*

12. How we learned to speak has been for centuries a subject of interest and conjecture for linguists and philosophers. One school of thought looks upon speech as gesture made audible. According to Sinclair:

> Speech is simply gesture that can be listened to, instead of watched. Speech is an extremely complex system of more or less standardized and conventionalized noises, and writing is an even more highly standardized and conventionalized system of visible marks upon a surface, but, in principle, speech and writing are as much gesture as is pointing with the finger.
>
> The origin of language appears to have been roughly as follows. Our remotest human ancestors, when they attempted to draw the attention of others of their kind to anything in particular . . . pointed and gesticulated in its direction. These movements were accompanied by various movements in the flexible tissues in other parts of the body, especially when any high degree of vigour was put into the action. Among these were movements in the tongue, lips, windpipe and associated parts. This was further accompanied in cer-

tain cases by contraction of the walls of the chest and movements of the diaphragm, which led to the expulsion of air
from the lungs through the windpipe over the tongue and
between the teeth and lips, thereby creating noises. The ges-
tures and the noises together resulted in drawing attention to
the object or situation in question, and then in course of time
the noises alone served to do so, i.e. the noises became significant speech. Later, after thousands upon thousands of
years, conventionalized marks upon surfaces came to be employed to represent the conventionalized noises.

w. a. sinclair—*An Introduction to Philosophy,*
London: Oxford University Press, 1944, pp. 118–119.

13. We may speculate on how many good scientists may have
died mute, inglorious, and bitter because their work was too ad-
vanced to be understood. This is the standard defense of the ill-
prepared and the crackpot. Yet the failure to recognize a brilliant
man is only partly due to the stupidity or stubbornness of the scien-
tific community; it is also partly his own fault.

For brilliance has an obligation not only to create but also to communicate. A scientist cannot really go "voyaging through strange
seas of thought alone." The more penetrating eye will see him to be
surrounded by a cloud of witnesses. He takes from others; he gives
to others. He must address the problems of his time. He must translate his thoughts into the language of his contemporaries. He must
scatter them abroad for interaction. A thought which has not pene-
trated to other minds will die unfruitful.

john rader platt—"Style in Science,"
Harper's, October, 1956.

14. The essence of folklore . . . is something that cannot be
contained in a definition but that grows upon one with folklore
experience. Old songs, old stories, old sayings, old beliefs, customs,
and practices—the mindskills and handskills that have been handed
down so long that they seem to have a life of their own, a life that
cannot be destroyed by print but that constantly has to get back to
the spoken word to be renewed; patterned by common experience;
varied by individual repetition, inventive or forgetful; and cherished

because somehow characteristic or expressive: all this, for want of a better word, is folklore.

B. A. BOTKIN—*A Treasury of American Folklore,*
New York: Crown Publishers, 1944, p. xxi.

[ʃ] (sh) As in *She, Ashore,* and *Ash*

With the consonant [s] as a basis for comparison, the [ʃ] (sh) should be easy to master. The sound is produced with the entire tongue drawn a little further back than for the [s]. The tongue surface is broadened and flat so that there is no groove or channel as is required for [s]. The stream of breath is forced over the flat tongue surface and emitted between the rows of teeth. [ʃ] is usually pro-

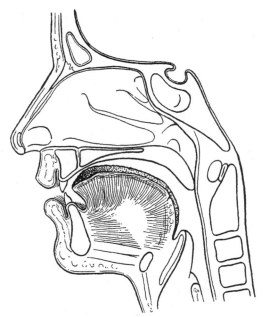

Fig. 21. Articulatory Adjustments for [ʃ] *and* [ʒ].

duced with slight lip rounding. Acoustically, the principal concentration of acoustic energy is in a lower-frequency band than that of [s]. Phonetically, [ʃ] may be described as a voiceless, orally emitted, blade-tongue fricative sound.

[ʃ] has several spellings. The most frequent is the combination *sh* as in *she*. Other frequent spellings include *ti* as in *nation, si* as in *tension, ci* as in *precious, ch* as in *machine,* and *s* as in *sure*.

For some speakers with a foreign language background and for some who may have a high-frequency hearing loss, the similarities in spelling and in manner of articulation may cause confusion between the [ʃ] and the [s]. Emphasis on lip rounding and on the more retracted and flattened tongue for the [ʃ] should help to contrast it with and distinguish it from the [s].

Practice Materials

Practice before a mirror with the word pairs that follow should be helpful.

she	sea	shoe	sue
sheik	seek	shoot	suit
sheep	seep	show	sew
shield	sealed	shawl	Saul
ship	sip	shore	sore
shin	sin	shop	sop
shay	say	shot	sot
shake	sake	shock	sock
shad	sad	shy	sigh
shall	sal	shed	said
brash	brass	gash	gas
clash	class	plush	plus
mesh	mess	rushed	rust
leash	lease	fashion	fasten

Initial

she	shoe	shirt	shriek
sheen	shoot	shirk	shrimp
ship	should	shut	shred
shin	shook	shun	shrewd
shay	shone	shout	shrub
shame	show	shower	shrine
shell	shawl	shine	shroud
shed	shore	shy	shrank
shall	shop	sugar	shrink
shaggy	shock	shark	shrug

Medial

leashing	lashes	pressure	fission
wishing	passion	quashed	hushing
ashamed	fashion	machine	Flushing
glacier	pushing	pension	national
nation	cushion	delicious	fractious
patient	lotion	conscience	washed
precious	ocean	anxious	crashed
dashes	caution	mission	rushing

Final

leash	hash	hush	Danish
wish	crash	harsh	blemish
fish	bush	marsh	English
dish	push	rush	garnish
mesh	burnish	tarnish	Flemish
flesh	furnish	varnish	brandish
flash	punish	Amish	gnash
cash	blush	vanish	lush

Sentences

1. Ocean fishing furnishes a livelihood for many British fishermen.

2. The shaggy Prussian brandished his tarnished sword.

3. Hamlet had an anxious and disturbed conscience.

4. Shaw was not ashamed to be fractious.

5. The chef earned a pension for his well-garnished dishes.

6. Sheila shrugged her shoulders as she added sugar to her milk shake.

7. The motion of the ship on the ocean made a patient of the man from Flushing.

8. A flash flood transformed the shrubless field into a marsh.

9. Some nations have a passion for peace; others seem to have a passion for aggression.

10. Ship-to-shore communication is available for most of our nation.

Selection

Daniel Shays was a captain of the militia during our Revolution against the British. Later, during the period of the Confederation and in a time of financial depression, Shays led an armed insurrection against the Massachusetts government. The insurrectionists were made up substantially of farmers. They protested that the salaries of public officials were too high. In addition they petitioned against the imposition of high taxes. Shays' petitions, protestations, general dissensions, and finally his insurrection are believed to have hastened the ratification of the Federal Constitution by Massachusetts.

[ʒ] (zh) As in *Measure* and *Pleasure*

The sound [ʒ] is a voiced, postdental, fricative. It is produced like the [ʃ] with accompanying vocal-fold vibration. [ʒ] occurs medially or finally in English words. The most frequent spellings for this consonant are *z* as in *seizure*, *s* as in *treasure*, and *ge* as in *garage*.

Practice Materials

Medial

azure	intrusion	delusion	persuasion
casual	measure	composure	incision
confusion	pleasure	explosion	derision
conclusion	treasure	erosion	precision
contusion	seizure	lesion	exposure
decision	usual	adhesion	illusion
division	vision	collision	occasion
explosion	glazier	invasion	abrasion

Final

garage	beige	camouflage	corsage
mirage	entourage	persiflage	rouge

Sentences

1. The Persian found nothing more pleasurable than an azure sky.

2. The collision occurred as the cars left the garage.

3. Soil erosion wastes the treasures of our land.

4. A mirage is a visual delusion.

5. Because he was given to persiflage, his decisions always seemed casual.

6. The invasion by an infantry division was preceded by an explosion of the camouflaged air field.

7. The glazier won prestige by the precision of his work.

8. Confusion resulted in numerous contusions among members of the treasure-hunting entourage.

9. Joe yielded to his wife's persuasion and accepted her decision to paint his garage beige.

10. The intrusion of the police prevented the seizure of the gold.

Selections

1. One man with a dream, at pleasure,
      Shall go forth and conquer a crown;
    And three with a new song's measure
      Can trample an empire down.
                A. W. E. O'SHAUGHNESSY—*Ode*

2. Rich the treasure,
    Sweet the pleasure,
    Sweet is pleasure after pain.
                JOHN DRYDEN
                —*Alexander's Feast*

3. Frazier was given to visual illusions and to occasional delusions. Unfortunately, he also acted in the light of these visionary aberrations. Frazier's demise was a result of this inclination. On the final and fatal occasion, Frazier was confronted with an escaped tiger which had hidden in his garage. Because of a visual illusion, Frazier insisted that the tiger was a house cat. In the light of this decision, he began to pat the animal. The beast, not sharing the illusion and having no delusions about himself as a domestic treasure, attacked and devoured Frazier. The job was done with dispatch and precision. Thus poor Frazier was consumed, a victim of a visual illusion and of delusionary behavior.

[tʃ] (ch) As in *Chest, Orchard,* and *Match*

The sound [tʃ] (ch) is a blend or compound of [t] followed immediately by [ʃ]. It may occur initially, medially, or finally. The blend, a combination of a stop-plosive and a voiceless fricative sound, is classified phonetically as an *affricate*. This voiceless affricate is regularly represented by the letters *ch* in spelling.

The sound may be troublesome for speakers for whom English is not a first language and in whose native language the [tʃ] does not occur. For example, it may be troublesome to native French speakers because it does not occur in French. For such persons, the most frequent tendency is to substitute the second element [ʃ] for the blend [tʃ].

Practice Materials

The exercises that follow should be of help in differentiating between [tʃ] and [ʃ].

cheer	sheer	hatch	hash
cheat	sheet	latch	lash
choose	shoes	march	marsh
chairs	shares	match	mash
chin	shin	much	mush
catch	cash	witch	wish
crutch	crush	watching	washing
ditch	dish	catching	cashing

Sentences

1. The sailors had to chip the paint from the ship.
2. Fido liked to chew on an old shoe.
3. The sheik had a scar on his cheek.
4. It may be pleasant to share a chair.
5. Tom bruised his chin and his shin.
6. Charles insisted that it does not take too long to have too much of mush.
7. The marines went on a march through the marsh.
8. Macbeth hoped that the witch would help him realize his wish.

Initial

cheese	chance	churn	chore
chief	chant	chug	change
chill	chewed	chum	Charles
chimp	choose	chunk	chirp
chain	choke	chowder	choice
chafe	chose	chide	chat
check	chalk	China	chicken
chess	chuck	chive	chin
channel	chop	chime	Chester
champ	char	child	chap

Medial

reaching	brooches	marching	bachelor
beeches	broaching	urchin	batches
pitcher	coached	birches	paunches
kitchen	encroaching	lurching	parched
exchange	orchard	searching	righteous
hatchet	launched	bunched	preaching

Final

each	match	staunch	couch
teach	dispatch	porch	slouch
speech	blotch	scorch	pouch
ditch	watch	torch	touch
witch	pooch	lurch	clutch
fetch	encroach	birch	such
wrench	coach	bunch	research
detach	reproach	hunch	squelch

Sentences

1. Charles was taught by his pupils to observe the difference between teaching and preaching.
2. After searching in the orchard, we found the chart under the beech tree.
3. Chop suey is sold by the Chinese, but rarely in China.
4. The church supper featured chicken and chowder.
5. The child was chided for chewing his chalk.

6. The chess contest was won by the Chilean champion.
7. Some children like their steak charred.
8. Birches are a climbing challenge for many urchins.
9. Chester was partial to chowder.
10. Charlton remained a bachelor because he could find no churned butter to match his mother's.

Selections

1. When I was a child, I spake as a child, I understood as a child, I thought as a child; but when I became a man, I put away childish things.

I Corinthians

2. Choice word and measured phrase, above the reach of ordinary men.

WILLIAM WORDSWORTH—*Resolution and Independence*

[dʒ] (dzh) As in *Age, Adjust,* and *Budge*

[dʒ] is the voiced counterpart of [tʃ]. This voiced sound blend may occur either initially, medially, or finally. In *judge* and *George* it occurs both initially and finally. In *agent* and *engine* the affricate [dʒ] occurs medially. The most frequent spellings for [dʒ] are *g, j,* and *dg* as in *wage, jam,* and *ridge.*

Many American and English speakers tend to unvoice [dʒ] when the blend occurs in final positions. French, Spanish, and German speakers may have difficulty with the voiced affricate because the sound does not occur in their native languages.

Speakers who have difficulty in deciding whether a given word calls for [dʒ] or [tʃ] should be helped by the relative frequency of the *ch* spelling for the unvoiced sound and the inclusion of the letter *j* or *g* for the voiced affricate.

Practice Materials

The first set of exercise materials is for the purpose of establishing the distinction between the two affricates.

gin	chin	jigger	chigger
jar	char	jug	chug
jeer	cheer	bridges	breeches

jest	chest	badge	batch
jump	chump	ridge	rich
jeep	cheap	surge	search
joke	choke	liege	leech

Initial

jeans	jewel	germ	junior
jib	June	jar	jury
giraffe	judicial	journey	just
gipsy	joke	jowl	jute
jig	jovial	jug	jade
jail	Jonah	jump	jilt
jay	jaunt	giant	general
jet	jaw	jibe	germane
gem	job	joint	genius
jack	jog	join	gentle

Medial

besieged	agent	adjust	larger
regent	changed	adjourn	margin
imagine	ranging	surgeon	region
regenerate	major	urgent	disjoint
hedging	stranger	merger	enjoin
wedged	ajar	legion	lounging
ledger	rajah	soldier	gouging
badger	plunged	budget	rejoin

Final

liege	huge	nudge	sponge
siege	sledge	grudge	bilge
ridge	forge	oblige	discharge
bridge	engorge	gouge	dirge
rage	barge	singe	grange
stage	large	fringe	strange
edge	urge	surge	derange
wedge	merge	emerge	average
carriage	bulge	orange	peerage
marriage	fudge	revenge	steerage

Sentences
1. Judge Jones adjourned the jury.
2. A legion of soldiers landed by jet plane.
3. Dr. Julian, a surgeon, adjusted Joe's disarranged jaw.
4. Jonah had a strange journey in a giant whale.
5. The gentleman of the peerage once traveled by steerage.
6. Justice cannot always be determined by jurists.
7. Jargon is a strange form of language usage.
8. June was in a rage because she was rudely nudged.
9. The merger of the companies resulted in a huge corporation specializing in surgical supplies.
10. Sturgeon is a major Russian item exported in jars.
11. The hedge under the bridge was edged with geraniums.
12. Junk jewelry is not likely to be made with jade.

The sentences that follow should be practiced with a view to maintaining vocalization for the final [dʒ]. Make certain that vocalization continues so that there is no substitution of [tʃ] for the voiced affricate.

Sentences
1. George and Marge were married by a judge.
2. Madge would not budge from her strange position.
3. John stood at the edge of the ridge.
4. Jones yielded to his urge and ate a large orange.
5. At two years of age the average child can speak his language.
6. A large suspension bridge was built over the gorge.
7. The grange was the scene of a battle of revenge.

In the following sentences make certain that you distinguish between the [dʒ] and the [ʒ]. The first italicized word will include the blend [dʒ]; the second will have the voiced fricative [ʒ].

Sentences
1. A *general* commands a *division*.
2. Charles *pledged* himself to a life of *pleasure*.
3. A *jury* found Wilson guilty of *usury*.
4. *Agile* Peter climbed a hill to admire the *azure* sky.
5. *Drudgery*, in *measure*, is part of living.

6. Ted *objected* to any form of *intrusion*.
7. *Judge* Thompson weighed all the evidence before announcing his *decision*.
8. Helen could not *imagine* inheriting a *treasure*.

Selections

1. Casey Jones was a railroad engineer and a figure legendary for his courage. Casey had a predecessor, an engineer named Jimmie Jones, for whom the following verses were written:

> On a Sunday mornin' it began to rain,
> 'Round the curve spied a passenger train,
> On the pilot lay poor Jimmie Jones,
> He's a good old porter, but he's dead and gone.

This verse for Casey Jones varies somewhat:

> On a Sunday morning it begins to rain,
> 'Round the curve spied a passenger train,
> Under the cab lay poor Casey Jones,
> He's a good engineer, but he's dead and gone—

Casey, born John Luther Jones, for all the legend built about him, was a real engineer who worked for the Illinois Central Railroad. When he had his fatal collision, Jones headed engine Number 638 out of the Memphis yards. The switchmen "knew by the engine's moans that the man at the throttle was Casey Jones." Casey, cannon-balling through the rain, knew that he was about to pile up into a freight train on the siding. He ordered his fireman to jump, and Casey himself died an engineer's death, one hand on the brakes and the other on the whistle cord.

JOHN A. and ALAN LOMAX (eds.)—Adapted from "The Legend of Casey Jones," *American Ballads and Folk Songs*

2. And what's a life?—a weary pilgrimage,
   Whose glory in one day doth fill the stage
   With childhood, manhood, and decrepit age.
   FRANCIS QUARLES—*What Is Life?*

[n] As in *No, Any,* and *Again*

[n] is a voiced, nasal, tongue tip to upper gum ridge sound. In common with the other nasal consonants, [n] requires nasal reinforcement and is emitted nasally. [n] is a continuant sound.

To produce the [n], the tongue should be elevated and the entire tongue tip should be in contact with the upper gum or alveolar ridge. The soft palate is relaxed (see Fig. 22).

In spelling, [n] is represented by the letter *n*. In some words a silent letter precedes the *n* as in *know, gnat,* and *pneumatic*.

The sound [n] presents little difficulty except that it may be slurred or replaced by a nasalized vowel in medial positions, especially in unstressed syllables as in *contact, infer,* and *inform*. The [n] is likely to be treated with greater articulatory respect in initial and final positions. Because of the high frequency of occurrence of the sound in American-English speech, careful articulation of the [n] is strongly recommended.

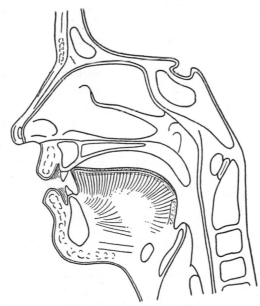

Fig. 22. Articulatory Adjustments for [n]. *Note relaxed (lowered) soft palate.*

Practice Materials

[m], we recall, is produced with the lips in gentle contact and, like [n], with the soft palate lowered. For [m] the tongue usually lies relaxed at the floor of the mouth. You may increase your awareness of the difference between the [n] and [m] by practice with the word pairs that follow.

knee	me	knob	mob
need	mead	note	mote
nude	mood	neat	meat
nail	mail	night	might
net	met	nice	mice

Initial

knee	natal	node	nut
niece	knell	notary	knuckle
neat	neck	gnome	number
kneel	nebula	gnaw	knife
near	knack	naughty	nice
knit	gnash	nautical	noise
nip	narrow	knob	now
nimble	natural	nocturn	notch
nape	nasty	nurse	pneumonia
name	nook	nerve	knew
nail	noose	nurture	knoll
nasal	nose	nub	knowledge

Make certain that an articulatory contact is made between your tongue tip and the upper gum ridge for the medial [n]. Prolong the contact, and the sound, in the word list that follows.

Medial

anneal	grinning	plaintive	fender
menial	spinnet	fainting	rented
screening	sinful	feigned	banded
dinner	hinted	fence	handed
sinner	tainted	fend	landing
thinner	saintly	defence	standing

blandish	demanded	intoned	spondee
vanish	cannibal	morning	respond
candy	stoned	dawning	despondent
dandy	telephoned	bonfire	fonder

bundle	bind	joining	pinch
trundle	kindly	connect	bench
cunning	miner	intact	branch
hunted	finer	instead	launch
gunner	ground	confer	munch
burning	hound	consume	lynch
turned	pound	confess	binge
furnace	frowning	definite	strange
burnish	lounge	inflect	lounge
furnish	coined	infest	sponge

Final

bean	amen	cone	spurn
lean	main	hone	stern
scene	lane	drone	burn
dean	grain	moan	run
mean	can	roan	done
sin	fan	brawn	stun
win	plan	faun	fine
tin	began	scorn	dine
hen	span	barn	down
ten	spoon	darn	frown
again	loon	gone	crown
when	dune	turn	brown

The consonant [n], like [m], can sometimes have syllable value without the "help" of a vowel. [n] is or may be pronounced as a syllabic sound when it occurs in a final unstressed position. This is the case in the words that follow.

button	kitten	mutton	seven
cotton	leaden	open	sudden
deaden	maiden	oven	token
heaven	mitten	rotten	leaven

Additional Materials for [n]

1. Nancy and Dan were fond of walking in the green fields.
2. Katherine, as a token of affection for her husband Neil, started her oven going at seven in the morning.
3. Nathaniel wondered why anyone, like his friend Ned, who could own a ninety-foot launch, could ever find reason to frown.
4. The missionary convinced the cannibal that eleven pounds of candy were every bit as dandy as the carnal dinner he (the cannibal) was anticipating.
5. The wounded gunner moaned but continued to direct the firing of his guns.
6. An artful use of pins and needles may be as significant in the winning of a husband as culinary acumen.
7. Nine towns were joined by the new net of highways.
8. Pine trees can grow along the ocean front as well as along mountain slopes.
9. At dawning Ben was fond of intoning plaintive tunes.
10. Quaint inns are frequently found in many parts of New England.
11. Trundle beds were in wide use in the early American colonies.
12. When the tenor suddenly showed signs of stage fright, some cynics insisted that at last he had heard the sound of his own voice.

Selections

1. Method is not less requisite in ordinary conversation than in writing, provided a man would talk to make himself understood.

JOSEPH ADDISON—*The Spectator*

2. A moral, sensible and well-bred man
   Will not affront me,—and no other can.
   WILLIAM COWPER—*Conversation*

3. On deck beneath the awning,
   I dozing lay and yawning;
   It was the grey of dawning,
      Ere yet the sun arose;
   And above the funnel's roaring,
   And the fitful wind's deploring,

I heard the cabin snoring
With universal noise.

WILLIAM MAKEPEACE THACKERAY
—*The White Squall*

4. I have met with women who I really think would like to be married to a Poem and to be given away by a Novel.

JOHN KEATS—*Letters to Fanny Braun*

5. Yet half the beast is the great god Pan,
   To laugh as he sits by the river,
   Making a poet out of a man:
   The true gods sigh for the cost and pain—
   For the reed which grows nevermore again
   As a reed with the reeds of the river.

ELIZABETH BARRETT BROWNING
—*A Musical Instrument*

6. When Nan was young and had no sense
   She bought a horn for eighteen pence,
   But the only tune that Nan could learn
   Was "High on a Hill and Around a Turn."

—Adapted from an old English ballad

Selections for [m] *and* [n]
   1. Who would be
      A mermaid fair,
      Singing alone,
      Combing her hair
      Under the sea,
      In a golden curl,
      With a comb of pearl,
      On a throne?

I would be a mermaid fair;
I would sing to myself the whole of the day;
With a comb of pearl I would comb my hair;

And still as I comb'd I would sing and say,
"Who is it loves me? who loves not me?"
ALFRED, LORD TENNYSON—*The Mermaid*

2. Life's a pudding full of plums;
   Care's a canker that benumbs,
   Wherefore waste our elocution
   On impossible solution?
   Life's a pleasant institution,
   Let us take it as it comes!
   W. S. GILBERT
   —"Life's Tangled Skein,"
   The Gondoliers

3. To be honest, to be kind—to earn a little and spend a little less,
to make upon the whole a family happier for his presence, to renounce when that shall be necessary and not to be embittered, to
keep a few friends, but these without capitulation—above all, on
the same grim conditions, to keep friends with himself—here is a
task for all that a man has of fortitude and delicacy.
   ROBERT LOUIS STEVENSON—*Christmas Sermon*

4. Know then thyself, presume not God to scan;
   The proper study of mankind is man.
   ALEXANDER POPE—*Essay on Man*

5. O Shenandoah, I long to hear you,
   Away, you rolling river,
   O Shenandoah, I long to hear you
   Away, I'm bound away,
   Across the wide Missouri.

   Missouri, she's a mighty river,
   Away, you rolling river,
   The Indians camp along her borders.
   Away, I'm bound away,
   Across the wide Missouri.

The white man loved an Indian maiden,
Away, you rolling river,
With notions his canoe was laden,
Away, I'm bound away,
Across the wide Missouri.
                    Shenandoah—American ballad

Additional review selections for [m] and [n] will be found in our earlier discussion of nasal reinforcement (see pages 77–80).

[l] As in *Late, Alone,* and *Bell*

[l] is a lingua-alveolar, voiced, lateral sound. This vowel-like consonant may occur initially, medially, or finally. As may be noted from the spellings of several of the words in the first two sentences of this paragraph, [l] is represented in spelling by the letter *l* or the letters *ll*.

[l], like [t] and [d], is produced with the tongue tip in contact with the upper gum ridge. Unlike the plosives [t] and [d], the [l]

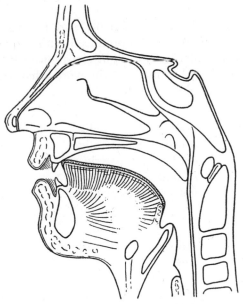

Fig. 23. Articulatory Adjustments for [l].

has a continuant and vowel-like quality. To achieve this quality, the blade of the tongue (the portion just behind the tongue tip) is lowered to permit vocalized breath to escape over the sides. The soft palate is raised to prevent nasal emission of sound. Vocal-fold vibration regularly accompanies the articulatory action for the [l].

Practice Materials

In producing the sound [l] make certain that the *tip* and *not the blade* of your tongue is in contact with the gum ridge. Avoid contact between the tongue tip and teeth.

Initial

leap	lute	learn	lake
lip	loom	lug	lower
late	load	lie	lapse
let	lawn	like	lane
lack	lot	low	linger
laugh	lost	lout	loin

In some contexts, before consonants and in final positions, a variant of the [l] sound may be produced with a quality referred to as "dark." This results from a slight elevation of the back of the tongue. It may be heard in many of the words that follow.

Medial

heels	pooled	alike	allow
hills	pulse	align	pallid
hailed	cold	sleep	palace
held	stalled	ballad	tailor
gals	gold	elope	tilt

Final

keel	tool	earl	gale
till	full	gull	ball
pale	foal	foil	guile
fell	hall	tile	eel
pal	doll	cowl	pearl

[l] Preceded by [p] or [b]

Some persons produce an "infantile" sound in contexts in which the [l] is immediately preceded by a [p] or [b]. This effect is frequently a result of failure to make the tongue tip to gum ridge contact for [l]. A [w]-like sound is produced as a carry-over of the lip movement of the [p] or [b].

Practice Materials

For the following practice materials, avoid lip movement for the [l]. Make certain that there is a definite tongue tip to gum ridge contact for the sound.

please	plume	bleed	blue
Pliocene	pluck	blame	blood
pleasant	plausible	blink	bloat
play	plot	blend	bluff
plan	plunder	bland	blot
pledge	plight	black	blind

The following word pairs should help to establish a clear distinction between [l] and [w].

weep	leap	wade	laid
wack	lack	wit	lit
wag	lag	way	lay
wax	lacks	wear	lair
went	lent	wet	let

Additional practice words follow.

lean	loom	glide	claw
lip	law	glaze	clue
lace	lock	glower	club
left	log	glimpse	cloy
lance	learn	glue	clan
glance	lunch	glutton	climb
loot	lion	clean	clutter
lose	glow	class	cluster

Sentences
1. Lila was fond of lilting lyrics.
2. The tall glasses sparkled and gleamed in the sunlight.
3. The lodge was built on the slope of a hill.
4. Eloquence was Paul's long suit.
5. Linda longed for a knight and his protective lance.
6. The fallen petals held the scent of the flower.
7. Preelection spellbinders are loath to employ logic.
8. An eel may display an electrifying personality.
9. Not long ago children went to bed by candlelight.
10. Lillian fell asleep in class.
11. Cannibals do not always trouble to be artful.
12. Lyman and Leo haggled over the bottle of glue.

Selections

1. I do not love thee, Doctor Fell,
   The reason why I cannot tell,
   But this alone I know full well:
   I do not love thee, Doctor Fell.
                THOMAS BROWN
   —paraphrase of Martial

2. There's a bear in yon hill, and he is a brave fellow,
   He's plenty in store, and lives at his ease,
   All he wants is a wife, and he's travelled all over,
   To find a companion his fancy to please.

                    · · · ·

   "Oh dearest possum, where are you a-goin'?
   It is a cold and blustery day.
   If you'll go with me, oh, how I will love you!
   I'll take you to my den, love, and there you may stay."

   With all these kind compliments, possum lie grinning,
   And then returned to her love and did say:
   "Go to my uncle on the banks of the river,
   And if he is willing, with you I'll agree."
            The Bear in the Hill—American ballad

3. In the New England village of Lyndale, Lyman Littleton was held to be a simple fellow who did not properly evaluate a dollar. This belief about Lyman began early in his life. When Lyman was ten years old, one of the wealthy villagers asked him to choose between a nickel and a silver dollar. Lyman, apparently foolishly, selected the nickel. The wealthy villager spread the tale about Lyman's failure to choose a dollar over a nickel. Before long, other Lyndale villagers put Lyman to the test. Even the nonaffluent ones were willing to try. Each time Lyman selected the nickel over the dollar.

When Lyman grew to be an adolescent, Leo, his closest friend, asked Lyman whether he would ever learn that a dollar had more value than a nickel. A sly look came into Lyman Littleton's eyes. He blinked at his pal Leo and explained, "Leo, how long do you believe I would be able to play the game of a nickel or a dollar if I didn't always select the nickel?"

4. Oft on the dappled turf at ease
   I sit, and play with similes,
   Loose type of things through all degrees.
   WILLIAM WORDSWORTH—*To the Daisy*

17 • The Vowel-Like Sound [r]

[r]

There is considerable variation in the production and pronunciation of [r] according to context and regional practice. In regard to the latter, as we indicated earlier, some persons in the areas of eastern New England, eastern Canada, New York City, and the southern coastal states pronounce [r] only when it is immediately followed by a vowel as in *reach, rise, grows, boring,* and *Marion* and omit [r] in other contexts. Most Americans, however, pronounce an [r] sound whenever the letter *r* appears in the spelling of a word regardless of whether the immediate next sound is a vowel or a consonant. The general tendency for most Americans is to produce an [r] in words such as *cart, bargain,* and *turn* as well as for contexts such as *around, through,* and *pour it.*

We will consider three varieties of [r]. Two of these call for the production of the *r* as a semi-vowel or vowel-like consonant. The third is a fricative, more characteristically consonant sound.

[r] As in *Rise, Rose,* and *Around*

We shall consider two ways of producing the [r] when the sound is immediately followed by a vowel in a stressed syllable. The first

264

method is to raise the tongue tip toward the roof of the mouth. The
tongue tip may be brought close to the gum ridge, but actual contact with the gum ridge should be avoided. The tongue tip may
also be flexed slightly toward the back of the mouth. Compare
Fig. 24 demonstrating production of this type of [r] with Fig. 13
illustrating the [t], [d], and [l] sounds.

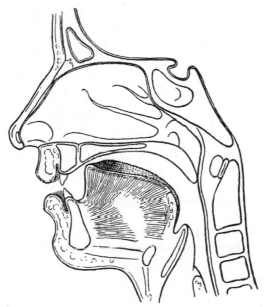

Fig. 24. Articulatory Adjustments for Retroflex [r].

The second method of articulating an [r] before a vowel in a
stressed syllable more nearly approximating the production of a
vowel sound. The tip of the tongue is lowered and the central
portion of the tongue is raised toward the roof of the mouth about
where the hard palate ends and the soft palate begins. This is
illustrated in Fig. 25. For both of these varieties of [r], the sound is
produced with accompanying vocal-fold vibration.

If you have no difficulty with either variety of [r], there is no
need for concern or consistency as to manner of production. If you
have difficulty with the sound, however, and tend to produce the

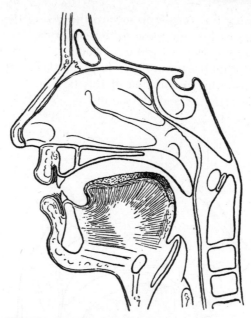

Fig. 25. Articulatory Adjustments for Velar [r].

[r] so that the effect is much like a [w], then you should analyze
your efforts for tongue tip and central [r] and try to produce consistently your best [r] sound. Experience suggests that persons who
tend to confuse [w] and [r] usually improve by establishing and
regularly using a tongue-tip [r]. Persons who tend to confuse [l]
and [r] are likely to do better by establishing and consistently producing a central position [r]. Whichever variety you produce, do
not prolong the sound excessively and do not convert the [r] into a
distorted vowel.

Practice Materials

Initial

reach	rage	rude	rope
ream	red	rule	raw
rid	rest	rook	wrought
rim	rack	roof	rock
rate	rap	rote	rod

rug	rice	royal	wren
rough	rise	roam	wreck
run	rhyme	rook	roast
rout	ripe	raucous	wrangle
round	real	road	wrestle

Medial (followed by a vowel)

breeze	brood	brunt	grime
green	group	grunt	brine
grim	broom	grub	bride
brim	brooch	broken	grind
dray	grope	grass	grouse
grade	gross	aroma	around
berry	brown	arise	awry
bread	brought	grave	peril
brand	grog	grail	very
marry	lorry	brig	bereave

For the medial [r] followed by a consonant check your practice and pronunciation with what is current in your community. Do you include or omit the [r]?

Medial (followed by a consonant)

pierce	art	smart	mourn
fierce	part	dart	dormitory
beard	warm	swarm	wired
seared	wart	forlorn	tired
chart	farm	orphan	hired
charm	unharmed	scarf	Martha
storm	absorb	dwarf	Marvin
alarm	fork	north	York
harm	pork	forth	inform
ark	hard	ward	torn

For the final [r], is your practice for the omission or inclusion of the final [r] consistent with that for medial [r] followed by a consonant? It is, for most speakers.

Final

dear	are	four	bother
hear	bar	more	mother
fear	car	lore	ignore
near	far	core	father
care	mar	soar	sister
dare	star	ire	tower
fair	boor	dire	shower
mare	moor	sire	paper
their	cure	sour	plumber
lair	tour	flower	summer

For special medial [r] words review the discussion of the [ɜ] and [ɝ] vowels (see pages 164–166).

Special medial words

birth	burn	turf	curl
mirth	stern	shirt	curtain
terse	girl	girth	certain
first	whirl	nerve	lurch
nurse	heard	serve	church
purse	hurl	spurn	yearn

Distinction between [r] and [w]

Persons who tend to produce [r] so that it resembles [w] should work to establish a clear acoustic difference between these sounds. The [r] should be produced without lip activity and, preferably, with the tongue tip raised toward the gum ridge. The [w] should be produced with lip movement and without front of the tongue activity (see page 193).

Practice Materials

The following materials should help to establish the distinction. Use a mirror to see what you do, and listen carefully to hear what happens with and without lip movement.

Distinguish between [r] and [w]:

reap	weep	roof	woof
read	weed	run	won
reek	week	ring	wing
red	wed	rue	woo
wren	wen	room	womb
rest	west	row	woe
rag	wag	ride	wide
rage	wage	rise	wise
rate	wait	rare	wear

Difficult [r] Combinations

Words beginning with [p] and [b] followed by [r], as in *prize* and *breeze,* may be troublesome because of the lip activity required for the first sounds. The fault is similar to the one discussed earlier in our discussion of the [l] preceded by [p] or [b].

Practice Materials

Avoid lip movement for the [r] as you practice with the materials that follow.

preach	praise	prude	sprawl
preen	press	prove	proud
prince	precious	probe	prow
print	prank	prone	pride
pray	prattle	prawn	price

breech	braise	brood	brought
breeze	breast	brew	broad
brick	break	broke	brow
bring	brain	broth	bride
bray	brash	brawn	brine

Some persons find the combinations [gr] and [kr], as in *green* and *cream,* somewhat difficult. If you are one of those who do, we suggest that you establish a central tongue [r], the second of the [r] sounds described, for the [gr] and [kr] combinations.

Practice Materials

The following materials should be of help.

cream	crest	crew	crock
creek	crept	crude	crowd
crib	cram	crow	crown
crayon	crash	croak	crime
cradle	craft	crawl	scribe

green	grew	grind	grist
greet	group	grape	grief
grin	grope	grime	grace
grit	grow	groom	grade
grate	gross	gruel	grant
grain	groan	groove	graze
grenadine	grog	grand	growl
grass	grotto	grunt	grudge
grapple	grub	grasp	gruff

Sentences

1. Pride sometimes brings grief.
2. The green crock was full of cream.
3. The crude craft crashed in the gray fog.
4. The driver stepped on the brakes and his car came to a grinding halt.
5. Grog poured out of the broken crock.
6. The wrestlers grunted and groaned through their performance.
7. Grass grows best in partly shaded areas.
8. The gruff dogs growled as they guarded their grub.

Another combination causing some difficulty is [r] preceded by [f]. Practice with the following words.

free	freckle	fruit	from
freeze	fresh	frugal	frock
frigid	friend	fro	front
frail	fragile	froze	fry
freight	frank	frog	frought

Sentences
1. Frozen fruit makes a good frappé.
2. Frank and his friend were freckled.
3. Fred, though frugal, bought his wife a French frock.
4. Frogs have short front legs.
5. Freda enjoyed fried foods.

Selections

    1. Freedom all solace to man gives:
        He lives at ease that freely lives
           JOHN BARBOUR—*The Brus*

2. A man's friendship's are, like his will, invalidated by marriage
—but they are no less invalidated by the marriage of his friends.

           SAMUEL BUTLER—*The Way of All Flesh*

[r] As in *True, Through,* and *Dry*

A third variety of [r] approximates a fricative sound in manner of production. It is articulated by placing the tip of the tongue close to but not quite touching the gum ridge. When air is forced over the tongue tip, a fricative [r] is produced (see Fig. 26). When this variety of [r] occurs in the initial position, the sound is vocalized. When it occurs after a voiceless sound, as in *three* and *tree,* the [r] may be completely or partly unvoiced. This [r] is not as frequently produced by American speakers as the other varieties earlier considered.

This variety of [r] is described as a postdental fricative. It is most likely to be produced after tongue-tip consonants such as [t], [d], and [θ] (th).

Practice Materials

Practice with the material that follows:

treat	tread	true	trot
tree	track	troop	trouble
trip	trap	truce	trunk
trigger	trash	trout	tripe
train	tram	trophy	try
trade	transit	tropic	trowel

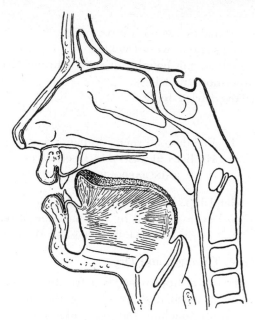

Fig. 26. Tongue position for Fricative [r].

three	thrash	throttle	throng
thrift	through	thrush	Thrace
thrill	throne	thrall	threaten
thresh	throw	thrive	throat
thread	throb	thrombus	thrust

Sentences
1. The troops arranged a truce.
2. The triple victory earned the team of three a trophy.
3. A thrush hid behind the trunk of the tree.
4. Trams are no longer popular in transit.
5. Tripe is a substantial if not a thrilling food.
6. The train, engineer on throttle, sped through the night.

Linking [r] and Intrusive [r]

Earlier, we discussed the regional tendencies in words in which the letter *r* is final in the spelling. The [r] in contexts such as *far away, near us, for it, for old,* and *bear it* is usually heard as a linking sound between vowels. If you listen closely to the production of the linking [r], you will note that it is produced with less vigor and is of shorter duration than the initial [r] or the medial [r] in stressed positions. Acoustically, the sound is much like the [r] in unstressed syllables, as in the words *berry, marry, carry,* and *ferry.*

Occasionally, an [r] sound is intruded where the spelling of the word does not include the letter *r*. It is most likely to be intruded in combinations such as *law and order, idea of, America is,* and *vanilla ice.* It is apparently easier to maintain speech fluency by inserting an [r] between words when one ends and the next begins with a vowel than to produce two vowels in succession. The intrusive [r] is generally considered substandard and its use is therefore not recommended.

Practice Materials

Practice the following sentences. Read each slowly and avoid the intrusive [r].

Sentences
1. North America is a large continent.
2. Law and order must be maintained.
3. The essential idea of a theme should be apparent.
4. Vanilla ice cream is my favorite flavor.
5. I am fond of sliced banana in my breakfast cereal.
6. The play was a drama in three acts.

The material following should provide practice for [r] in various positions.

Sentences
1. Harrigan boasted of his Irish breeding and his proud name.
2. The graceless criminal broke out of the brig.
3. Nitrogen is used freely as a fertilizer.
4. The fearful lover did not know whether to bring his darling flowers or a fragrant perfume.
5. Random thoughts do not necessarily produce reasonable free verse.

6. The real estate broker exercised no scruples when he appropriated the poor widow's property.

7. The rustle of crisp red leaves was carried by the autumn breeze.

8. The air we breathe contains considerably more nitrogen than oxygen.

9. The growling mongrel was tested for rabies.

10. Three policemen broke up the unruly rally.

11. Many foreign-born persons have difficulty in pronouncing *r* sounds.

12. For reasons not always clear, persons named Harry are reputed to be mirthful characters.

13. Though many have inquired, we have not learned the answer to "Who threw the overalls in Mrs. Murphy's chowder?"

14. More theories die than survive their theorists.

15. Theresa and Rose wanted to marry Fred and Robert, and they hoped that there would be no need to tarry.

16. Long-range weather forecasts are becoming increasingly accurate.

Additional Selections for [l] *and* [r]

1. Albert Einstein, in telling of his religious belief, held that "My religion consists of a humble admiration of the illimitable superior spirit who reveals himself in the slight details we are able to perceive with our frail and feeble minds."

LINCOLN BARNETT—*The Universe and Dr. Einstein*

2. James MacGregor Burns wrote a political biography of Franklin Delano Roosevelt. Some critics characterized this literary effort as forthright, dramatic, and critical. The underlying theme of the biography is borrowed from Machiavelli's *The Prince*. Machiavelli, in the year 1513, wrote that "A prince must imitate the fox and the lion, for the lion cannot protect himself from traps, and the fox cannot defend himself from wolves. One must therefore be a fox to recognize traps, and a lion to frighten wolves." Burns' biography of Roosevelt brings out that politics is America's most alluring game in which Franklin Delano Roosevelt was a prince of players.

3. Leo Nicholas Tolstoy's *War and Peace* is a vast book that flows for more than 600,000 words like a great river, twisting, turning and full of literary whirlpools as it tells of the historic duel between the French emperor Napoleon and the Russian czar Alexander I. Considered by many the greatest novel ever written, it is a stupendous panorama of battles and how they were fought, of imperial pageantry, aristocratic society, tender romances, prodigious sins, religious and patriotic fervor, of the burning of Moscow and the destruction of Napoleon's Grande Armée in the snows on the Smolensk road. *War and Peace* has 23 main characters, 47 minor ones and nearly 500 more appear briefly. It is suffused with love for them all and hate for war and death. Tolstoy took six years (1863–1869) to write it and people usually take months to read it.

Life, August 20, 1956

4. Alas, my love, you do me wrong
   To cast me out thus discourteously
   When I have loved you so long
   Delighting in thy company.

   Greensleeves is all my joy
   And Greensleeves is my delight
   Greensleeves is my heart of love
   And who but my lady Greensleeves.

   I sent to thee a dress of red
   Embroidered with gold finery
   And sent thee kerchers to thy head
   Which cost my purse well favouredly.

   Oh, Greensleeves, now farewell, adieu
   God I pray to prosper thee,
   Yet I am still thy lover true
   Come once again my lover be!

   Greensleeves
   —16th century English ballad

5. There I sat on Buttermilk Hill
   Who could blame me, cry my fill,
   And every tear would turn a mill,
   Johnny has gone for a soldier.

   Me oh my, I loved him so
   Broke my heart to see him go,
   And only time will heal my woe,
   Johnny has gone for a soldier.

   I'll sell my flax, I'll sell my wheel
   Buy my love a sword of steel,
   So it in battle he may wield
   Johnny has gone for a soldier.
             Johnny Has Gone for a Soldier
                —American version of
                17th century Irish song

6. Come all you fair and tender ladies,
   Be careful how you court young men,
   They're like a star of summer's morning,
   They'll first appear and then they're gone.

   They'll tell to you some loving story,
   They'll declare to you their love is true;
   Straightway they'll go and court some other,
   And that's the love they have for you.

   I wish I was some little sparrow,
   That I had wings, could fly so high;
   I'd fly away to my false lover,
   And when he's talkin' I'd be by.

   But I am not a little sparrow,
   And neither have I wings to fly;
   I'll sit down here in grief and sorrow
   To weep and pass my troubles by.

   If I'd a-known before I courted,
   I never would have courted none;

I'd have locked my heart in a box of golden,
And pinned it up with a silver pin.
Come All You Fair and Tender Ladies
—American ballad

7. It is manifestly impossible to discuss language quite separately
and distinctly without considering, by implication at least, thought,
of which language might be said to be the instrument. In the most
primitive animals there is nothing that corresponds to thought.
These animals are truly systems of reflexes. In them action follows
immediately on the heels of stimulus. There is no hesitation, no
intervening delay. The translation from stimulus to reaction is immediate, smooth and effective.

As we advance in the course of evolution to more complex, higher
types this immediate translation of stimulus into action is ever more
and more interrupted until, not only the interval between the two
is or may be considerable but the resulting reaction becomes less
and less predictable. It is in this interval between stimulus and
action that thought occurs, that ideas and concepts are formed, and
formulated into symbols.

WILLIAM A. WHITE—"The Language of Schizophrenia,"
Archives of Neurology and Psychiatry,
October, 1926, *16*:4, 396–398.

8. Dr. Arnold Gesell has become world famous for his observations and research on the mental and physical development of children. Gesell believes in the "ontogenetic patterning of behavior."
According to this line of thinking, the child's mind develops in an
orderly and natural manner in stages of growth that repeat and
parallel the experiences of the race.

9. To most English speaking persons who know of Richard III,
this king who reigned briefly from 1483 to 1485 is reputed to be a
villain. Shakespeare is probably responsible for Richard's characterization. In his melodramatic historical play about the allegedly
arch-Machiavellian monarch, Shakespeare has Richard utter the
following:

I, that am curtail'd of this fair proportion,
Cheated of feature by dissembling nature,

Deform'd, unfinish'd, sent before my time
Into this breathing world, scarce half made up,
And that so lamely and unfashionable
That dogs bark at me as I halt by them;

. . . .

I am determin'd to prove a villain

Plots have I laid, inductions dangerous.

A more kindly and generous characterization of this English king
is presented by Paul Murray Kendall in his biography *Richard the
Third*. Kendall holds that Richard tried to enforce laws that were
proper and just; that his brief reign is remarkable for enlightened
legislation that safeguarded the rights of individuals against abuse.
Richard tried to be a just and humane sovereign. Unfortunately, he
alienated some of the nobility by curtailing their rights to abuse
others, and in doing so lost their military support.

10. . . . Women like women fine. The more feminine she is, the
more comfortable a woman feels with her own gender. It is only the
occasional and therefore noticeable rake or adventuress among our
sex who refuses to make friends with us. I speak now merely of genu-
ine friendship. Our love we reserve for its proper object, Man. How
could we help loving men, the dear, romantic, illogical, timid, sen-
timental things? Their hearts are so tender, their trusts so deep; and
they are often such good cooks too! Uncertain, coy and hard to
please they may be, but it is woman's duty to cosset and protect
them. And she has done so to the best of her considerable ability
for a long, long while. In addition, men make the best possible
fathers for our children.

What man has misconstrued, perhaps, is woman's behavior during
what I must bluntly call the hunting season. We are immensely practical. If the race is to continue, we like to provide a second parent.
So we go about the serious business of finding husbands in a serious
manner which allows no time for small luxuries like mercy toward
competitors. Nature turns red in tooth and claw, every method is
fair and rivals get no quarter.

PHYLLIS MC GINLEY—"Women Are Wonderful,"
Life, December 24, 1956

18 · The Palatal Sounds and the Laryngeal Fricative

[k] As in *Key, Because,* and *Luck*

[k] is a voiceless, velar, plosive sound. It is produced by raising the back of the tongue to the elevated soft palate so that a firm contact is made between these articulators (see Fig. 27). In contexts in which the [k] is followed immediately by a vowel, air is impounded at the place of contact and suddenly and completely released when the contact is broken. The sound is then said to be aspirated.

The sound of [k] has several representations in spelling. The most frequent include *k* as in *key, c* as in *cat, ch* as in *chasm, qu* as in *quick,* and one element of the sound blend of *x* as in *fix* and *six.*

The [k] sound must be produced with energetic action of the articulators. Persons with normal control of their articulatory organs should find the [k] sound an easy one to make, whether in initial, medial, or final position.

Practice Materials

Initial

key	keel	kill	came
keep	keen	kit	kale

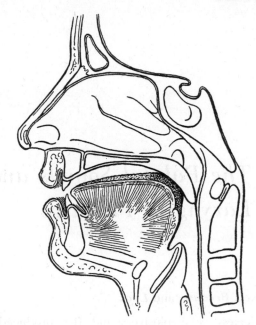

Fig. 27. Articulatory Adjustments for [k] *and* [g].

kennel	coolie	cod	coin
kept	could	cog	quoit
keg	cook	quash	cow
camp	cope	qualm	cowl
cap	comb	curl	queer
cash	coach	curve	quit
quack	call	come	quiz
calf	caught	cut	quail
cool	chorus	quiet	quaint
coop	corn	choir	chord

Medial

beaker	sticker	checker	lacquer
weaker	baker	wrecker	booked
speaker	raked	basket	looked
liquid	waking	blacken	joker
milking	shaking	cracker	poker

stoker	uncle	requite	anxious
because	percolate	uncrown	flanks
recourse	lurking	record	six
mocked	murky	second	manx
honking	turkey	extra	thanks
drunkard	recoil	fix	boxed
buckle	require	tricks	knocks

Final

beak	deck	joke	Turk
teak	back	stoke	jerk
seek	lack	poke	like
meek	bank	talk	hike
pick	rank	stalk	bike
tick	flank	balk	buck
sick	knack	chalk	tuck
make	attack	stork	luck
lake	prank	fork	duck
take	duke	torque	amuck
flake	fluke	clock	shock
wake	book	frock	stock
neck	hook	rock	spook
wreck	forsook	sock	
fleck	mistook	lurk	

Initial [kl]

clean	close	clergy	clip
cleat	claw	clerk	climax
clash	clause	clumsy	Klondike
clan	clod	cloister	kleptomania
cleanse	clog	climb	clatter
clue	clown	club	cloth

Initial [kr]

cream	crane	crawl	crowd
creep	crag	crop	cry
crib	crest	cross	crime
crisp	crude	crust	critic
crape	crow	crown	crystal

Sentences

1. Kurt was grateful to Kate because she calmed his qualms.
2. Uncle Frank liked percolated coffee.
3. The Yankees have their ball park in the Bronx.
4. Carl stalked the wild turkeys until he bagged six of them.
5. A cargo of Turkish goods was sent to the Congo.
6. The drunkard considered it bad luck to dilute either alcohol or coffee with cream.
7. The picnic basket contained crackers, cakes, and black bread.
8. The choir sang in the quiet of the cool night.
9. Queen Catherine established a record for wicked killings.

Selections

1. Current among men,
    Like coin, the tinsel clink of compliment.
    ALFRED, LORD TENNYSON—*The Princess*

2. I've never any pity for conceited people, because I think they carry their comfort about with them.
    GEORGE ELIOT—*The Mill on the Floss*

3. But screw your courage to the sticking-place
    And we'll not fail.
    WILLIAM SHAKESPEARE—*Macbeth*

4. He was in Logic, a great critic,
    Profoundly skill'd in Analytic;
    He could distinguish, and divide
    A hair 'twixt south and south-west side.
    SAMUEL BUTLER—*Hudibras*

5. Nor all that heralds rake from coffin'd clay,
    Nor florid prose, nor honied lies of rhyme,
    Can blazon evil deeds, or consecrate a crime.
    LORD BYRON—*Childe Harold*

6. Such dupes are men to custom, and so prone
    To rev'rence what is ancient, and can plead

A course of long observance for its use,
That even servitude, the worst of ill,
Because deliver'd down from sire to son,
Is kept and guarded as a sacred thing!

WILLIAM COWPER—*Task*

7. By the pricking of my thumbs,
Something wicked this way comes.
Open, locks,
Whoever knocks!

WILLIAM SHAKESPEARE—*Macbeth*

8. The whole difference between construction and creation is exactly this: that a thing constructed can only be loved after it is constructed; but a thing created is loved before it exists.

G. K. CHESTERTON—Preface to Dicken's *Pickwick Papers*

9. Nice customs curtesy to great kings.

WILLIAM SHAKESPEARE—*Henry V*

[g] As in *Go, Forget, Aghast, Egg,* and *Rogue*

[g], the voiced counterpart of [k], is a velar, stop sound. It is produced like the [k], except that a less vigorous contact is required for the [g].

[g] is usually represented by the letter *g* in spelling; less frequently it is represented by *gh*. The sound is also part of the consonant blend represented by the letter *x* in words such as *examine* and *exact*. The sound may occur initially, medially, or finally.

Initial

gear	guest	ghoul	gall
geese	gelding	goose	gaunt
greed	gap	good	gauze
green	gaff	gloom	got
give	gaze	groom	goblin
gift	game	grew	guard
grin	gate	goat	gird
guilt	gale	gloat	girth

gull	growl	grind	glue
gust	glower	gripe	glaze
gout	goiter	glide	glass
ground	guide	guise	gleen

Medial

eagle	regale	regard	beguile
eager	regain	unguarded	disguise
meager	vaguely	vanguard	misguided
begin	forget	bargain	gargoyle
rigging	regret	regulate	vigor
signal	began	cargo	regress
finger	begat	embargo	ingrain
linger	aghast	luggage	ingrown
figure	beggar	struggle	ungraded
tingle	haggle	burglar	magnify

Final

league	egg	rogue	hog
big	plague	jug	jog
fig	hag	lug	dog
pig	rag	shrug	log
rig	stag	hug	fugue
leg	crag	fog	morgue
beg	tag	frog	iceberg
peg	vogue	flog	erg

Contrasting [k] and [g]

There are two elements of contrast for the [k] and [g]. The first is the readily apparent element of voice which is present for the [g] and absent for the [k]. The second is the less obvious aspect of vigor of articulation which characterizes the [k] more than the [g].

Practice Materials

Observe these contrasts in the word pairs that follow.

cam	gam	pick	pig
cat	gat	rack	rag

kill	gill	hack	hag
coat	goat	tack	tag
coast	ghost	sack	sag
cool	ghoul	buck	bug
cull	gull	tuck	tug
cut	gut	chuck	chug

Sentences

1. The ghost was said to haunt the coast.
2. The surgeon had to cut the animal's gut.
3. Robinson Crusoe wore a coat of goat skin.
4. A tack kept the price tag in place.
5. An empty sack will sag.

Sentences for [g]

1. The Englishman's girth grew out of control because of his fondness for cooked goose.
2. The misguided burglar left his fingerprints on the luggage.
3. Greta was fond of bargains, be it eggs or frog's legs.
4. Gordon, perhaps because of guilt, thought that the gargoyle regarded him with a glower.
5. The beggar magnified his hunger as he begged for his breakfast.
6. Goodhue was a rogue, a matter he did not struggle to have well-groomed persons forget.
7. Big league baseball players must regulate their eagerness for food.
8. Ghosts are not supposed to groan nor look as though they have gout.
9. On Hallowe'en the goblins are eager to get you if you are not on guard.
10. A fugue is not a vaguely organized composition.

Selections for [k] and [g]

1. What? Was man made a wheel-work to wind up,
   And be discharged, and straight wound up anew?
   No! grown, his growth lasts; taught, he ne'er forgets;
   May learn a thousand things, not twice the same.
   ROBERT BROWNING—*A Death in the Desert*

2. "Ay," quoth my uncle Gloucester,
"Small herbs have grace, great weeds do grow apace;"
And since, methinks, I would not grow so fast,
Because sweet flowers are slow, and weeds make haste.
                    WILLIAM SHAKESPEARE—*Richard III*

3.   The gods
Grow angry with your patience, 'Tis their care,
And must be yours, that guilty men escape not:
As crimes do grow, justice should rouse itself.
                          BEN JONSON—*Catiline*

4. The gift, to be true, must be the flowing of the giver unto me,
correspondent to my flowing unto him.
                    RALPH WALDO EMERSON—*Of Gifts*

5. His presence haunts this room to-night,
A form of mingled mist and light
    From that far coast.
Welcome beneath this roof of mine!
Welcome! this vacant chair is thine,
    Dear guest and ghost!
          HENRY WADSWORTH LONGFELLOW
                    —*Robert Burns*

6. Great is the art of beginning, but greater
the art is of ending:
          HENRY WADSWORTH LONGFELLOW
                    —*Elegiac Verse*

[ŋ] (ng) As in *Wing* and *Singer*

[ŋ] is a velar nasal sound. It is produced, as indicated in Fig. 28,
by raising the back of the tongue so that it is in contact with the
lowered soft palate while the vocal folds are in vibration. [ŋ] is a
continuant sound which is reinforced and emitted nasally. In
American-English speech the [ŋ] occurs either medially or finally
but never initially.

The [ŋ] is represented by the letter *n* or the letters *ng*. The sound

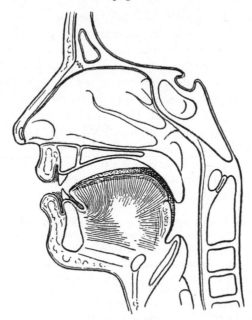

Fig. 28. Articulatory Adjustments for [ŋ]. *Note relaxed (lowered) soft palate.*

occurs usually in words in which the letter *n* is followed by either a *k* or a *g* in the same syllable. [ŋ] is generally not heard in standard speech in combinations where the *n* and the *g* which follows are in different syllables, as in *ingrate* and *congratulate*.

Except for possible confusion between the [n] and the [ŋ], there is seldom any difficulty in the actual articulation of the velar nasal sound. There is some tendency, however, for some speakers to add either a [g] or a [k] following the [ŋ] so that all words containing the velar nasal sound are pronounced either [ŋg] or [ŋk]. This tendency may frequently be traced to the influence of a foreign dialect. A second influence may be attributed to the speaker's failure to remember the pronunciation of the particular word relative to the omission or inclusion of the [g] or [k]. A third influence is a direct result of the manner of articulating the [ŋ]. If the soft palate is raised before the contact between the tongue and palate is broken, a [k] or [g] sound is produced. To avoid adding either of these sounds when only the velar nasal is required, the speaker must watch his articulatory timing. Specifically, he must make certain that the back of his tongue is moved away from his soft palate before he raises his soft palate to block off the entrance to the nasal passage.

To know how to produce an [ŋ] is not enough. We must also know whether the velar nasal is to be followed by a velar stop [k] or [g], or by some other sound. There is, of course, only one reliable way to learn the pronunciation of a word with velar nasal consonants. The reliable way is to study each word individually, using an up-to-date large dictionary as a pronunciation guide. A second approach of general help is to learn the so-called "rules" for the use of the velar consonants in English speech.

1. When a word ends with the letters *ng* or *ngue*, the pronunciation calls for the [ŋ]. Examples include *wing, rang, tongue,* and *meringue.*
2. Usually, when a suffix is added to a root word that is pronounced with the [ŋ], the pronunciation calls for the [ŋ]. Examples include *swings, rings, singer, longing,* and *stinging.* The exceptions to this general tendency include the comparative and superlative forms of the adjectives *long, young* and *strong;* e.g., *longer, longest; younger, youngest; stronger, strongest.* These have the [ŋ] followed by [g].
3. Where the letters *ng* are medial in a root word, as in *finger, tingle, hunger, angle, extinguish* and *single,* standard pronunciation calls for the use of [ŋg]. An exception is the pronunciation of *gingham* as [giŋəm].
4. In combinations in which the letter *n* is immediately followed by *k, c,* or *x* in the same syllable, the [ŋk] is used. Examples include *link, hank, distinct, anxious,* and *larynx.*

Note that not all words which include the letters *ng* in their spelling call for [ŋ] in their pronunciation. For example, words such as *range, singe,* and *longevity* are pronounced with the combination [ndʒ] rather than with either the [ŋ] or the [ŋg].

Apply these rules to the list of words which follow.

[ŋ]	[ŋg]	[ŋk]
wing	tingle	link
rang	spangle	anchor
young	younger	wink
harangue	elongate	sank
evening	anger	bunk
ringing	bungalow	trinket

[ŋ]	[ŋg]	[ŋk]
longing	longest	lynx
sings	tangle	length *
strong	stronger	strength *
banging	youngest	tanker

Practice to Establish a Final [ŋ]

Speakers who tend to add a [g] or [k] to words that should properly end with the [ŋ] should be helped by contrasting the plosives [g] and [k] with the nasal continuant [ŋ]. The plosive sounds call for an abrupt stopping of the breath and the emission of a puff of air. The [ŋ] should be produced so that the nasally emitted sound dies away gradually. At the outset, exaggerate the length of the sound so that it is prolonged to two or three times the length of what it might be in normal conversational speech.

Practice Materials

In practicing with the material that follows, establish your timing and control. Prolong the [ŋ] and move, without stopping, to the next word.

long ago	coming and going	King of England
going away	running away	swing along
bring it	sitting up	hang it up
Long Island	sing a song	spring is here
strong one	ring a bell	tang of fall

Sentences

1. Merely counting money is not conducive to increasing its amount.
2. Browning indicated a yearning for meringue pie.
3. The young husband longed in vain for his mother's cooking.
4. Long ago we learned that running away solves few problems.
5. Several adolescents were heard complaining about the problem of bringing up their parents.

*The words *strength* and *length* are accceptably pronounced with or without a [k] before the final sound.

Practice the following individual words and then incorporate them in phrases in which the [ŋ] is immediately followed by a vowel.

bring	hang	song	sung
sing	rang	wrong	glowing
wing	bang	tong	flowing
thing	sang	young	growing
sting	long	tongue	knowing
fling	thong	lung	towing
gang	prong	swung	sewing
fang	throng	flung	blowing

Medial [ŋ]

The words which follow conform to rule 2; a suffix is added to a word ending with *ng*.

Practice Materials

bringing	fangs	thronging	prolonging
brings	hangs	youngster	twangy
singing	banged	songbird	hangman
sings	hanged	tongueless	clangs
things	hanger	kingly	strings
stings	songs	pronged	longhorn
wings	longing	tongs	gangster
gangs	wronging	strongly	Wingdale

Sentences for Medial and Final [ŋ]

1. The sword was hung on a high ring to keep it away from the young child.

2. Many stories pleasing to children have their beginning with the words "long ago."

3. The bellringer longed to ring his bells.

4. Molly was a fishmonger who sang while selling her fish.

5. In the spring many birds wing their way from the South.

6. Some gangs are reputed to have their own hangmen.

7. Young children will not be tongueless if their mothers are fond of singing.

8. Jones banged on the door because his ringing was not heard.

9. When a bee stings he may have to give up his longing for living.

10. The orang-outang lived a kingly life.

[ŋg]

When the letters *ng* occur within the root of a word, the pronunciation is [ŋg].

Practice Materials

Practice with the following words.

single	shingle	languor	jungle
mingle	wrangle	spangle	Congo
tingle	angle	tangle	linguist
finger	anger	language	languid
England	anguish	hunger	English
jingle	jangle	bungle	distinguish

The following suffix words are pronounced [ŋg] and are exceptions to the *ng* rule.

younger	longer	stronger	prolongate
youngest	longest	strongest	diphthongal

[ŋg]

The following words are pronounced with [ŋ] followed by [k].

wink	pharynx	dank	slunk
ink	yank	shank	flunk
sink	bank	plank	donkey
pink	thank	lanky	monkey
blink	rank	monk	conquer
shrink	spank	honk	bronco
rink	drank	trunk	Bronx
clink	frank	sunk	honked
lynx	swank	dunk	junked
larynx	blank	uncle	flanked

Sentences for [ŋg] *and* [ŋk]

1. The larynx is just below the pharynx in the throat.
2. Frank was fond of attending banquets.
3. Uncle Joe believed in keeping in the pink of condition.
4. The lanky Yank came from the Bronx.
5. The lynx slunk away in the jungle.
6. The Englishman knew many languages, including those of the Congo.
7. A donkey is considered to be one of our strongest animals.
8. The baby kangaroo dangled from his mother's pouch.
9. Susan was thankful for the gift of trinkets.
10. It is important to distinguish between mushrooms and other inedible fungus plants.

Sentences for [ŋ]

1. Fielding observed the swinging of the pendulum and knew that his time was running out.
2. Long Island trains are not noted for their great speed during either the day or evening.
3. Though he was a stranger to the fast-running brook, the angler was successful in his fishing.
4. Many roads are being lengthened and widened to take care of ever increasing traffic.
5. Instead of moaning in anguish, Molly looked proud as she saw her husband swinging aloft from the gallows in Reading Jail.
6. King, the Birmingham Englishman, spoke nine languages.
7. At long last, Young's strivings were rewarded with the things for which he had been yearning.
8. Wilding worked with singular purpose even after some of his New England friends no longer tried.
9. The hungry donkey showed his unfailing strength to earn his feeding.
10. The kingfisher is better known for his fishing ability than for his singing.
11. Ingram's younger brother was stronger than he, but his oldest brother was the strongest of them all.
12. While the opera singer was suffering from an infection of the larynx, his neighbors, though wishing him well, were enjoying the strange quiet.

Selections

1. Topping left his little English town of Springfield when he was still a young man. He left to go fishing and hunting in the Congo jungles. Now, in his middle years, Topping found himself yearning to return home. In his mind's eye, he was ever seeing and reliving the scenes of his younger days. He saw quiet streets and roads with crooked turnings. He heard sounds of droning bees and bird's singing. The nightingale sang his favorite song. So Topping got ready for his returning. And return he did! But what he found was disillusioning. Springfield was now a bustling town. Speeding cars and honking horns were the sights and the sounds. After a few days of disturbed thinking, Topping did some concluding. He repacked his belongings and returned to the Congo jungle where he could peacefully live out the remaining years of his life.

2. As I went out one morning to breathe the morning air
   I heard a dear old mother saying, "O my daughter fair,
   You better go wash them dishes and hush that flattering tongue,
   You know you want to marry and that you are too young."
   Adapted from *Lolly-Too-Dum*—American ballad

8. I wish I were single again,
   I wish I were single
   My pockets would jingle,
   I wish I were single again.

   I got me a wife, O then,
   I got me a wife
   She's the plague of my life,
   I wish I were single again.

   She beat me, she banged me O then,
   She beat me, she banged me,
   She swore she would hang me,
   I wish I were single again.
   Adapted from *I Wish I Was Single
   Again*—American ballad

4. Sweeter than any sung
   My songs that found no tongue;
   Nobler than any fact
   My wish that failed to act.

   Others shall sing the song,
   Others shall right the wrong,—
   Finish what I begin,
   And all I fail of win.
                    JOHN GREENLEAF WHITTIER
                        —*My Triumph*

5. It's every Monday morning
   When the blue birds begin to sing,
   You can hear those hammers a mile or more,
   You can hear John Henry's hammer ring,
   O Lord! John Henry's hammer ring.

   John Henry was hammering on the mountain
   And his hammer was striking fire,
   He drove so hard he broke his poor heart
   And he put down his hammer and he died,
   Lord, Lord, he stopped his hammering and he died.

   They took John Henry to the graveyard
   And they buried him in the sand
   And every locomotive comes roaring by,
   Says, "There lays a steel driving man,"
   Lord, Lord, says, "There lays a steel driving man."
                    John Henry—American ballad

The Glide Consonant [j] (y) As in *Year*, *Unite*, and *Loyal*

[j] is a vocalized, palatal glide sound. In acoustic effect, because it is an unobstructed and continuant sound, it is vowel-like in quality. [j] glides or moves from the initial position of the vowel [i] to a final position determined by the sound that immediately follows it. The initial articulatory position calls for the tongue to be arched toward the front of the hard palate and for the lips to be

parted and retracted as though for a smile. The soft palate is raised and the vocal folds are in vibration throughout the production of the sound.

When the [j] sound is represented by a single letter in spelling it is by the letter *y*. In medial positions [j] may be represented in spelling by the letters *io, ie,* and *ia.* Frequently, however, in both initial and medial positions, there is no spelling representation for the [j]. The sound often becomes part of vowel blends as in *unite* and *unify.*

Practice Materials

Initial

yield	yam	yoho	Europe
yeast	Yankee	yacht	young
year	you	yonder	yowl
yes	youth	yard	yellow
yen	your	yule	yesterday
yet	yawn	yearn	usual
yell	yawl	use	usurp
yank	yoke	unit	eulogy

Medial

Daniel	companion	accuse	volume
genial	familiar	refuse	collier
genius	billiard	confuse	review
senior	canyon	amuse	stallion
vineyard	million	onion	argue
lanyard	abuse	bunion	opinion

[j] Preceded by an Initial Consonant

The inclusion of a [j] after an initial consonant varies according to context and regional practice. It is optional in words such as *Tuesday, tune,* and *new* and in many other words that begin with the sounds [t], [d], or [n]. If there are no special influences to direct your choice, regional usage should be followed.

Practice Materials

[j] is regularly included after the first consonant in the word list that immediately follows. It is optional for the second word list.

pure	fuel	cute	music
pupil	few	future	futile
beauty	feud	huge	fusion
muse	humane	view	mule
mute	humorous	cupid	puny

Tuesday	due	knew	nuisance
new	tube	nuclear	nude
tune	numerous	duke	Nubian
tuba	duty	tumult	Newt
constitute	reduce	institute	gratuity
destitute	annuity	plume	restitute
induce	platitude	acumen	enduring

Sentences

1. Few knew the origin of the feud.

2. Cupid sometimes takes a dim view of the wishes of human beings.

3. Even the puny may muse on things of beauty.

4. Americans have a duty to study their Constitution.

5. Because of his acumen, the duke considered the compliments gratuitous platitudes.

6. The Yale student was fond of billiards.

7. Daniel, though not a millionaire, preferred riding a stallion to a mule.

8. Opinions vary as to whether onions and yams make a congenial dish.

9. Avoid speaking in platitudes if you wish to express gratitude.

10. The young New Yorker enjoyed yachting and sailing a yawl.

Selections

1. *To-morrow!*—Why, Tomorrow I may be
   Myself with Yesterday's Sev'n thousand Years.
   OMAR KHAYYÁM—*Rubáiyát*

2. These passengers, by reason of their clinging to a mast,
   Upon a desert island were eventually cast.
   They hunted for their meals, as Alexander Selkirk used,
   But they couldn't chat together—they had not been introduced.
   W. S. GILBERT—*Etiquette*

3. It's one to a million
   That any civilian
   My figure and form'll surpass.
   w. s. GILBERT—*Patience*

4. Does he study the wants of his own dominion?
   Or doesn't he care for public opinion?
   EDWARD LEAR—*The Akond of Swat*

5. After a man has sown his wild oats in the years of his youth,
he has still every year to get over a few weeks and days of folly.
   JEAN PAUL—*Flower, Fruit, and Thorn Pieces*

[h] As in *He* and *Who*

The sound [h] lacks fixed or distinctive articulatory position. The
sound which immediately follows the [h] determines the position
assumed by the lips and tongue for this voiceless fricative.

[h] consists of a stream or puff of breath made discernible by
the degree of contraction and vocal-fold vibration in the larynx.

Few persons are likely to have difficulty in the actual production
of the [h]. The most likely basis for difficulty is that of determining
whether, despite or because of the spelling of the word, an [h] is
to be produced or omitted in the pronunciation. It may be of help
to know that in American-English speech the [h] is appropriately
included chiefly before vowels in stressed syllables as in *he, hot,* and
hate. Some speakers also include the sound in words that begin with
a *wh* as in *which* and *whale.* [h] is usually not pronounced in
medial, unstressed syllables.

Practice Materials

Initial

he	hen	hoof	harm
heat	ham	hoe	harsh
hit	hag	host	her
hill	hoot	haughty	hurl
haste	who	halt	hurt
hate	whom	hog	heard
head	hood	hot	hearse

hut	height	house	humid
hum	hire	howl	huge
hunt	hoyden	humane	humor

Medial (note its position in stressed syllables before vowels)

unheeded	unhealthy	unharmed	behind
reheat	rehash	unheard	dishearten
inhibit	inhuman	rehearse	inherit
inhale	overhaul	uphold	upheaval
behave	rehone	rehouse	prehistoric
behead	cohort	somehow	exhale

Sentences

1. Haters are often more harmed than those who are hated.
2. High humidity is common in Ohio.
3. Helen was disheartened by the heat.
4. Mount Hood has one of the highest peaks on this whole continent.
5. The hog who entered the hut soon became a ham.
6. The owls hooted and the dogs howled as the hunters hastened up the hill.
7. The smith inhaled deeply as he shod the horse's hoof.
8. Rehearsals were held in the converted hen house.
9. The hoe hit a huge stone and put the farmer in a bad humor.
10. Who will be the host for the hoyden and her uninhibited cohort?
11. Hiram learned to enjoy whale meat while on his fishing trip.
12. Harold did not know when or where he lost his heavy coat.

Selection

Harry, who worked in Soho, came from a part of London where human beings were somewhat variable about their *h's*. Harry himself was a harried husband because he would not always make it clear whether *ham* was something he ate or something he preferred to hate. When you heard Harry, you could not be sure whether *honey* was what he had or what he would like to add to his butterhorns. The result was that Harry was often hungry, because his wife Helen was never entirely sure whether it was time to heed him or feed him.

Index